Communications in Computer and Information Science 857

Commenced Publication in 2007
Founding and Former Series Editors:
Phoebe Chen, Alfredo Cuzzocrea, Xiaoyong Du, Orhun Kara, Ting Liu,
Dominik Ślęzak, and Xiaokang Yang

More information about this series at http://www.springer.com/series/7899

Yuanguo Bi · Gang Chen
Qingxu Deng · Yi Wang (Eds.)

Embedded Systems Technology

15th National Conference, ESTC 2017
Shenyang, China, November 17–19, 2017
Revised Selected Papers

Springer

Editors
Yuanguo Bi
Northeastern University
Shenyang
China

Qingxu Deng
Northeastern University
Shenyang
China

Gang Chen
Northeastern University
Shenyang
China

Yi Wang
Northeastern University
Shenyang
China

ISSN 1865-0929   ISSN 1865-0937   (electronic)
Communications in Computer and Information Science
ISBN 978-981-13-1025-6   ISBN 978-981-13-1026-3   (eBook)
https://doi.org/10.1007/978-981-13-1026-3

Library of Congress Control Number: 2018947567

Printed on acid-free paper

This Springer imprint is published by the registered company Springer Nature Singapore Pte Ltd.
The registered company address is: 152 Beach Road, #21-01/04 Gateway East, Singapore 189721, Singapore

Preface

The Embedded Systems Technology Conference (ESTC) is an annual conference sponsored by the Embedded System Specialized Committee of the China Computer Federation (CCF), and it has been held 14 times since 2001. ESTC has become one of the most important academic conferences for experts, scholars, engineers, and graduate students in the fields of embedded systems and related areas for academic exchanges, technical seminars, and interaction. ESTC 2017 was held in Shenyang, China, during November 17–19, 2017. This conference was jointly sponsored by the CCF, the CCF Embedded System Specialized Committee, and the School of Computer Science and Engineering, Northeastern University.

ESTC 2017, with the theme of "Embedded Systems and Intelligent Computing," aimed to provide a venue for discussing the latest research results and development trends in the field of embedded systems, hosting extensive academic exchanges and discussions. ESTC 2017 received 63 submissions (45 submissions in English and 18 in Chinese) from experts, academics, engineers, industry professionals, and postgraduates in the related fields of embedded systems. We invited a large number of local and international experts to serve as the Program Committee and reviewers. Each paper received three reviews, and finally 24 full papers including 18 papers in English and six papers in Chinese were accepted.

May 2018

Yuanguo Bi
Gang Chen
Qingxu Deng
Yi Wang

Organization

Technical Program Committee

Yuanguo Bi	Northeastern University, China
Gang Chen	Northeastern University, China
Xue-Yang Zhu	Institute of Software, Chinese Academy of Sciences, China
Qingxu Deng	NEU, China
Xiaoli Gong	Nankai University, China
Kai Huang	Sun Yat-sen University, China
Lei Bu	Nanjing University, China, China
Mingsong Chen	East China Normal University, China
Duo Liu	Chongqing University, China
Weichen Liu	Nanyang Technological University, Singapore
Wang Quan	Xidian University, China
Liu Xue	Northeastern University, China
Jianfeng Yang	Wuhan University, China
Lanshun Nie	Harbin Institute of Technology, China
Zonghua Gu	Zhejiang University, China
Dakai Zhu	University of Texas at San Antonio, USA
Yong Xie	Xiamen University of Technology, China
Liqian Chen	National University of Defense Technology, China
Hanhua Chen	Huazhong University of Science and Technology, China
Yi Wang	Shenzhen University, China
Wei Dong	National University of Defense Technology, China
Jian Guo	East China Normal University, China
Wanwei Liu	National University of Defense Technology, China
Yu Hua	Huazhong University of Science and Technology, China
Bing Guo	Sichuan University, China
Guan Nan	Hong Kong Polytechnic University, SAR China
Ji Wang	National University of Defense Technology, China
Jian-Jun Han	Huazhong University of Science and Technology, China
Xixin Cao	Peking University, China
Mingsong Lv	Northeastern University, China
Chuanwen Li	NEU, China
Geguang Pu	East China Normal University, China
Guitao Cao	East China Normal University, China
Xiebing Wang	Technical University of Munich, Germany
Long Cheng	Technical University of Munich, Germany
Nan Cheng	University of Waterloo, Canada
Kuan Zhang	University of Nebraska-Lincoln, USA
Kan Yang	University of Memphis, USA

Organizing Committee

General Chair

Zhonghai Wu   Peking University, China

Technical Program Chairs

Yi Wang   Northeastern University, China
Nan Guan   Northeastern University, China
Gang Chen   Northeastern University, China

Publications Chairs

Xixin Cao   Peking University, China
Yuanguo Bi   Northeastern University, China

Local Arrangements Chair

Qingxu Deng   Northeastern University, China

Publicity Chairs

Mingsong Lv   Northeastern University, China
Chuanwen Li   Northeastern University, China
Xue Liu   Northeastern University, China

Reviewers

Zhuangyi Jiang   Technical University of Munich, Germany
Mingchuan Zhou   Technical University of Munich, Germany
Biao Hu   Technical University of Munich, Germany
Yuanguo Bi   Northeastern University, China
Gang Chen   Northeastern University, China
Xue-Yang Zhu   Institute of Software, Chinese Academy of Sciences, China
Qingxu Deng   NEU, China
Xiaoli Gong   Nankai University, China
Kai Huang   Sun Yat-sen University, China
Lei Bu   Nanjing University, China, China
Mingsong Chen   East China Normal University, China
Duo Liu   Chongqing University, China
Weichen Liu   Nanyang Technological University, Singapore
Wang Quan   Xidian University, China
Liu Xue   Northeastern University, China
Jianfeng Yang   Wuhan University, China
Lanshun Nie   Harbin Institute of Technology, China
Zonghua Gu   Zhejiang University, China
Dakai Zhu   University of Texas at San Antonio, USA
Yong Xie   Xiamen University of Technology, China

Liqian Chen	National University of Defense Technology, China
Hanhua Chen	Huazhong University of Science and Technology, China
Yi Wang	Shenzhen University, China
Wei Dong	National University of Defense Technology, China
Jian Guo	East China Normal University, China
Wanwei Liu	National University of Defense Technology, China
Yu Hua	Huazhong University of Science and Technology, China
Bing Guo	Sichuan University, China
Guan Nan	Hong Kong Polytechnic University, SAR China
Ji Wang	National University of Defense Technology, China
Jian-Jun Han	Huazhong University of Science and Technology, China
Xixin Cao	Peking University, China
Mingsong Lv	Northeastern University, China
Chuanwen Li	NEU, China
Geguang Pu	East China Normal University, China
Guitao Cao	East China Normal University, China
Xiebing Wang	Technical University of Munich, Germany
Long Cheng	Technical University of Munich, Germany
Nan Cheng	University of Waterloo, Canada
Kuan Zhang	University of Nebraska-Lincoln, USA
Kan Yang	University of Memphis, USA

Sponsors

Neusoft®

Contents

Context Aware Computing

Traffic Sign Recognition
Based on Convolutional Neural Network

Zhuo Cai[1], Jian Cao[1]([✉]), May Huang[2], and Xing Zhang[1]

[1] School of Software and Microelectronics, Peking University, Beijing, China
{caojian,zhx}@ss.pku.edu.cn
[2] International Technological University, San Jose, USA

Abstract. With the progress of science and technology and the development of social economy, intelligent transportation came into being. Traffic signs recognition, as an important part of intelligent traffic, has been widely researched. The problem of traffic signs identification is complicated and changeable, and it is easy to be affected by the factors such as weather, illumination, occlusion and shooting angle. Convolutional neural network has a strong robustness for image translation, scaling, rotation and other deformation. Based on this, we use an improved convolutional neural network to recognize traffic signs to meet the needs of practical applications. This method can automatically extract the features of the image by convolution and pool processing, and then make classification of them, so as to realize the recognition of traffic signs. The correct rate of the algorithm which is used in this paper is 98.13%, by processing the experiment on the GTSRB data set.

Keywords: Traffic signs recognition · Convolutional neural network
Intelligent transportation · Classification

1 Introduction

With the development of urbanization and the popularity of cars, the number of cars has increased dramatically, the traffic congestion has increased, the traffic accidents have occurred frequently, and the road traffic safety and transportation efficiency have become more and more serious. The driver assistance system [1] based on computer vision is one of the important measures to solve the problem of traffic safety and transport efficiency. As a result, it is applied in the field of intelligent transportation step by step. Its related research mainly involves three aspects: road recognition, collision detection and traffic sign recognition. The research on road recognition and collision detection started earlier and achieved a lot of results, but the research on traffic sign recognition is relatively small. The traffic sign contains some important traffic information, such as road changes, speed limits, driving behavior constraints and so on. By identifying the traffic signs, and timely providing the driver with the road information to help them make the correct operation can ensure traffic safety, so as to avoid the occurrence of traffic accidents. Therefore, this research has important practical significance.

© Springer Nature Singapore Pte Ltd. 2018
Y. Bi et al. (Eds.): ESTC 2017, CCIS 857, pp. 3–16, 2018.
https://doi.org/10.1007/978-981-13-1026-3_1

The image of the traffic sign is usually the real road information taken in the natural environment. The background environment is quite complex, greatly affected by weather conditions and road conditions. Moreover, the moving of the camera at the time of shooting can also have certain influence on the picture quality of the images. All of these have a great impact on the recognition effect and reliability of the algorithm. Now the effective and commonly used recognition algorithms are feature matching classification, support vector machine classification, neural network classification method and so on.

In the classification and recognition algorithm of traffic signs, the feature matching method is a simple one. Sompoc [2] et al. used the original color image and the standard Euler distance of traffic signs for classification and recognition, this method is also called the nearest neighbor method. As the distance between different kinds is not independent, the final classification result has a certain occasionality. Betk [3] et al. compared the similarity between the original images and the standard templates of the traffic signs, judging the classification of the traffic signs according to the similarity. The principle of support vector machine (SVM) is simple, and it has a strong ability to adapt. Arroyo [4] Lafuente et al. use support vector machine to identify traffic signs. The nonlinear support vector machine is trained to classify the traffic signs, while the whole image is used as the training sample data set. However, the whole image is characterized by high feature dimension, complex network structure, large amount of computation and slow speed. Using neural network to classify traffic signs is a method frequently used, the effect of the classification is also relatively good. De La EScalera [5] et al. first detected the original image, extracting the local images which contain traffic signs, and then unified them to the size of 32*32. The images of the uniform size are used as the input sample training set. Nguwi [6] et al. also used the images of the uniform size as the training sample data set, training a neural network binary classifier for each type of traffic signs. Finally, a large multiple classifier is composed of these binary classifiers using the method of cascade. This method is simple to use, but the structure of the neural network is not fixed, which needs to be designed according to the characteristics of the training samples, and it will have a certain impact on the classification effect.

In this paper, we use the convolutional neural network to identify traffic signs. Convolutional neural network is a kind of deep artificial neural network, which extracts the feature of the images by doing convolution and pool operation to the local region in the image, enhancing target information and weakening the noise information. As a result, the images are shift invariant and have very strong robustness.

2   The Basic Structure and Principle of Convolutional Neural Network

Convolutional neural network [7,8] is designed according to the principle of visual nerve. In 1962, receptive fields were proposed by Hubel and Wiesel [9] in the study of the visual cells of the cat. Neocognitron proposed by Fukushima [10] in 1980, can be said to be the first to realize convolutional neural network. It is based on receptive field, and it is also the first application of receptive field in artificial neural network. Convolutional neural network has two characteristics, namely, sparse connectivity and weight sharing(shown in Figs. 1 and 2). With respect to the general neural network, these two features make the convolutional neural network have the advantages that the parameter is reduced, the network complexity is reduced and the adaptability is enhanced.

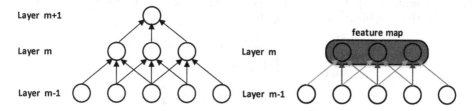

Fig. 1. Sparse connectivity   **Fig. 2.** Shared weights

2.1 Forward Propagation

The characteristic of the image is extracted by the convolution and pool processing of the input image. Convolution processing of the feature map of previous layer will obtain convolution layer. Convolution operation is an operation form of mathematical analysis, which can be expressed with the formula below:

$$\int_{-\infty}^{+\infty} f(\tau) \cdot g(x - \tau)d\tau \tag{1}$$

In the formula above, $f(x)$ and $g(x)$ are integrable on R. Discrete convolution operation of the image can be expressed by the following formula:

$$x_j^l = f(\sum_{i \in M_j} x_i^{l-1} \times W_{ij}^l + b_j^l) \tag{2}$$

In the formula above, M_j represents the set consisting of all the input feature maps, x_j^l represents the feature graph j in the convolution layer l after the operation of convolution, W_{ij}^l represents the weight of the convolution kernel j in the layer l, b_j^l represents bias. The convolution operation of the image can enhance the original signal and reduce the noise.

The pooling layer usually does no overlap sampling and gets the local average or the maximum value to reduce the amount of the data, which can be expressed with the following formula:

$$x_j^l = down(x_j^{l-1}) \tag{3}$$

In the formula, x_j^l represents the jth pool output in the pool layer l, x_j^{l-1} represents the jth feature map in the layer $l-1$.

Softmax regression classification is used as the output layer. Softmax regression [11] is a generalization of the *Logistic* two classification regression. Softmax processing is a multi classification problem, the number of categories h can be taken to the value of more than 2. For input sample data sets $\{(x^{(1)}, y^{(1)}), ..., (x^{(m)}, y^{(m)})\}$, there is $y^{(i)} \in \{1, 2, ..., h\}$.

In the Softmax regression classification, the final output is the probability that the input sample belongs to a particular class, that is $p(y = j \mid x)$. Set $h_\theta(*)$ be the classification function, then:

$$h_\theta(x^{(i)}) = \begin{bmatrix} p(y^{(i)} = 1 \mid x^{(i)}; w) \\ p(y^{(i)} = 2 \mid x^{(i)}; w) \\ \cdots \\ p(y^{(i)} = k \mid x^{(i)}; w) \end{bmatrix}$$

$$= \frac{1}{\sum_{j=1}^{k} e^{w_j^r x^{(i)}}} \begin{bmatrix} e^{w_1^r x^{(i)}} \\ e^{w_2^r x^{(i)}} \\ \cdots \\ e^{w_k^r x^{(i)}} \end{bmatrix} \tag{4}$$

$w_1, w_2, ..., w_k \in R^{n+1}$ are model parameters in the above formula. $\frac{1}{\sum_{j=1}^{k} e^{w_j^r x^{(i)}}}$ is to make the sum of the output value be 1.

2.2 Back Propagation

Convolutional neural network use back propagation method [12,13] to train parameters. First, the sample data is used for forward propagation, and the output value is calculated, then the error is calculated, and the parameters are adjusted. Using the squared error cost function as an error function E^N, when there are C classes and N input samples, E^N can be expressed with the formula below:

$$E^N = \frac{1}{2} \sum_{n=1}^{N} \sum_{k=1}^{c} (t_k^n - y_k^n)^2 \tag{5}$$

In the above formula, n represents the number of samples, k indicates the dimension, t^n is the sample value and y^n is the output value. After the error of all individual samples is summed up, then the overall error of the sample data set is got. The error of a single sample can be expressed in the following formula:

$$E^n = \frac{1}{2}(t_k^n - y_k^n)^2 = \frac{1}{2} \parallel t^n - y^n \parallel_2^2 \tag{6}$$

Sensitivity of the Output Layer. We see the partial derivative of the bias of the back propagation error on neurons as the sensitivity of the error to neurons bias. With chain derivative method we can get:

$$\frac{\partial E}{\partial b} = \frac{\partial E}{\partial u}\frac{\partial u}{\partial b} = \delta \tag{7}$$

By formula (1) $\frac{\partial u}{\partial b}$ can be obtained 1, so $\frac{\partial E}{\partial b} = \frac{\partial E}{\partial u} = \delta$. Thus, the sensitivity and error of the bias are equivalent to the partial derivation of the full input of a unit. The output layer is set to be the layer l, and the sensitivity of the neurons is:

$$\delta^l = f'(u^l) \times (y^n - t^n) \tag{8}$$

$$u^l = W^l x^{l-1} + b^l \tag{9}$$

In which t^n is the sample value, y^n is the output value, x^{l-1} is the input value of the current layer, W^l and b^l are respectively the weight and bias of the layer.

The derivative of the weight and the bias of the output layer are:

$$\frac{\partial E}{\partial W^l} = x^{l-1}(\delta^l)^T \tag{10}$$

$$\frac{\partial E}{\partial b^l} = \delta^l \tag{11}$$

Sensitivity of the Pool Layer. The layer l is set to be the pool layer, and if the next layer is the output layer, the sensitivity is:

$$\delta_i^l = W_{ij}^T \delta_j \tag{12}$$

If the next layer of the pool layer is the convolution layer, we set the sensitivity of the convolution layer be δ^{l-1}. There are M feature maps, then the sensitivity of the layer l is:

$$\delta_i^l = \sum_{j=1}^{M} \delta_j^{l-1} * W_{ij}^{l-1} \tag{13}$$

In which δ_i^l is the sensitivity of the feature map i in the layer l, δ_j^{l-1} is the sensitivity of the feature map j in the layer $l-1$ and W_{ij}^{l-1} represents the weight of the layer l.

Sensitivity of the Convolution Layer. Layer l is set to be the convolution layer and layer $l-1$ is set to be the pool layer. The sensitivity of the layer $l-1$ is δ^{l-1}, then the sensitivity of layer l is:

$$\delta_j^l = up(\delta_j^{l-1}) \tag{14}$$

$$up(\delta_j^{l+1}) = \delta_j^{l+1} \otimes 1_{n \times n} \tag{15}$$

For a given characteristic graph, the gradient of the weight and the bias of the convolution layer are:

$$\frac{\partial E}{\partial b_j^l} = \sum_{u,v} (\delta_j^l)_{uv} \tag{16}$$

$$\frac{\partial E}{\partial W_{ij}^l} = \sum_{u,v} (\delta_j^l)_{uv} (P_i^{l-1})_{uv} \tag{17}$$

Among them, $(P_i^{l-1})_{uv}$ is a regional block, which is multiplied by elements in x_i^{l-1} and W_{ij}^l. The size of $(P_i^{l-1})_{uv}$ is the same as the size of the convolution kernel, and the value of the (u,v) of the convolution layer feature map x_i^l is obtained through the convolution operation of $(P_i^{l-1})_{uv}$ and the weight of W_{ij}^l.

The Parameter Adjustment. By using the gradient of the above weight and bias, the adjustment is carried out according to the following formula.

$$\Delta W_{ij}(k+1) = \eta \Delta W_{ij}(k) + \alpha(1-\eta)\frac{\partial E}{\partial W_{ij}(k)} \tag{18}$$

$$\Delta b_j(k+1) = \eta \Delta b_j(k) + \alpha(1-\eta)\frac{\partial E}{\partial b_j(k)} \tag{19}$$

In the formula above, k is the training times, ΔW_{ij} and Δb_{ij} are the adjustment value of the weight and bias, α represents the learning efficiency and η is the momentum factor.

3   Contributions and Innovations

In this paper, the final output of the convolutional neural network for traffic sign recognition is 44 kinds, of which 43 kinds of traffic signs and a negative sample. Compared with traditional neural network, this paper has increased multilayer perceptron in the convolution layer, improving the abstraction of the extracted feature, also using a linear correction function as the activation function at the same time.

3.1 Convolution Layer

Feature abstraction refers to obtain the invariant features of the changing object. The higher the degree of the invariant features, the more accurate the identification of the object and the stronger the robustness of the object. In traditional convolutional neural networks, the convolution filter is a generalized linear model (GLM). For linear separable objects, the linear model can obtain better abstract results. However, it is not good for the nonlinear object. The traditional convolutional network can make up for this problem by increasing the number of convolution kernel and obtaining more kinds of abstract features. But doing so will make the network more complex and need to train a large number of parameters. The use of nonlinear function instead of GLM, can enhance the abstract ability of the model to the input characteristics. Lin [14] et al. proposed the use of nonlinear multilayer perceptron instead of GLM, and enhance the abstraction ability of the convolution neural network to extract the feature. Figure 3 is the traditional linear convolution process. Figure 4 is the convolution with the increased multilayer perceptron.

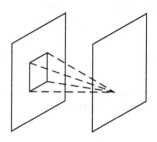
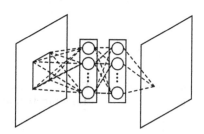

Fig. 3. Linear convolution   Fig. 4. Nonlinear convolution

The traditional convolutional neural network use the following formula to calculate the convolution process:

$$P_{i,j,k} = f(W_k^T x_{i,j} + b, 0) \tag{20}$$

In the formula, (i, j) represents the position coordinates of the pixels in the feature map, $x_{i,j}$ represents the local area in the output feature map at (i, j). k represents the number of feature maps.

The convolution procedure of the convolutional neural network using multilayer perceptron is represented by the following formula:

$$P_{i,j,k_1}^1 = f(w_{k_1}^{1T} x_{i,j} + b_{k_1}, 0) \tag{21}$$

$$P_{i,j,k_n}^n = f(w_{k_1}^{uT} P_{i,j}^{n-1} + b_{k_n}, 0) \tag{22}$$

The number of neurons in a multilayer perceptron is represented with n in the above formula. In this paper, the multilayer perceptron in use has 3 layers.

3.2 Linear Correction Unit

The activation function in the traditional convolution neural network generally used *Sigmoid* function or *tanh* function. In this paper, the non negative linear correction (*Rectifier*) function [15] $max(x, 0)$ is used as the activation function. In 2001, neuroscientists Dayan and Abott simulated a more accurate activation model of neurons on receiving signals from the point of view of biology, that is, Fig. 5. This model with respect to the *Sigmoid* function has three changes: 1, unilateral inhibition, 2, relatively broad exciting boundary, 3, sparse activation (the state of the front section in the red box is not activated). From Fig. 6 and Fig. 7, we can see that the *Softplus* function has two characteristics, which are unilateral inhibition and relatively broad exciting boundary, but it does not satisfy the sparse activation. However, the *Rectifier* function has three characteristics of the signal activation model of brain neurons.

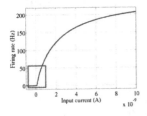 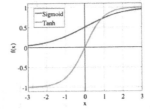 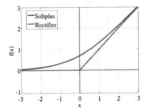

Fig. 5. Signal activation model of brain neurons

Fig. 6. Sigmoid and Tanh function images

Fig. 7. Softplus and Rectifier function images

At the same time, the *Rectifier* function can reduce *Vanishing Gradient Problem* with respect to the *Sigmoid* function. For the *Sigmoid* function, its derivative is less than 1. Using the recursive method to reverse the error, the gradient will continue to decay, slowing down the learning speed, or eventually leading to the disappearance of the gradient. But the gradient of the *Rectifier* function is 1, in the process of the reverse propagation, the gradient can flow well, greatly speed up the training speed.

3.3 Increase the Negative Sample

In this paper, the final output of the convolutional neural network for traffic sign recognition is 44 kinds, of which 43 kinds of traffic signs, namely positive samples, and a negative sample. The negative sample is a variety of external environmental images, which does not contain traffic signs. The traffic sign is outside. In the outdoor scene, especially in the city's road, the background environment is complex and diverse, and it has great influence on the identification of traffic signs. During the training process of the network model, increasing a kind of negative samples can reduce the probability of non traffic signs identified as traffic signs, improving the recognition accuracy.

3.4   Algorithm Flow

The flow chart of the algorithm is shown in Fig. 8. In the GTSRB data set, the size of the image is not uniform, and it is not necessarily square. In this paper, the image processed by the network structure is square image with the size of 52×52. So the first is the normalization of the images in the data set.

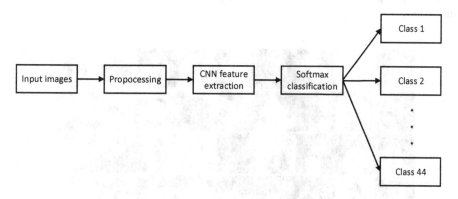

Fig. 8. Flow chart of classification algorithm

The processed image is used as the input of the convolutional neural network, and the feature of the image is extracted through the convolution process. In this paper, the used convolutional neural network has added the multilayer perceptron, that is to add the convolution layer with 1×1 convolution kernel. After the operation, the image feature abstraction degree is higher and the size of the feature map is unchanged.

In convolutional neural networks, the size and the size of the moving step of the convolution and the pool kernel can be adjusted manually. The size of the convolution kernel determines the size of the receptive field of neurons, the too large convolution kernel size may cause the too large amount of image feature, so that it can not be expressed. If its size is too small, it will affect the effect of feature extraction. Therefore, the adjustment of the convolution kernel size is a difficult problem of parameter adjustment in the neural network. The method to solve this problem is to be involved in a great number of experiments. After the input image is processed by convolution and pool, the output is a one-dimensional vector. Input the vector to the Softmax classification layer to do the classification recognition and finally output the probability of each type of the original image.

4   Test Results and Analysis

The experimental data used in this paper is the GTSRB data set. GTSRB data set is collected in the real road environment in Germany. There is only one kind of traffic signs in each picture and the category is a total of 43. Figure 9 is a random selection of the traffic signs from each category. In each picture of the data set, there is only one traffic sign. As the data set is taken in the real environment, the image in the data set is the same as the image in the real environment, containing the following situation such as: image blurring, low resolution, different light illumination, obscured by other objects, deformation, distorted perspective and so on. As a result, we can better test the effect of the algorithm.

Fig. 9. GTSRB data set

In this paper, the structural parameters of the convolutional neural network used in the experiment are shown in Table 1.

The architecture of the convolutional neural network used in this test include nine convolution layers and three pool layers. The convolution layer is from the layer of C1 to the layer of C9 and the pool layer is from the layer of P1 to the layer of P3. Layer C1 and layer C4 use the 5×5 filter on the feature map to do the convolution operation with a step size of 1, while the filter of the layer C7 has the size of 3×3. The filter of the rest convolution layer has the size of 1×1, which is a layer in the multilayer perceptron. The pool size of the pool layer P1 and P2 is 3×3, while the pool size of the pool layer P3 is 7×7. The mobile step size of the pool window is 2, which can be adjusted manually.

As we have 44 output classes (43 types of traffic signs and a class of negative samples), the final output of the P3 layer is a vector of 1×44, which serves as the input for the Softmax classification layer.

This paper is a model training in the environment of matlab, while the test system environment is Windows2008 operating system and the processor is Xeon E5 - 2063 v3 1.6 GHz and 8G memory. There are about 39000 pictures in GTSRB data set. In our experiment, we have divided the data set into two parts with the proportion of 2:1. Among them, one part is the training set with approximately

Table 1. The structural parameters of the network.

Layer	Type	Feature maps	Kernel size
I1	Input		
C1	Convolution	192	5×5
C2	Convolution	160	1×1
C3	Convolution	96	1×1
P1	Pooling	96	3×3
C4	Convolution	192	5×5
C5	Convolution	192	1×1
C6	Convolution	192	1×1
P2	Pooling	192	3×3
C7	Convolution	192	3×3
C8	Convolution	192	1×1
C9	Convolution	44	1×1
P3	Pooling	44	7×7
S1	Softmax		

26000 pictures, while the other part is the validation set with about 13000 pictures. When we start to train the data set, only the training set is used for training, while the validation set is not involved. As a result, this can effectively prevent overfitting. 30 rounds were trained in the training model and the trend of the error rate of each round in the training process is shown as in Fig. 10.

In the training process of the classification model, with the increase of the number of training, the classification accuracy is also gradually increased, and the time it takes is also increased. In Fig. 10, the error rate of the first five turns classification model is falling fast, and the rate of decline is decreased with the increase of training times. After the twenty-fifth turn, the error rate of the model is almost no longer decreased. Based on the accuracy of the model classification and the training time, we set the number of training turns to 30.

The classification model of this method is tested on the reserved validation data set of GTSRB data set, and the final classification accuracy is 98.13%. The main causes of the error classification include that the image is too vague, the image of the resolution is too low, motion blur, a shadow or other objects occlusion and so on. In order to compare the performance of this algorithm with other algorithms, the classification results of several representative methods are listed in Table 2.

Compared with the traditional convolutional neural network, the classification accuracy of the proposed algorithm is greatly improved. The classical pattern recognition theory is used in the random forest method and the LDA method. First, the image features are extracted to find the characteristic of traffic sign. They have human experience and subjective awareness in feature

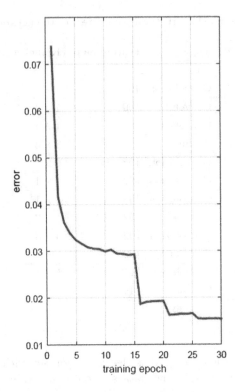

Fig. 10. Error diagram

extraction and selection. In this paper, the original image is directly used as the input, and the image features are extracted automatically without manual participation, and the influence of human factors is reduced.

Table 2. Comparison of precision with other algorithms.

Method	Accuracy(%)
Proposed algorithm	98.13
Random forest	96.14
LDA(HOG2)	95.68
CNN	92.51
LDA(HOG3)	92.34

5   Conclusion

In this paper, an improved convolutional neural network is used for classification and recognition of traffic signs. The original image is directly used as the input of the network, and the image is processed by convolution and pool processing. Then, we get the combination of advanced features of the images. Finally, we will do image recognition. After the experimental test on the reserved validation data set of GTSRB [16] data set, the correct rate of the algorithm used in this paper is 98.13%. The experimental data was collected in Germany. If we want the domestic traffic sign recognition, we still need to acquire domestic traffic signs, establish a database and have a model training, which is the content that can be further studied in the future. In addition, other factors such as model recognition speed will be optimized and verified in the future, so that it can be used in the actual traffic scene.

References

1. Euler, G., Robertson, H.D. (eds.): National Intelligent Transportation Systems Program Plan. ITS America, Washington, D.C. (1995)
2. Sompoch, P., Xiaoyangv, C., Michiro, K.: Automatic recognition and location of road signs from terrestrial color imagery. In: Geoinformatics & DMGIS, Bangkok, Thailad, pp. 238–247 (2001)
3. Betke, M., Makris, N.C.: Fast object recognition in noisy images using simulated annealing. In: International Conference on Computer Vision, IEEE Computer Society, pp. 523–530 (1995)
4. Maldonado-Bascon, S., Lafuente-Arroyo, S., Gil-Jimenez, P., et al.: Road-sign detection and recognition based on support vector machines. IEEE Trans. Intell. Transp. Syst. 8(2), 264–278 (2007)
5. De La Escalera, A., Moreno, L.E., Salichs, M.A., et al.: Road traffic sign detection and classification. IEEE Trans. Ind. Electron. 44(6), 848–859 (1997)
6. Nguwi, Y.Y., Kouzani, A.Z.: Detection and classification of road signs in natural environments. Neural Comput. Appl. 17(3), 265–289 (2008)
7. Dalal, N., Triggs, B.: Histograms of oriented gradients for human detection. In: IEEE Society Conference on Computer Vision&Pattern Recognition, vol. 1, pp. 886–893 (2005)
8. Simard, P.Y., Steinkraus, D., Platt, J.C.: Best practices for convolutional neural networks applied to visual document analysis. In: International Conference on Document Analysis and Recognition, Proceedings IEEE, p. 958 (2003)
9. Hubel, D.H., Wiesel, T.N.: Receptive fields, binocular interaction and functional architecture in the cat's visual cortex. J. Physiol. 160(1), 106–154 (1962)
10. Fukushima, K.: Neocognitron: a self-organizing neural network model for a mechanism of pattern recognition unaffected by shift in position. Biol. Cybern. 36(4), 193–202 (1980)
11. Rao, S.J.: Regression modeling strategies: with applications to linear models, logistic regression, and survival analysis. Am. Stat. Assoc. 98(461), 257–258 (2005)
12. Cirean, D., Meier, U., Masci, J., et al.: Multi-column deep neural network for traffic sign classification. Neural Networks 32(1), 333–338 (2012)

13. Giusti, A., Dan, C.C., Masci, J., et al.: Fast image scanning with deep max-pooling convolutional neural networks, pp. 4034–4038 (2013)
14. Lin, M., Chen, Q., Yan, S.: Network in network. In: Computer Science (2013)
15. Glorot, X., Bordes, A., Bengio, Y.: Deep sparse rectifier neural networks. In: International Conference on Artificial Intelligence and Statistics, pp. 315–323 (2011)
16. Sermanet, P., Kavukcuoglu, K., LeCun, Y.: Traffic signs and pedestrians vision with multi-scale convolutional networks. Snowbird Mach. Learn. Workshop **2**(3), 8 (2011)

A Novel RGB-T Based Real-Time Road Detection on Low Cost Embedded Devices

Wenquan Zhang[1,2], Xing Cai[1,2], Kai Huang[1,2(✉)], and Zhiguo Zhang[1,2,3]

[1] Key Laboratory of Machine Intelligence and Advanced Computing,
Sun Yat-sen University, Ministry of Education, Guangzhou, China
{zhangwq35,caix9}@mail2.sysu.edu.cn, huangk36@mail.sysu.edu.cn
[2] School of Data and Computer Science, Sun Yat-sen University, Guangzhou, China
[3] School of Biomedical Engineering, Health Science Center,
Shenzhen University, Shenzhen, China
zgzhang@szu.edu.cn

Abstract. Road detection plays an important role in autonomous driving and driving assistant system. However, the performance of existing methods still suffers from illumination change or bad illumination. In this paper, a novel method is presented which fuses RGB and thermal features to solve these problems. Our method is accurate as well as light-weighted. Evaluating on our RGB-T dataset, the method can achieve 92.01% accuracy and real-time performances on low cost embedded devices.

Keywords: RGB-Thermal · Road detection · Illumination-robust
Driver assistant system

1 Introduction

Autonomous driving, or Advanced Driving Assistant System (ADAS), can reduce traffic accidents and enhance the driving comfort. To date, there are two major paradigms implementation on autonomous driving system [6]: explicit decomposition of detection, path planning and control, i.e. mediated perception, and implemented through end-to-end deep Convolutional Neural Network (CNN) by mapping an input image to driving actions, i.e. behavior reflex [3,4]. While the level of abstraction of behavior reflex is too high to cooperated with other modules in ADAS, mediated perception encompassed the current state-of-the art approaches [6]. Therefore, road detection still plays an important role in ADAS.

Road detection can be used for Lane Departure Warning (LDW) and Lane Keep Assistant System (LKAS). And detected road area can limit the search space, i.e. region of interest, and improve the speed and accuracy of object detection. The main task of road detection is to detect the road area from an image captured by camera mounted on the vehicle. Although many feature-based methods have been devoted in this area, most detection methods still suffer from

© Springer Nature Singapore Pte Ltd. 2018
Y. Bi et al. (Eds.): ESTC 2017, CCIS 857, pp. 17–26, 2018.
https://doi.org/10.1007/978-981-13-1026-3_2

the interference of shadow and illumination [2]. While shadow removal methods can be used for improving performance, it's too time-consuming for such real-time road detection application [13].

In this paper, we propose a novel real-time and illumination-robust RGB-Thermal feature based road detection method. Thermal features are used to find the adaptive region of interest (ROI) using the vanish point of road, and to perform road area masking. RGB features are then fused for the mask road area refinement. Experiments on our RGB-T dataset show that road surfaces can be detected accurately and efficiently on low-cost embedded devices with the proposed method. It achieves 92.01% accuracy, and runs 23 fps on a Raspberry Pi 3, 55 fps on Nvidia TX 1 and 230 fps on a laptop with Intel i7-4702MQ CPU.

2   Related Work

Many approaches have been proposed in recent decades, including monocular vision based methods, stereo vision based methods and 3D LiDAR point cloud based methods.

Monocular Road Detection. With the development of deep learning, and public human road annotations image datasets [8], current advances in the field of computer vision have made clear that visual perception is going to play a key role in the development of self-driving cars. One typical approach is to perform road detection by using labeled datasets to train a CNN [11]. Although such data-driven methods perform well in road detection, to apply these methods to new scenarios is hard, because they require considerable human efforts to produce new training annotations. And deep neural network is still time-consuming and energy-consuming for mobile devices mounted on vehicle.

Other traditional monocular vision road detection techniques can be divided into two broad categories: feature-based methods [9], which use local features such as gradient, color, and orientation; and model-based methods [2], which utilize global road models to fit local features, and are thus sensitive road shapes. Although some shadow-free feature extractors have been introduced, only monocular based road detection methods still suffer from low illumination.

Road Detection with Depth Information. To efficiently deal with illumination changes and shadow, some researches take advantages of 3D scene information, including stereo vision [7], and 3D LiDAR point cloud [5,12]. However, high accuracy stereo image requires lots of computation and is time-consuming. And currently, 3D LiDAR is still expensive and far from commercial usage.

3   Proposed Method

In this section, we proposed the first RGB-Thermal feature based illumination-robust real-time road detection method as shown in Fig. 1. For the object saliency in RGB-T image [10], the road area and non-road area are salient in thermal image.

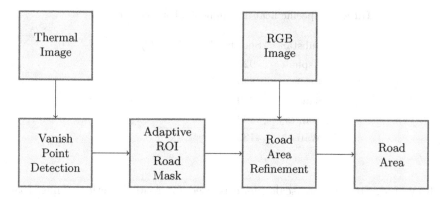

Fig. 1. Proposed RGB-Thermal based road detection

3.1 Road Thermal Feature

The RGB and thermal image of asphalt road and non-road area can be seen in Appendix A in Fig. 7, which starts from 5:30 and ends at 22:30, the time interval is an hour. Because homogeneous surface have the same thermodynamic characteristics, it can be seen that regions in road area are at almost the same temperature, while regions in non-road area are at other temperature. While at night, road and non-area are still salient in auto scale thermal images. The thermal feature is also salient in heavy rain, as shown in Sect. 4.

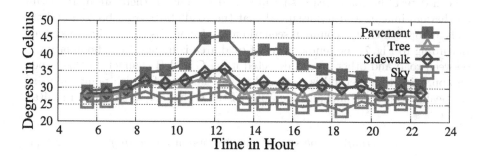

Fig. 2. Temperature-time distribution of road surface on a summer day. Sun rises at 5:40. It rains at 12:30 and then turns cloudy. (Color figure online)

The distribution of temperature of asphalt road can be seen in Fig. 2. The temperature of asphalt road area is higher than non-road area as shown in Figs. 7 and 2. Specific heat of common substances[1] on road can be seen in Table 1. The specific heat of asphalt is higher than brick, thus the temperature of asphalt road is changing stably, as Fig. 7 shows. The road area in auto scale mode image

---

[1] http://www.engineeringtoolbox.com/specific-heat-capacity-d_391.html.

Table 1. Specific heat of common substances on road

Substance	Specific Heat (J/kg°C)
Asphalt	920
Brick	840
Sand	710
Soil, dry	800
Water	4182

is always red. So the auto scale mode is used for road detection. Thus, road detection can also be performed at night with the help of thermal image.

3.2 Rough Detection

In this section, the road rough detection is performed in two steps: adaptive region of interest and road area masking.

Adaptive Region of Interest. The row number of the road vanish point is acquired in this part to adapt the region of interest (ROI). As the color palette of thermal image for this paper is rainbow, the high temperature area is displayed in red and the low temperature area is displayed in blue. Figure 3 shows the RGB channel of thermal image in gray scale. It can be observed that in R channel we can detect the road area easily; in G and B channel, there are more details on thermal image. And it's assumed that the road starts from bottom and the ends at top, which is a common scenario for autonomous driving image system. According to Fig. 7, the temperature of road area is highest. The boundary line between road and other area is detected using G and B channel. In this paper, an approximation method is proposed to get the row of vanish point, by using the peak of the G channel and the valley of the B channel, as shown in Fig. 4(a). Let's set:

$$\gamma(img) := \text{the sum of row vectors on image } img \qquad (1)$$

$$\omega_k(\gamma) := \text{the } k^{\text{th}} \text{ smallest item of } \gamma \qquad (2)$$

$$\Omega_k(\gamma) := \text{the } k^{\text{th}} \text{ largest item of } \gamma \qquad (3)$$

$$\lambda(\omega_k) := \text{the row number of } \omega_k \qquad (4)$$

The approximation algorithm is proposed to find the vanish line. For robustness K rows are picked, which means the sum of row is largest in G channel and lowest in B channel, in G and B channels. The average row number of these K rows will be regarded as the vanish row, as Eq. 5 mentions, and the results and be seen in Fig. 4. The row of vanish point is then used to limit the ROI in R channel for road area masking.

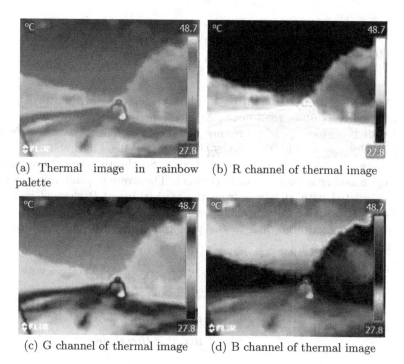

(a) Thermal image in rainbow palette

(b) R channel of thermal image

(c) G channel of thermal image

(d) B channel of thermal image

Fig. 3. Thermal image in rainbow palette, and the RGB channel (Color figure online)

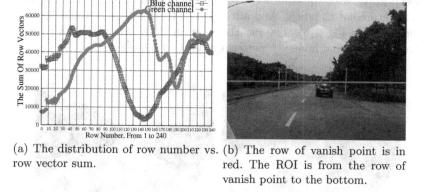

(a) The distribution of row number vs. row vector sum.

(b) The row of vanish point is in red. The ROI is from the row of vanish point to the bottom.

Fig. 4. The distribution of row number vs. the sum of row vectors, and the row of vanish point. (Color figure online)

$$vanish\_row := avg \sum_{i=1}^{2k} (\lambda(\omega_k(\gamma(B\ channel\ img))) + \lambda(\Omega_k(\gamma(G\ channel\ img)))) \tag{5}$$

Road Area Masking. An adaptive threshold is calculated within the adaptive ROI and used to perform road mask. As mentioned above, the road pavement and sidewalk is bottom-up, which means the bottom of image is road and the top of image is sky. And as Fig. 3(b) shows, the gray scale pixel in R channel change sharply between road area and non-road area. So the threshold computation and image masking is perform in R channel. The average pixel value of road area is calculated with all pixels from the vanish line of R channel image to the bottom, as an adaptive threshold, mentioned in Eq. 6. And the road area masking is performed according to the pixels in R channel and the threshold value, mentioned in Eq. 7.

$$Threshold := avg \sum_{i=vanish\_row}^{rows} \sum_{j=0}^{cols} R(i,j) \tag{6}$$

$$mask(i,j) = \begin{cases} 0 & \text{if } R(i,j) < threshold \\ 1 & \text{if } R(i,j) \geq threshold \end{cases} \tag{7}$$

3.3 Road Area Refinement

Only thermal feature based road detection may include some plants and humans around the road. In this section, features in RGB image is taken using the method proposed in [1], with the equation $r := log(\frac{R}{G})$ and $b := log(\frac{B}{G})$ while R, G, B is the standard color channels. And after that, a morphology hole filling step will be performed in Fig. 5(b). The masked area on RGB image is then fused with road area on thermal image to perform road area refinement.

(a) The original image   (b) After green color removal

Fig. 5. Road area masking on RGB image before refinement (Color figure online)

The RGB-thermal feature based road detection method is summed up as Fig. 1.

4   Results

RGB-Thermal Dataset. Our RGB-T image dataset is acquired by a FLIR C2 full-feature thermal imaging camera, with resolution 320×240. There are 70 RGB and corresponding thermal images of various scenes, road types, different illumination conditions, and different weathers. The road area ground truth is manually labeled with Labelme.

To evaluate the performance of road detection, we adopt pixel-wise measurements [13] shown in Table 2 (TN: True Negative, FN: False Negative, FP: False Positive, TP: True Positive) and set the $K = 5$. While processing images taken at night, the road refinement step is not taken for the bad quality of RGB images. Quantitative evaluation are performed using four error measurements: quality $\hat{g}$, precision DR (known as detection rate), recall DA (known as detection accuracy) and effectiveness F. The road detection results is shown in Table 2(b) and Fig. 6. The proposed method performs well with detection rate 94.69% and detection accuracy 92.01% on our RGB-T dataset. It also works well on rainy day in our RGB-T dataset see Fig. 6(c).

Table 2. Pixel-wise measures and performance

(a) Pixel-wise measure entries

		Ground-truth	
		Others	Road
Results Road Others		TN	FN
		FP	TP

(b) Performance on our RGB-T Dataset

Measure	Definition	Performance
Quality	$\hat{g} = \frac{TP}{TP+FP+FN}$	.8750
Precision	$DR = \frac{TP}{TP+FP}$	.9469
Recall	$DA = \frac{TP}{TP+FN}$	.9201
Effectiveness	$F = \frac{2DR \times DA}{DR+DA}$	.9333

Table 3. Frame rate performance on CPU

Platform	CPU model	Frequency	Frame rate
Laptop	Intel i7-4702MQ	2.2 GHz	230
Nvidia TX 1	Cortex-A57	-	55
Raspberry Pi 3	Cortex-A53	1.2 GHz	23

As Fig. 6 shows, our proposed RGB-T feature based road detection algorithm is illumination-robust and works well under shadow Fig. 6(d) and even at night Fig. 6(e). Figure 6(a) and (b) shows the corresponding results running on Kitti-Seg. And the proposed method does not require any landmarks on road surface. Thus, the proposed method can used for urban unmarked road.

The method is measured on three different platforms, i.e., a laptop computer and two embedded devices. The reported frame rates are mean values of

(a) Results of proposed method

(b) Results of Kitti-seg

(c) Proposed method in rain

(d) Proposed method in shadow

(e) Proposed method at night

Fig. 6. Road detection results: the detected road area is in red. (Color figure online)

50 independent runs. The results are shown in Table 3. On the laptop equipped with an Intel i7-4720MQ 2.2 GHz CPU, we can achieve 230 frame per seconds (fps) on average. We also measured our dataset on Nvidia Jetson TX1 and Raspberry Pi 3 and obtained 55 and 23 fps, respectively. These experiments demonstrate the light-weightness of our method and show our method can be applied to real-world ADAS systems.

5   Conclusions

In this paper, we proposed the first RGB-T feature based illumination-robust real-time road detection method. The road area is detected and masked with an adaptive ROI with thermal features, and refined with RGB features. It runs efficiently on low-cost embedded devices, and achieves high accuracy. And it even works well on dusk, and night. The proposed real-time method can be used as image pre-processing for other object detection tasks. It can be easily extent to other homogeneous road surface such as sand or brick.

Acknowledgments. This work was supported by Zhuhai Specially Appointed Scholar Program (No. 67000-42070001).

Appendix

A   Thermal Images In a Day

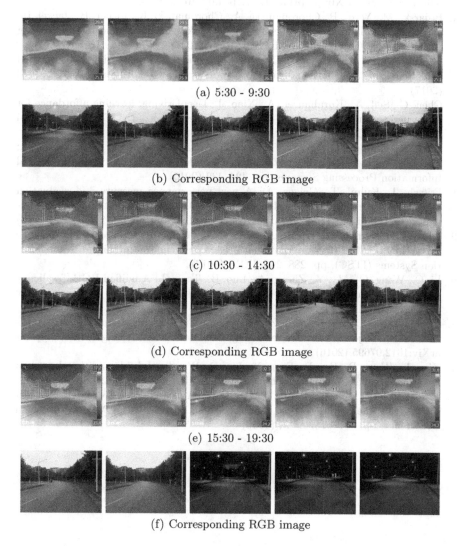

(a) 5:30 - 9:30

(b) Corresponding RGB image

(c) 10:30 - 14:30

(d) Corresponding RGB image

(e) 15:30 - 19:30

(f) Corresponding RGB image

Fig. 7. Thermal images in rainbow color palette and corresponding RGB images from 5:30 to 19:30. (Color figure online)

References

1. Alvarez, J.M.Á., Lopez, A.M.: Road detection based on illuminant invariance. IEEE Trans. Intell. Transp. Syst. **12**(1), 184–193 (2011)
2. Bar Hillel, A., Lerner, R., Levi, D., Raz, G.: Recent progress in road and lane detection: a survey. Mach. Vis. Appl. **25**, 727–745 (2014)
3. Bojarski, M., Del Testa, D., Dworakowski, D., Firner, B., Flepp, B., Goyal, P., Jackel, L.D., Monfort, M., Muller, U., Zhang, J., et al.: End to end learning for self-driving cars. arXiv preprint arXiv:1604.07316 (2016)
4. Bojarski, M., Yeres, P., Choromanska, A., Choromanski, K., Firner, B., Jackel, L., Muller, U.: Explaining how a deep neural network trained with end-to-end learning steers a car. arXiv preprint arXiv:1704.07911 (2017)
5. Caltagirone, L., Scheidegger, S., Svensson, L., Wahde, M.: Fast LiDAR-based road detection using convolutional neural networks. arXiv preprint arXiv:1703.03613 (2017)
6. Chen, C., Seff, A., Kornhauser, A., Xiao, J.: DeepDriving: learning affordance for direct perception in autonomous driving. In: Proceedings of the IEEE International Conference on Computer Vision, pp. 2722–2730 (2015)
7. Chen, X., Kundu, K., Zhu, Y., Berneshawi, A.G., Ma, H., Fidler, S., Urtasun, R.: 3D object proposals for accurate object class detection. In: Advances in Neural Information Processing Systems, pp. 424–432 (2015)
8. Fritsch, J., Kuhnl, T., Geiger, A.: A new performance measure and evaluation benchmark for road detection algorithms. In: 2013 16th International IEEE Conference on Intelligent Transportation Systems-(ITSC), pp. 1693–1700. IEEE (2013)
9. Kühnl, T., Kummert, F., Fritsch, J.: Spatial ray features for real-time ego-lane extraction. In: 2012 15th International IEEE Conference on Intelligent Transportation Systems (ITSC), pp. 288–293. IEEE (2012)
10. Li, C., Wang, G., Ma, Y., Zheng, A., Luo, B., Tang, J.: A unified RGB-T saliency detection benchmark: dataset, baselines, analysis and a novel approach. arXiv preprint arXiv:1701.02829 (2017)
11. Teichmann, M., Weber, M., Zoellner, M., Cipolla, R., Urtasun, R.: Multi-Net: real-time joint semantic reasoning for autonomous driving. arXiv preprint arXiv:1612.07695 (2016)
12. Xiao, L., Wang, R., Dai, B., Fang, Y., Liu, D., Wu, T.: Hybrid conditional random field based camera-LiDAR fusion for road detection. Inf. Sci. **432**, 543–558 (2017)
13. Ying, Z., Li, G., Zang, X., Wang, R., Wang, W.: A novel shadow-free feature extractor for real-time road detection. In: Proceedings of the 2016 ACM on Multimedia Conference, pp. 611–615. ACM (2016)

An Access Point Filtering Method Based on CRLB in Indoor Localization Technology

Qingwei Duan[✉] and Minmin Liu

College of Computer Science, Inner Mongolia University, Hohhot, China
{duanqingwei,liuminmin}@mail.imu.edu.cn

Abstract. With the rapid development of Mobile Internet and the popularity of mobile terminal equipment, demands on the Location-Based Services (LBS), especially the indoor localization are growing. The Access Point (AP) Filtering work is a very critical part in the indoor localization technology. Aiming at the problems which exist in the present AP filtering algorithms which include the low positioning accuracy, the long computation time and the high computational complexity, in this paper, we proposed an AP filtering algorithm based on the Cramer-Rao Lower Bound (CRLB) and Gradient standard. The AP filtering algorithm can effectively remove the APs with large noise to avoid them from negative effect to the results of localization, then to achieve the goals that reducing the calculation complexity in the positioning phase and improving the positioning accuracy. The experiment results show that the AP filtering algorithm proposed in this paper is superior to the traditional AP filtering algorithms in positioning performance, especially, it is applicable to the case of AP number limited and practical public places with multiple APs at the same time.

Keywords: Wi-Fi indoor localization · Fingerprint database
Access Point filtering · Cramer-Rao Lower Bound

1 Introduction

With the rapid development of mobile computing, location-based services have attracted the extensive attention of numerous researchers. All location-based service systems work properly with the premise that precise positioning is completed. At present, the service of outdoor location is mainly based on GPS positioning, but in the dense area or indoor environment, GPS signal transmission is vulnerable to the building blocks, the wall reflection and other interference. The received signal strength (RSS) is greatly attenuated which results in low positioning accuracy, poor positioning results and even making the positioning uncompleted. In recent years, in order to improve the accuracy and stability of the indoor positioning, a large number of indoor positioning technologies based on LBS are emerged in the field, which include RFID [1], Ultrasound [2], Inertial

© Springer Nature Singapore Pte Ltd. 2018
Y. Bi et al. (Eds.): ESTC 2017, CCIS 857, pp. 27–42, 2018.
https://doi.org/10.1007/978-981-13-1026-3_3

Navigation [3,4], Wi-Fi [5,6], and so on. Among these technologies, Wi-Fi fingerprint positioning technology has great prospects and has been unanimously approved by a great many users. Its advantage is to take full advantage of the existing wireless infrastructure without need for additional deployment of hardware equipment to save infrastructure costs. The typical Wi-Fi fingerprint positioning technology is divided into two phases [7], the offline construction phase and the online query phase. In the offline phase, Wi-Fi information from multiple APs is collected at a known geographic location (i.e., a reference node). Each fingerprint is a set of vectors of the RSS from multiple APs, and the set of vectors and their corresponding position coordinates are stored in the location fingerprint database. In the online phase, the mobile user handles the device collects the RSS vectors from APs at the unknown node and uploads the data to the server. The server performs the position resolution algorithm to return the coordinates of the most similar position fingerprint to the client, and displays the coordinates on the client interface ultimately [8].

Wi-Fi fingerprint positioning technology also has some drawbacks, such as the propagating RSS is greatly changed by the object occlusion, multi-path effects [9], reflection and other factors, resulting in the large positioning error and positioning results deviated, so the positioning accuracy and robustness is the key issue in the Wi-Fi fingerprint positioning [10]. A large number of studies have shown that indoor positioning accuracy of existing wireless sensor equipment is high, but its high cost leads to the low applicability. Therefore, we use the RSS information obtained from existing APs to estimate the location of users. The research in this paper mainly focuses on the offline phase which includes filtering APs based on Cramer-Rao Lower Bound criterion, removing APs with unstable RSS, and reducing the number of fingerprints stored in the database, with the purpose of improving the quality of fingerprint database, and improving the accuracy of indoor positioning system while reducing the amount of calculation and the response time of the indoor positioning system.

The rest of this paper is organized as follows. In Sect. 2, we provide a brief description of related work about AP filtering algorithms. In Sect. 3, we discuss the fingerprint acquisition and preprocessing phase before the filtering, and provide much more details about the Access Point filtering algorithm. Section 4 describes our experiments, presents and analyzes the results. Finally, we depict in Sect. 5 the conclusions drawn and prospects for further work.

2   Related Works

The current research on AP filtering algorithms is described as below.

In [11], selecting a number of APs with large signal coverage and strong signal strength, however, since the propagation of wireless signals is susceptible to environmental changes, the RSS fluctuates up and down. Even in the same fixed position, the number of APs covering the same area is also varied, when received RSS from an AP is weaker, the number of samples collected at that location is less; when received RSS from an AP is stronger, the number of samples collected at that location is more, and the higher probability that the AP will appear in the set of received APs used for positioning. So it is possible that selecting APs with the stronger signal strength will reduce the positioning accuracy. In addition, it leads to the adjacent location points to be more difficult to distinguish.

Chen *et al.* [12] proposes a new strategy, by calculating the information gain of the entropy to measure the identification ability of the APs to the location, and select the APs with the larger gain to position. Compared with other access point filtering algorithms with the highest average RSS, the algorithm distinguishes the position by the size of the entropy, and the positioning performance is obviously improved. However, the selecting AP step in this paper is performed during the offline sampling phase and is not associated with the signal acquired in the real-time positioning phase.

Kushki *et al.* [13] proposed that APs can be selected by calculating the dispersion between access points. There are two ways to calculate the dispersion, Bhattacharyya Distance and Information Potential. The Bhattacharyya Distance measures the difference between two probability density functions. The information potential is a non-parametric method of measuring the distance between two probability density functions. When calculating the Bhattacharyya Distance, Kushki uses the Gaussian distribution as the approximate probability distribution of RSS, so only the second order moments of the RSS distribution are needed. But its calculation takes a long time to collect a number of signal strength samples, resulting in poor real-time positioning.

Deng *et al.* [14] proposed a joint AP selection method. This method use the correlation between AP signals, that is, Location nearby, the same AP has the closer RSS, and feature selection of APs is based on maximizing mutual information criterion. However, with the increase of the number of APs and reference points, the computational complexity of mutual information gain of AP sets is also increased, and the computational complexity and the energy consumption are high.

Aiming at the problems in the above research work, the paper we proposes a new AP filtering algorithm. This algorithm analyzes the contribution of each AP to the position by calculating the traces of all the AP fitting surface CRLB matrices at each reference point, and selects the AP with large contribution as the basis for positioning. This algorithm can improve the positioning accuracy, reduce the calculation of the system and shorten the operation time at the same time.

3   The AP Filtering Algorithm

In this section, we discuss the AP filtering algorithm, which includes the fingerprint acquisition and preprocessing, and the description of the AP filtering algorithm.

3.1   The Fingerprint Acquisition and Preprocessing

In the process of fingerprint acquisition and preprocessing, firstly, a plurality of reference points are set in the area to be positioned(rasterization), the reference coordinate system is selected and the coordinate of each reference point is indicated in the coordinate system. Then, the information is collected by using the handled device carried by the users at different reference points, including MAC Address, RSS, Time stamp, and Location Coordinates. At last, collected information is stored into the database [15] to construct a database that represents the relationship between signal strength and position coordinates.

After the acquisition process is completed, the fingerprint information in database will be preprocessed. The preprocessing consists of two steps, namely, the processing of singular points and the calculation of the mean fingerprint information. The processing of the singular points is for a single AP, by calculating the standard deviation of all RSS collected over a period of time, removing the information that the RSS deviates from the normal fluctuation range due to the noise or other interference factors. We use the following methods [16] to remove information during the process, for a single AP: (a) If the standard deviation of the collected RSS is much larger than the mean of the standard deviation for the given position, then remove the data. (b) If the RSS of one location is very different from the RSS of its two adjacent locations, then remove the data. (c) If the two consecutive RSS are very different from the RSS of their two adjacent locations, then that the two RSS are singular points, remove the data. (d) At the boundary of the building, the measured values of RSS drops sharply. If there is a sudden increase in value before descent, the value is considered to be singular and the data is removed. The calculation of the mean value of the fingerprint information is for a single AP. It is to calculate the mean of all the RSS of the APs collected over a period of time, and the calculated mean value is used to replace all the information collected in the time period, thus reducing the amount of fingerprint information in the fingerprint data.

After the fingerprint information preprocessing is completed, the obtained mean value, the corresponding MAC address and location coordinates are stored into the database. The next step is to filter the APs according to the processed fingerprint database.

3.2   The AP Filtering Algorithm

In the process of indoor positioning, the continuous change of AP signal may result in different positioning results in the same test point at the different time, that is, the instability of positioning results. Although we can improve the positioning accuracy by collecting as many APs as possible, but in the complex indoor environment, some APs signal fluctuates, or its establishment of the map with the location is vague, the resolution and judgment of the location can not be provided, so only part of the APs can be used for the actual positioning calculation. With the number of APs increasing, as the number of fingerprint RSS sampling increases, the difficulty to establish the fingerprint database also increases, which leads to the increasing online positioning calculation and poor positioning time. So we need to filter out the appropriate number of APs in a large number of APs for RSS data sampling. The AP filtering algorithm is an important part of the Wi-Fi fingerprint positioning method. Its main purpose is to reduce the input dimension of the RSS data by reducing the number of APs used for positioning and reduce the positioning calculation while maintaining the positioning accuracy.

The AP filtering algorithm proposed in this paper forms the fitting surface according to the position coordinates and signal strength of the same AP received from several neighboring points, calculates the gradient from the fitting surface function, and filters APs preliminary according to the gradient. A plurality of AP combinations are obtained from the selected APs, and the trace of the CRLB matrices of the multiple AP combinations are obtained for each reference point. At last, the AP combinations with small traces are selected for positioning. The algorithm can effectively remove the APs with large noise, reduce the complexity in the calculation positioning phase, and improve the positioning accuracy. This algorithm can select the optimal combination of APs when the number of APs is limited, consider the correlation between the different APs for position discrimination, and take the optimal AP combination at each location point to consider the whole positioning area.

First, the formation of fitting surface is introduced. The position coordinates of each reference point obtained in the offline stage are discrete. After the position coordinates are continuous, the fitting function between the signal strength X and the position coordinates is obtained, and fitting function includes interpolation fitting, non-parametric fitting and polynomial fitting. The experiment results show that the surface formed by the polynomial fitting is the most closest to the realistic condition, so we get the following fitting function between X and (u_1, u_2).

$$X(u_1, u_2) = \alpha_0 + \alpha_1 u_1 + \alpha_2 u_2 + \alpha_3 u_1^2 + \alpha_4 u_2^2 + \alpha_5 u_1 u_2 \qquad (1)$$

The formula contains six parameters, which are $(\alpha_0, \alpha_1, \alpha_2, \alpha_3, \alpha_4, \alpha_5)$, therefore, we select the data of the six reference points with the smallest distance from the current reference point to fit the surface and solve the surface equation. A fitting surface of an AP is showed as Fig. 1.

Followed by the introduction of AP filtering, we use 6 APs as an example. AP filtering includes two steps. The first step, the gradient of the surface fitting function is calculated according to the formula (2) for a rough AP filtering work. The module of the fitting surface gradient is calculated according to formula (3) and the 15 APs with the largest gradient module are selected.

$$L = \frac{\partial X(u_1, u_2)}{\partial u_1} \vec{i} + \frac{\partial X(u_1, u_2)}{\partial u_2} \vec{j} \qquad (2)$$

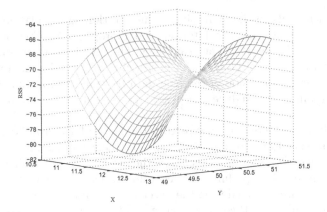

Fig. 1. A fitting surface of an AP.

$$S = \sqrt{(\frac{\partial X(u_1, u_2)}{\partial u_1})^2 + (\frac{\partial X(u_1, u_2)}{\partial u_2})^2} \tag{3}$$

The second step, 15 APs selected for each reference point are arranged in combination, and 6 APs are selected to calculate the CRLB matrix of these 6 APs. The traces of the CRLB matrix are obtained, and the 6 APs with the smallest traces are the APs used by the current reference point. The smaller the trace of the CRLB matrix of the APs, the better the positioning performance of the APs used, the greater the contribution the APs made to the position, and the more obvious distinction is. Finally, the optimal 6 APs selected from each reference point are taken together to represent the APs used by all reference points in the area. The calculation of the trace of the APs' CRLB matrix at each reference point is as follows.

The CRLB matrix of the AP combination is calculated first, as is followed

$$Fim(u) = I(u) = \frac{1}{\sigma^2} \cdot \frac{\partial M^T(u)}{\partial u} \cdot \frac{\partial M(u)}{\partial u} \tag{4}$$

In formular (4), u represents the position coordinates, $u = (u_1, u_2)$; σ represents the standard deviation; M(u) is the mean of the values of the multiple $X(u_1, u_2)$ functions in formular (1). In general, CRLB is the lowest bound of the unbiased estimate variance, so the obtained CRLB is the lowest bound of the positioning accuracy error. However, in the AP filtering algorithm proposed in this paper, the $Fim(u)$ is a matrix because $u = (u_1, u_2)$ represents the set of position coordinates, and the matrices can not be compared, so we use the trace of the matrix to measure the size of the AP contribution, and the trace of the matrix is used as the lowest bound of the positioning accuracy error. The trace of the matrix is obtained from the following calculation.

$$\frac{\partial M^T(u)}{\partial u} \cdot \frac{\partial M(u)}{\partial u}$$

(5)

$$= \begin{bmatrix} \frac{\partial M^T(u)}{\partial u_1} \\ \frac{\partial M^T(u)}{\partial u_2} \end{bmatrix} \cdot \begin{bmatrix} \frac{\partial M(u)}{\partial u_1} & \frac{\partial M(u)}{\partial u_2} \end{bmatrix}$$

$$\begin{bmatrix} \frac{\partial M^T(u)}{\partial u_1} \\ \frac{\partial M^T(u)}{\partial u_2} \end{bmatrix} \cdot \begin{bmatrix} \frac{\partial M(u)}{\partial u_1} & \frac{\partial M(u)}{\partial u_2} \end{bmatrix}$$

(6)

$$= \begin{bmatrix} \frac{\partial M^T(u)}{\partial u_1} \cdot \frac{\partial M(u)}{\partial u_1} & \frac{\partial M^T(u)}{\partial u_1} \cdot \frac{\partial M(u)}{\partial u_2} \\ \frac{\partial M^T(u)}{\partial u_2} \cdot \frac{\partial M(u)}{\partial u_1} & \frac{\partial M^T(u)}{\partial u_2} \cdot \frac{\partial M(u)}{\partial u_2} \end{bmatrix}$$

$$\begin{bmatrix} \frac{\partial M^T(u)}{\partial u_1} \cdot \frac{\partial M(u)}{\partial u_1} & \frac{\partial M^T(u)}{\partial u_1} \cdot \frac{\partial M(u)}{\partial u_2} \\ \frac{\partial M^T(u)}{\partial u_2} \cdot \frac{\partial M(u)}{\partial u_1} & \frac{\partial M^T(u)}{\partial u_2} \cdot \frac{\partial M(u)}{\partial u_2} \end{bmatrix}$$

(7)

$$= \begin{bmatrix} \sum_i (\frac{\partial m_i(u)}{\partial u_1})^2 & \sum_i \frac{\partial m_i(u)}{\partial u_1} \cdot \frac{\partial m_i(u)}{\partial u_2} \\ \sum_i \frac{\partial m_i(u)}{\partial u_2} \cdot \frac{\partial m_i(u)}{\partial u_1} & \sum_i (\frac{\partial m_i(u)}{\partial u_2})^2 \end{bmatrix}$$

$$\begin{bmatrix} \sum_i (\frac{\partial m_i(u)}{\partial u_1})^2 & \sum_i \frac{\partial m_i(u)}{\partial u_1} \cdot \frac{\partial m_i(u)}{\partial u_2} \\ \sum_i \frac{\partial m_i(u)}{\partial u_2} \cdot \frac{\partial m_i(u)}{\partial u_1} & \sum_i (\frac{\partial m_i(u)}{\partial u_2})^2 \end{bmatrix}$$

$$= \sum_i \begin{bmatrix} m_{i1}^2 & m_{i1} \cdot m_{i2} \\ m_{i2} \cdot m_{i1} & m_{i2}^2 \end{bmatrix},$$

(8)

$$m_{i1} = \frac{\partial m_i(u)}{\partial u_1}, m_{i2} = \frac{\partial m_i(u)}{\partial u_2}$$

$$I(u)^{-1} = \sigma^2 \cdot \left\{ \sum_i \begin{bmatrix} m_{i1}^2 & m_{i1} \cdot m_{i2} \\ m_{i2} \cdot m_{i1} & m_{i2}^2 \end{bmatrix} \right\}^{-1}$$

(9)

$$Tr(\frac{1}{\sigma^2}I(u)^{-1}) = \frac{\sum_i (m_{i1}^2 + m_{i2}^2)}{\sum_i m_{i1}^2 \cdot \sum_i m_{i2}^2 - (\sum_i m_{i1} \cdot m_{i2})^2} \tag{10}$$

4 Experiments

In our experiments, the AP filtering algorithm based on Maximum Mean value (MM), the Random AP filtering algorithm and the AP filtering algorithm based on CRLB and gradient proposed in this paper are used as AP filtering algorithms, and the deterministic algorithms are used as the location solution algorithm to obtain the positioning results. In this section, we introduce the experimental setup, present and analyze the results, and draw the conclusions.

4.1 Experimental Setup

The experimental environment of this paper is the third floor of the computer academy of the Inner Mongolia University, the environmental structure of this floor is shown in Fig. 2. The room 316 in Fig. 2 is selected for experimental verification, as shown in Fig. 5. The room size is about $78\,\mathrm{m}^2$ ($13.5\,\mathrm{m}$ long, $6.0\,\mathrm{m}$ wide), which evenly deployed 78 reference points (RP), 40 random test points (TP), as shown in Fig. 6, black points for the RP, red points for the TP, and the acquisition interval is 1m. The collected time for each reference point is 5 min, the refresh rate of the handled device is 1s, RSS data from about 40 APs can be received in each collected time period, and the RSS reference for RP is the average of the data collected from 1: 00–3: 00 in one week. The TPs were also collected at 1: 00–3: 00, and 10 sets of data were collected at each TP, each containing RSS data of approximately 25 APs.

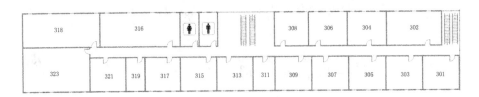

Fig. 2. Floor environmental structure.

We use the Red Note2 phone as the handled device [17, 18], the Wi-Fi information from multiple APs is displayed by the device as shown in Fig. 3 below, and the display interface of the data acquisition process is shown in Fig. 4 below.

Fig. 3. The Wi-Fi information from multiple APs.

Fig. 4. The display interface of the data acquisition Process.

4.2 Experimental Results

Each of the TP in Fig. 6 performs data collection according to the method described in Experiments Setup Section. After the data collection of the TPs is completed, the AP filtering algorithm based on Maximum Mean value (MM),

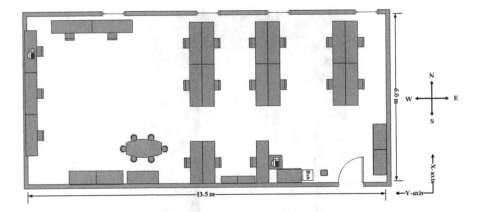

Fig. 5. The layout of experimental scene.

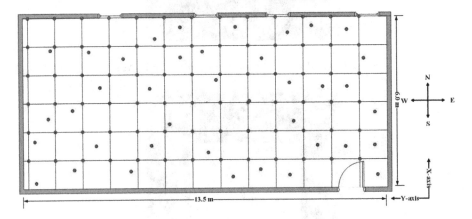

Fig. 6. The layout of reference Node and Test Node. (Color figure online)

Random AP filtering algorithm and the AP filtering algorithm based on CRLB and gradient proposed in this paper are used to select AP sample data, then the selected AP sample data is input to the position resolution algorithm to obtain the position coordinates. For the 40 TPs, the average of the error and the mean of the 10 sets of sample data on each TP represents the average error of this TP.

The Effect of the AP Number on the Positioning Accuracy. From the optional test point in Fig. 6, three different algorithms are used to filter the APs, and the number of AP is 1 to 25. After the AP filtering is completed, the WKNN (K = 5) [19] matching algorithm in the deterministic algorithms is used as the location solution algorithm to obtain the positioning results. This experiment verifies the effect of different numbers of AP on positioning accuracy, and the positioning accuracy is measured by the probability that the positioning results fall within 2 m of the distance from the TP, results are shown in Fig. 7.

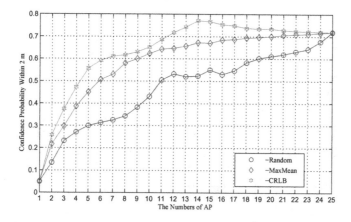

Fig. 7. The relationship between AP number and positioning error.

From the Fig. 7, we can draw the following two conclusions. The first one is that the AP filtering algorithm proposed in this paper has the highest positioning accuracy. When the number of APs is 14, the probability of falling within 2 m from the TP is the highest, which is 78.5%. When the number of APs is 1 to 14, the positioning accuracy increases with the increase of the number of APs, and our algorithm is the fastest one to achieve the highest positioning accuracy. When the number of APs is 14 to 25, the positioning accuracy decreases with the inclusion of some noise APs, but still higher than the other two algorithms. From the above results, we can see that with our algorithm, using the minimum number of APs can achieve the highest positioning accuracy. The second one is that when the number of APs is small, the accuracy of our algorithm is significantly higher than that of the other two algorithms, therefore, it is applicable to the case where the number of APs is limited. When the number of APs is large, our algorithm is also being applicable to the public places with a large number of APs.

The Effect of Different Filtering Algorithms on the Positioning Accuracy When the Number of APs Is Constant. In this experiment, three AP combinations selected by three AP filtering algorithms in experiment 1) were used, each combination includes 6 APs, and the distance from the TP coordinates is changed from 2 m to 1m to 10 m interval. After the AP filtering is completed, the WKNN (K = 5) matching algorithm in the deterministic algorithms is used as the positioning solution algorithm to obtain the positioning results. When the number of APs is constant, the cumulative probability distributions of the three AP combinations are shown in Fig. 8. As shown in Fig. 8, the point (2, 0.6), indicating that when the number of APs is 6, the probability of positioning falls within 2 m of the TP coordinates is 0.6.

The specific data of Fig. 8 is shown in Table 1, and from Fig. 8 and Table 1, we can get that he probabilities of 1 m, 2 m, 3 m, 4 m of our algorithm were 17.4%, 59.7%, 83.1% and 90.3%, respectively, which were significantly higher

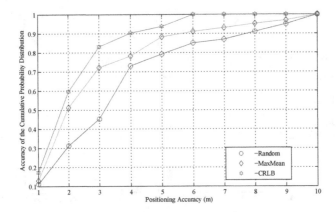

Fig. 8. The cumulative probability distribution of positioning accuracy under optimal AP set.

Table 1. The cumulative probability of positioning accuracy in 1 m to 4 m interval

Error (m)	Random	MaxMean	CRLB
	Probability (%)	Probability (%)	Probability (%)
1 m	11.2	13.1	17.4
2 m	31.3	51.3	59.7
3 m	45.3	72.2	83.1
4 m	73.1	78.2	90.3

than those of the other AP filtering algorithms. The results were higher than those of Random algorithm (6.2%, 28.4%, 37.8% and 17.2%), and higher than those of MM algorithm(4.3%, 8.4%, 10.9% and 12.1%). This indicates that our algorithm is more favorable than other algorithms to reduce the positioning error (error within 5 m). And our algorithm results in the localization of the probability of falling within 3 m to 83.3%, and the other two algorithms have to reach this probability for a range of 6–8 m, so our algorithm has a smaller positioning error range and higher positioning accuracy.

Comparison of Positioning Errors of the Same Positioning Solution Algorithm with Different Filtering Algorithms When the AP Number Is Constant. In this experiment, three AP combinations selected by three AP filtering algorithms in experiment 1) were used, each combination includes 6 APs. After the AP filtering is completed, the WKNN (K = 5) matching algorithm in the deterministic algorithms is used as the positioning solution algorithm to obtain the positioning results. Then we calculate the maximum error, minimum error, and average error for four sets of positioning data obtained by the three

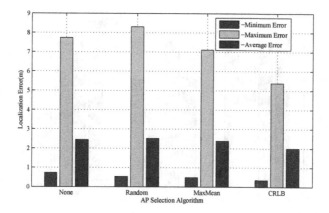

Fig. 9. Comparison of the maximum, minimum and mean positioning errors of multiple AP options.

AP combinations, plus a set of positioning data that has not been processed by any AP. The results are shown in Fig. 9.

From Fig. 9 we can get that the maximum error, minimum error, and average error of our algorithm are lower than the other AP filtering algorithms, and the range of the positioning error is much smaller than the other algorithms. The error range of our algorithm is 0.35 to 5.38 m, and the error range of None, Random and MM is 0.73 m to 7.73 m, 0.53 m to 8.3 m and 0.48 m to 7.1 m respectively. The average positioning error of our algorithm is 2.01 m, which is 17.4%, 19.9% and 15.7% lower than that of None, Random and MM algorithms respectively.

Comparison of Average Positioning Errors of Different Positioning Solution Algorithms with Different Filtering Algorithms When the AP Number Is Constant. In this experiment, three AP combinations selected by three AP filtering algorithms in experiment 1) were used, each combination includes 6 APs. After the AP filtering is completed, the NN, KNN and WKNN (K = 5) matching algorithms in the deterministic algorithms are used as the positioning solution algorithms to obtain the positioning results. Then we calculate the average errors for four sets of positioning data obtained by the three AP combinations, plus a set of positioning data that has not been processed by any AP. The results are shown in Fig. 10 below.

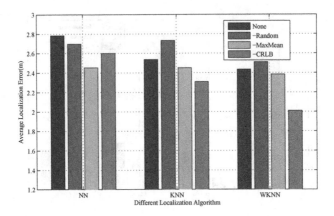

Fig. 10. The Multiple AP Selection Algorithms are compared with various Positioning Algorithms.

Table 2. The comparison of average localization error using various positioning algorithms

Algorithms	NN	KNN	WKNN
	Error (m)	Error (m)	Error (m)
None	2.7846	2.5361	2.4342
Random	2.6965	2.7325	2.5094
MaxMean	2.4535	2.4502	2.3837
CRLB	2.5998	2.3083	2.0111

The specific data of Fig. 10 is shown in Table 2, and from Fig. 10 and Table 2, we can get that the average error is the smallest when the AP algorithm proposed in this paper and the WKNN position matching algorithm are used simultaneously. We can also get that the error of our algorithm proposed in this paper is higher than that of the MaxMean algorithm, it may be due to the influence of other environmental factors, handled devices or human factors.

4.3   Experimental Conclusions

The experimental results in Figs. 7, 8, 9 and 10 show that the AP filtering algorithm based on CRLB criterion is superior to the other two AP filtering algorithms in terms of positioning accuracy and positioning error range. Figure 11 shows the results of the 40 sets of true positions and estimated positions, and the positioning results of the estimated locations are obtained by the AP algorithm proposed in this paper and the WKNN position matching algorithm. We can get the conclusion that using the AP filtering algorithm proposed in this paper, the average error interval of the area to be positioned is within 2 m. So our algorithm can achieve the highest positioning accuracy, reduce the data input dimension

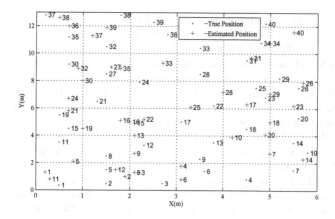

Fig. 11. Comparing with the true position and the estimated position.

and the amount of data calculation, avoid the dimension of disaster to a certain extent, and improve the efficiency of the algorithm in the meantime.

5   Conclusion

The AP filtering algorithm proposed in this paper performs a random combination according to the different degree of contribution from different APs on the location to filter out the APs used for the positioning. The AP filtering algorithm can effectively remove the APs with large noise, reduce the calculation complexity in the positioning phase, and improve the positioning accuracy. Compared with the traditional MM and Random AP filtering algorithms, the AP filtering algorithm proposed in this paper is superior to other algorithms in positioning performance, and especially applicable for the case of limited number of APs and actual public places with large number of APs. The next step is to increase the indicators of AP filtering, combine the RSS data with other data from sensors, such as barometer, geomagnetism, etc., and choose the APs with greater contributions. We can also minimize the fluctuation of signal strength due to environmental impact, and improve the positioning accuracy further.

Acknowledgment. This work is supported by the National Natural Science Foundation of China (Grant No. 61461037), and the Natural Science Foundation of Inner Mongolia Autonomous Region of China under Grant 2017JQ09.

References

1. Wang, J., Katabi, D.: Dude, where's my card?: RFID positioning that works with multipath and non-line of sight. In: ACM SIGCOMM. Conference on SIGCOMM 2013, pp. 51–62 (2013)

2. Nandakumar, R., Chintalapudi, K.K., Padmanabhan, V.N.: Centaur: locating devices in an office environment. In: International Conference on Mobile Computing and NETWORKING 2012, pp. 281–292 (2012)
3. Rai, A., Chintalapudi, K.K., Padmanabhan, V.N., Sen, R.: Zee:zero-effort crowdsourcing for indoor localization, pp. 293–304 (2012)
4. Huang, B., Qi, G., Yang, X., Zhao, L., Zou, H.: Exploiting cyclic features of walking for pedestrian dead reckoning with unconstrained smartphones. In: ACM International Joint Conference, pp. 374–385 (2016)
5. Yang, Z., Wu, C., Liu, Y.: Locating in fingerprint space: wireless indoor localization with little human intervention. In: International Conference on Mobile Computing and NETWORKING, pp. 269–280 (2012)
6. Abdellatif, M., Mtibaa, A., Harras, K.A., Youssef, M.: GreenLoc: an energy efficient architecture for WiFi-based indoor localization on mobile phones. In: IEEE International Conference on Communications, pp. 4425–4430 (2013)
7. Krishnakumar, A.S., Krishnan, P.: The theory and practice of signal strength-based location estimation. In: International Conference on Collaborative Computing: Networking, Applications and Worksharing, pp. 10–11 (2005)
8. Alawi, R.A.: RSSI based location estimation in wireless sensors networks. In: IEEE International Conference on Networks, pp. 118–122 (2012)
9. Zou, H., Huang, B., Lu, X., Jiang, H., Xie, L.: Standardizing location fingerprints across heterogeneous mobile devices for indoor localization. In: Wireless Communications and NETWORKING Conference (2016)
10. Kjargaard, M.B.: A taxonomy for radio location fingerprinting. In: International Symposium on Location- and Context-Awareness, pp. 139–156 (2007)
11. Youssef, M.A., Agrawala, A., Udaya Shankar, A.: WLAN location determination via clustering and probability distributions. In: IEEE International Conference on Pervasive Computing and Communications, pp. 143–150 (2003)
12. Chen, Y., Yang, Q., Yin, J., Chai, X.: Power-efficient accesspoint selection for indoor location estimation. IEEE Trans. Knowl. Data Eng. **18**(7), 877–888 (2006)
13. Kushki, A., Plataniotis, K.N., Venetsanopoulos, A.N.: Kernel-based positioning in wireless local area networks. IEEE Trans. Mob. Comput. **6**(6), 689–705 (2007)
14. Deng, Z.A., Lin, M.A., Yu-Bin, X.U.: Spatially localized and joint access point selection for WI-FI indoor positioning. J. Harbin Inst. Technol. **19**(6), 27–33 (2012)
15. Zou, H., Zhou, Y., Jiang, H., Huang, B., Xie, L., Spanos, C.: A transfer kernel learning based strategy for adaptive localization in dynamic indoor environments: poster. In: Wireless Communications and NETWORKING Conference, pp. 462–464 (2017)
16. Location fingerprint algorithm based on Wi-Fi indoor positioning. Industrial Control Computer (2015)
17. Qi, G., Huang, B.: Walking detection using the gyroscope of an unconstrained smartphone. In: International Conference on Communications and Networking in China, pp. 539–548 (2016)
18. Zou, H., Huang, B., Lu, X., Jiang, H., Xie, L.: A robust indoor positioning system based on the procrustes analysis and weighted extreme learning machine. IEEE Trans. Wireless Commun. **15**(2), 1252–1266 (2016)
19. Zhao, H., Huang, B., Jia, B.: Applying kriging interpolation for WiFi fingerprinting based indoor positioning systems. In: Wireless Communications and NETWORKING Conference (2016)

A Computationally Efficient Solution for LiDAR-Based Obstacle Detection in Autonomous Driving

Shengjie Chen[1,2], Rihui Song[1,2], Shixiong Chen[1], Wenjun Li[1,2], and Kai Huang[1,2(✉)]

[1] School of Data and Computer Science, Sun Yat-sen University, Guangzhou, China
huangk36@mail.sysu.edu.cn
[2] Key Laboratory of Machine Intelligence and Advanced Computing,
Sun Yat-sen University, Ministry of Education, Guangzhou, China
http://sdcs.sysu.edu.cn/

Abstract. Precise perception is essential for autonomous driving, where obstacle detection is a very important part. The vision-based approaches are susceptible to light, and other commonly used sensors in autonomous driving such as millimeter-ware radars are not satisfied in distance and range, while the LiDAR (Light Detection and Ranging) has strong adaptability to the environment, becoming a standard sensor on an autonomous vehicle. In this paper, we propose a computationally efficient obstacle detection method based on Velodyne HDL-32E, a 3D LiDAR which can generates 700,000 points per second. To overcome this challenge from such huge amount of data, dimensionality reduction through the projection is introduced, combined with efficient and highly available detection methods, to meet the accuracy as well as real-time requirements. Experiments show that our obstacle detection method can meet the real-time requirement on the vehicle devices with limited resources and provide reliable obstacles information for our autonomous driving vehicle.

Keywords: LiDAR · Cartesian/polar projection model
Obstacle detection · Autonomous driving

1 Introduction

This paper presents a computationally efficient solution for obstacle detection using 3D LiDAR data. Obstacle detection is a critical pre-processing step in a number of autonomous perception tasks. Douillard et al. [1] made a good summary of methods based on 3D point clouds' grid-based statistical characteristics. Mean elevation can be chosen as the basis for the ground extraction from 3D LiDAR data but it cannot capture overhanging structures. While Min-Max elevation, proposing by bias between maximum and minimum height, can be chosen as the basis for the obstacle detection, but sensitive to noise.

© Springer Nature Singapore Pte Ltd. 2018
Y. Bi et al. (Eds.): ESTC 2017, CCIS 857, pp. 43–62, 2018.
https://doi.org/10.1007/978-981-13-1026-3_4

Some other methods based on 3D point clouds' geometric features were introduced in the past several years. Line-fit ground plane segmentation was put forth by Himmelsbach et al. [2]. They treated the point clouds in polar model, instead of cartesian model mentioned above, and took advantage of the distribution of the points. On the other hand, a typical plane-fit technique was introduced from Zermas et al. [3] for the fast extraction of the ground points.

Recently, some deep learning techniques are applying to LiDAR-based detection tasks. BoLi used a single 2D end-to-end fully convolutional network, taking LiDAR bird view as input, to detect vehicle, leading to an excellent performance [4], followed by his new approach using 3D end-to-end fully convolutional network [5]. Chen et al. [6] proposed a Multi-View 3D object detection network (MV3D) which takes multimodal data, both LIDAR point cloud and RGB images as input, and predicts the full 3D extent of objects in 3D space.

All state-of-art obstacle detection methods using 3D LiDAR data mentioned so far, some cannot reach the real-time requirements even offline testing, some lack of challenges from online testing. Besides, most of them only consider about features in current scan, ignoring features in historical scans. With work presented in this paper, we put forward a computationally efficient solution for obstacle detection using 3D LiDAR data. In order to pull up the detection accuracy, we do fuse the results from historical scans. Experiments have been conducted to find the effect of two kinds of projection, both cartesian model and polar model, and several kinds of grid size, from small to large, on our approach. Optimal projection as well as grid size has been applied to our autonomous driving vehicle. Over 2,000 miles of road test shows that our obstacle detection approach is highly available for autonomous driving.

The remainder of the paper is organized as follows. We give a detailed description of our approach in Sects. 2 and 3, from obstacle detection in current scan to fusion with historical detection results. In Sect. 4 we provide experimental results and conclude the paper in Sect. 5.

2   Current Scan Processing

To meet the accuracy as well as real-time requirements, both spatial and temporal features of point clouds are considered. In spatial features, we need to put forth an efficient detection method in current scan processing.

2.1   Dimensionality Reduction Through the Projection

Formally, current scan at time t will be denoted by an unordered set $P_t = \{p_1, p_2, ..., p_{N_t}\}$ with 3D points $p_i = (x_i, y_i, z_i)$ given by LiDAR's cartesian coordinate and the number of points, N_t, in current scan.

For a greater flexibility in controlling the run-time of the algorithm, we project each 3D point p_i into corresponding grid cell in Cartesian Model or Polar Model. Thus, the complexity of our obstacle detection approach will not depend on the size of the point clouds, but our selected parameters.

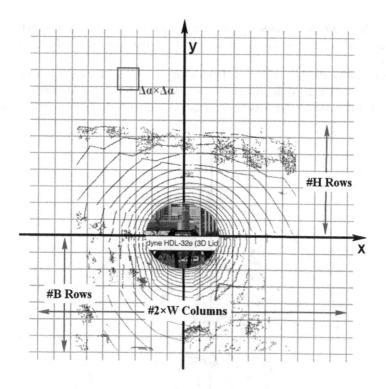

Fig. 1. Cartesian model projection

Cartesian Model Projection. This Cartesian Model projection has been applied in many grid-based segmentation since Stanley, an autonomous car from Standford, that utilized this strategy to build his 2D terrain occupancy map and won the DARPA Grand Challenge in 2005 [7]. As shown in Fig. 1, the xy-plane is divided into number of $\Delta\alpha \times \Delta\alpha$ squares, with number of front rows $H(ead)$, number of rear rows $B(ack)$, number of columns on both sides $2 \times W(idth)$ and W columns for each side.

H, B, W are configured for the focus field of view, influenced by navigation planner, like maximum control speed, etc. The focus field of view is $-W\Delta\alpha \leq x \leq W\Delta\alpha$, $-B\Delta\alpha \leq y \leq H\Delta\alpha$.

Given a 3D points $p_i = (x_i, y_i, z_i)$, the corresponding grid cell is (x_{idx}, y_{idx}), where,

$$x_{idx} = \frac{W\Delta\alpha - x_i}{\Delta\alpha}; \tag{1}$$

$$y_{idx} = \frac{y_i}{\Delta\alpha} + B, \tag{2}$$

from the lower left to the upper right.

Polar Model Projection. As shown in Fig. 2, the grid size is different, with inner ones smaller than outer ones. By contract, the Cartesian Model shares the same grid size.

The Polar Model is closer to LiDAR's physical model, and it treats distant and near objects with different resolution while reducing computations. Using smaller grid size, this Polar Model can capture close obstacles even little objects.

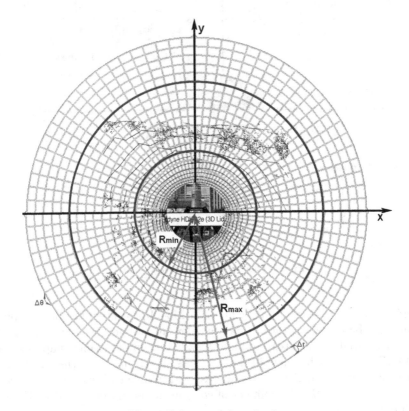

Fig. 2. Polar model projection

As shown in Fig. 2, the xy-plane is represented as a circle of radius between R_{min} and R_{max}, the focus field of view. You can even only care about the forward vision, $[-10°, 190°]$ in polar coordinate, or we say a 200° perspective. We introduce parameter $\Delta\theta$ to describe the angle one segment covers, so we come up with $M = \frac{2\pi}{\Delta\theta}$ segments. The index to a segment that a point $p_i = (x_i, y_i, z_i)$ maps to is,

$$segment_{idx} = \frac{atan2(y_i, x_i)}{\Delta\theta}. \tag{3}$$

Besides, we introduce parameter Δr to describe the radius one bin covers, also come up with $B = \frac{R_{max} - R_{min}}{\Delta r}$ bins. The index to its corresponding bin is,

$$
bin_{idx} = \begin{cases} \frac{\sqrt{x_i^2 + y_i^2} - R_{min}}{\Delta r}, & R_{min} \leq \sqrt{x_i^2 + y_i^2} \leq R_{max} \\ not\ exists, & otherwise \end{cases} \tag{4}
$$

By these two models projection mentioned above, the LiDAR's 3D point clouds are dimensionally reducted to $2\frac{1}{2}$D, with $\frac{1}{2}$ representing for following statistical features.

2.2 Obstacle Detection Based on Hybrid Statistical Features

Our obstacle detection approach consists of following three steps: firstly remove ground points; next, non-ground points are used to capture obstacles; last, some overhanging obstacles, which our autonomous vehicle can pass through, should be excluded.

Remove Ground Points. Points that belong to the ground surface constitute the majority of the point clouds and their removal significantly reduces the number of points involved in the proceeding computations.

After projection using Cartesian Model or Polar Model, statistical features in each grid cell such as elevation mean, elevation standard deviation, elevation variance, elevation Min-Max deviation are calculated. We use a simple but efficient way, the vertical mean, to extract the ground plane for removing ground points. Outliers should be eliminated as following way: where there are $N_{(x_{idx}, y_{idx})}$ points in grid (x_{idx}, y_{idx}) with maximum elevation z_{max}, minimum elevation z_{min}, its vertical mean is,

$$
z_{mean} = \frac{(\sum_{j=0}^{N_{(x_{idx}, y_{idx})} - 1} z_j) - z_{max} - z_{min}}{N_{(x_{idx}, y_{idx})} - 2} \tag{5}
$$

In common road scene, road curbs are little obstacles compared with cones, street lights, fences, greenbelt, street trees and so on. The typical height for road curbs is from 5 cm to 10 cm [8] and we use a critical vertical mean threshold $\delta = 5$ (cm) to avoid false positives but remove great majority of ground points.

Capture Obstacles. The Min-Max vertical distance is a widely used feature in many LiDAR-based segmentation tasks, like [1,2,7,9,10]. Similar to them, the maximum absolute difference in z coordinate of all points falling into the respective grid cell is calculated and a vertical distance threshold $\sigma = 10$ (cm) works well in our road scenarios. In addition, as mentioned above, z_{max} or z_{min} which has a large bias from the z_{mean} should be eliminated.

Fig. 3. The autonomous vehicle from Sun Yat-sen University, China

Exclude Overhanging Obstacles. Street trees are seen everywhere inside the campus and they always grow over the road. Some other overhanging structures like an open-style door, overbridge and so on that our autonomous vehicle can pass through and these should not be captured as obstacles using Min-Max feature.

Our autonomous vehicle (Fig. 3) is $H_v = 172$ (cm) high, hence point clouds referred to higher objects can be ignored. We count the point clouds $\{p_i \in P|\ \delta \leq z_i \leq H_v\}$ and calculate the proportion of P for each grid cell,

$$\phi(x_{idx}, y_{idx}) = \frac{|P|}{N_{(x_{idx}, y_{idx})}}, \qquad (6)$$

and 78% works well in our road scenarios.

3   Multi-scan Fusion

3.1   Historical Pose Transformation

For fusing historical scans, what have to do first is to transform those historical scans to current LiDAR base. Since the LiDAR scanner is mounted on our autonomous vehicle, the physical constraints like momentum are bound to the vehicle odometry.

Before transformation, we analyze the LiDAR data offline. The data was captured when the vehicle was driven at 20 kph or slower. Because the highest speed for our autonomous vehicle is 20 kph in auto mode. Using ICP (Iterative Closest Point)[11] algorithm to calculate the RT (Rotation matrix and Translation vector) from the current scan to the previous scan, we found that the rotation matrix are approximately equal to unit matrix and the translation vector are approximately equal to zero vector. "Approximately equal to" means that the differences between elements which are in the same position of matrix (or vector) are less than $1e-5$.

Since the difference is little, the points from the current scan and the previous scan which can be matched will be projected into the same grid cell, which means the historical pose transform can be ignored. For example, *Point a* is one point of the current scan and it is projected into grid cell A. *Point a'* is a point of previous scan and it is the point matches to *Point a* which means *Point a'* is very close to *Point a*. *Point a'* will be projected into grid cell A as we expected.

The validation of this hypothesis depends on the low speed of our autonomous vehicle (less than 20 kph) and high frequency of LiDAR (10 Hz). In other words, If the speed of vehicle is high, this hypothesis will be wrong.

3.2   Current-Historical Scans Fusion

Although there is little difference between two scans as we have discussed above, we can not fuse too many scans together. If we do, the differences between each two scans will product together and then it will become too large to be ignored. So we only fuse three scans: the current scan and two previous scans together.

Since the frequency of LiDAR is 10 Hz, LiDAR will output one scan every 0.1 s. Numbering the scan in order, we get a sequence of scans. And then use a sliding window with size three to select the data we want to fuse together, as shown in Fig. 4.

Processing strategy	Input	Output
Current-scan processing	1	1
	1 2	2
Multi-scan fusion	1 2 3	3
	1 2 3 4	4
	1 2 3 4 5	5
	...	...

Fig. 4. Multi-scan fusion using sliding window with size 3

For each scan, we firstly apply current scan processing to it, and store the 0–1 occupancy grid map. And then merge three 0–1 occupancy grid maps to get one probability occupancy grid map as following:

$$grid^t_{(x_{idx}, y_{idx})} = \sum_{i=1}^{3} \Omega_i \cdot grid^{t-i}_{(x_{idx}, y_{idx})}, \tag{7}$$

giving more accurate obstacles information for path planning.

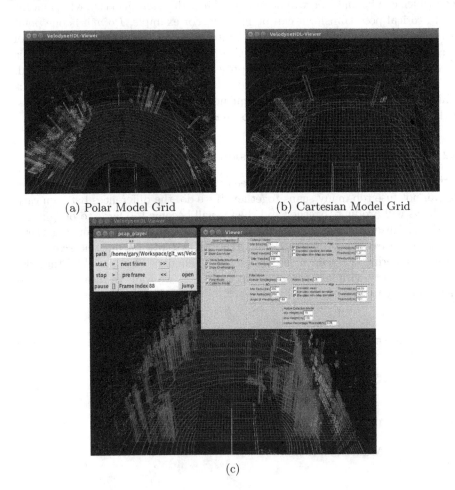

(a) Polar Model Grid   (b) Cartesian Model Grid

(c)

Fig. 5. *(a)* *(b)* is grid visualization of corresponding cell size for either model. grid of detection area is used for verification with ground truth. *(c)* is our visualization tool with algorithm configuration panel and replay tool. With *red* for obstacles higher than LiDAR, *green* for obstacles lower than LiDAR; *blues* are overhanging obstacles. (Color figure online)

4   Experiments

We analyze several typical scenarios offline to learn about the impact on different grid size in either projection model. Some available sizes are chosen in further online test and we analyze the detecting time inside both on our vehicle ECU (Electronic Control Unit) and raspberry pi 3. So far, over 2,000 miles of road tests for our autonomous vehicle also verify that approaches mentioned above can efficiently detect obstacles with high availability.

4.1   Offline Multi-scenarios Analysis

In this paper, we implement both models of projection and compare their detection results in following scenarios using different grid size. As shown in Fig. 5 We record the LiDAR data in each scenario as PCAP (Packet CAPture) files and replay offline using our self-implemented tools. Furthermore, landmarks in each scenario are manually marked and measured as ground truth.

Scenario I **Tree**

As illustrated in Fig. 6, our approach using Cartesian Model with grid size from 12×12 (cm) to 40×40 (cm) can detect well for tree overhanging structures as well as road curbs. Moreover, grid size using 25×25 (cm) and 30×30 (cm) perform best for the overhanging tree detection in the front of our autonomous vehicle in this scenario.

Compared with Fig. 7, smaller grid sizes not only upset the computations, but also lose the fineness of detection, missing some overhanging structures. As for larger grid sizes, the results, with obvious false positives, cannot be used for autonomous driving to pass through this road section.

Polar Model shares similar results as illustrated in Figs. 8 and 9, and azimuth with $1°$ resolution as well as 25 (cm) and 30 (cm) radius size are most suitable. Besides, Polar Model can capture more details of nearby road curbs than Cartesian Model, which is more available for nearby small obstacles.

Scenario II–IV **Flat Road**, *"toll gate"* and **Intersection**

We also analyze our detection results on following scenarios: Fig. 10. Both Cartesian Model and Polar Model with different grid size are evaluated following the way mentioned above. Grid size using 25×25 (cm), 30×30 (cm) and $1.0° \times 25$ (cm), $1.0° \times 30$ (cm) are most tolerant in these scenarios.

Detection results of grid size 25×25 (cm) and $1.0° \times 25$ (cm) are compared in Fig. 11. Once again, for nearby road curbs, Polar Model performs better. However, Polar Model cannot detect small obstacles far away, even false check obstacles for overhanging structures in toll gate scenario. In comparison, Cartesian Model always performs normally, though without too much detail.

Scenario V **Tilted Ground**

Tilted ground detection is a huge challenge for obstacle detection in autonomous driving, and many papers (including those mentioned above) chose to keep from talking about it. As shown in Fig. 12, Our approach can filter tilted ground during detecting, providing drivable messages for autonomous driving.

(a) Scenario: tree

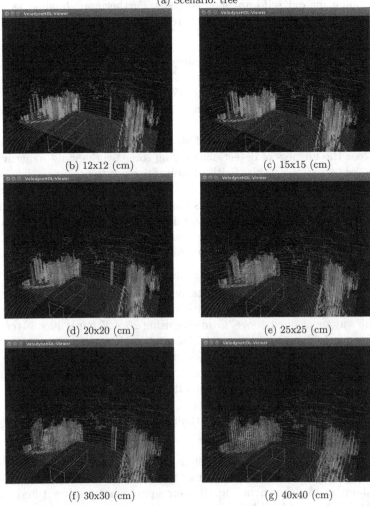

(b) 12x12 (cm)

(c) 15x15 (cm)

(d) 20x20 (cm)

(e) 25x25 (cm)

(f) 30x30 (cm)

(g) 40x40 (cm)

Fig. 6. Cartesian projection model using suitable grid size for tree overhanging detection

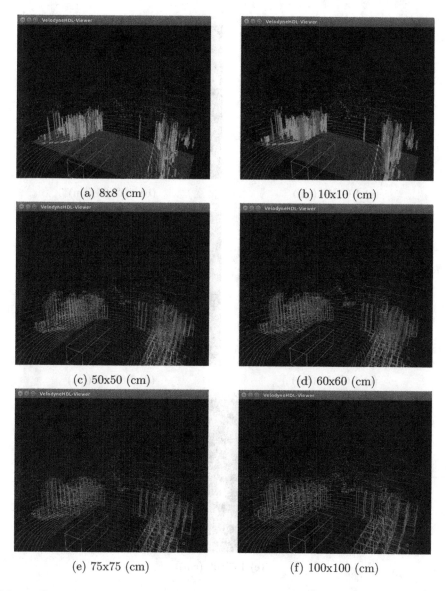

(a) 8x8 (cm)

(b) 10x10 (cm)

(c) 50x50 (cm)

(d) 60x60 (cm)

(e) 75x75 (cm)

(f) 100x100 (cm)

Fig. 7. Cartesian projection model using too small/large grid size for tree overhanging detection

A Brief Sum-Up. Based on the Cartesian Model projection, the whole space is divided into the same size of the grid cell, impartial for obstacles both nearby and far away.

Differently, in Polar Model projection, starting from the center to the outward, inner grids are small and dense, while the outsides become larger and larger. The advantage of this Polar Model is that it has a good precision for

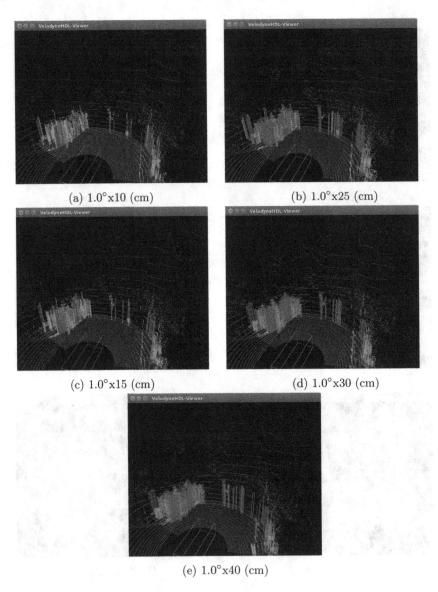

(a) 1.0°x10 (cm)

(b) 1.0°x25 (cm)

(c) 1.0°x15 (cm)

(d) 1.0°x30 (cm)

(e) 1.0°x40 (cm)

Fig. 8. Polar projection model using different grid size for tree overhanging detection

nearby objects, which can well distinguish small obstacles when reducing the amount of computations. Focus on some, we say. The disadvantage is that it may not be possible to identify small obstacles far away.

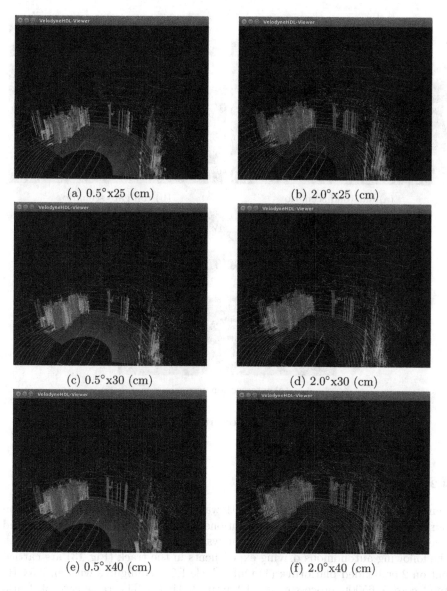

Fig. 9. Polar projection model using too small/large grid size for tree overhanging detection

(a) flat road scenario   (b) toll gate scenario

(c) intersection scenario

Fig. 10. Scenarios II–IV

4.2 Online Running Results

Our autonomous vehicle is qualified with way points following function, based on our obstacle detection approaches mentioned in this paper. Using available grid sizes learning from Multi-Scenarios Analysis offline in either projection model, the following autonomous driving experiments in the track (Fig. 13) are carried out on 2 embedded platforms: (1) Our vehicle ECU configures with an 2.5 GHz Intel core-i7 6500u processor and Ubuntu 16.04; (2) The raspberry pi 3 also runs Ubuntu 16.04, but has a A53 (BCM2837) processor, the basic frequency of which is only 1.2 GHz. Autonomous performances are evaluated referring to the degree of human intervention, comfort of passengers, etc. Besides, detecting time inside are analyzed on both embedded platform, especially in term of restrict-computation raspberry pi 3.

Time Analysis. As illustrated in Fig. 14, raspberry pi 3 needs greatly more time, typically 8 times, than high-performing vehicle ECU. Besides, detecting time is almost the same in Cartesian Model, even using different grid sizes on both

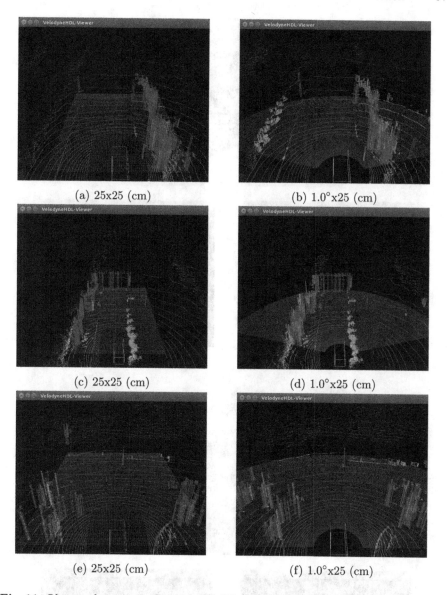

(a) 25x25 (cm)

(b) 1.0°x25 (cm)

(c) 25x25 (cm)

(d) 1.0°x25 (cm)

(e) 25x25 (cm)

(f) 1.0°x25 (cm)

Fig. 11. Obstace detection in Scenarios II–IV. *(a) (b)* is in flat road scenario, *(c) (d)* in toll gate scenario and *(e) (f)* in intersection scenario.

platform, which differs a lot in Polar Model. It costs more time using dense cells, that better matches the way we thought. The reason, we find that this Cartesian Model is more in line with this road section, filtering out the vast majority of obstacles except for curbs on both sides of the road. In addition, Polar Model is more stable due to its centralized detecting time.

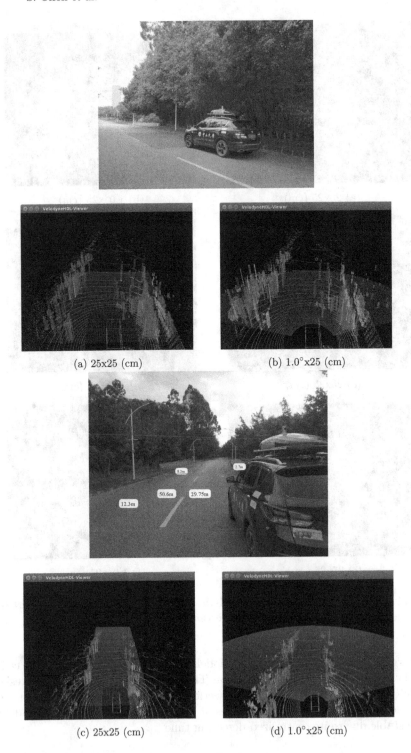

(a) 25x25 (cm)   (b) 1.0°x25 (cm)

(c) 25x25 (cm)   (d) 1.0°x25 (cm)

Fig. 12. Obstace detection in tilted ground scenario

Fig. 13. Test section environments in East Campus, Sun Yat-sen University, China. Our autonomous vehicle starts at ⎍1⎍, drives around 2 U-turns at ⎍2⎍ and ⎍3⎍, changes to left driveaway to pass the cones ⎍4⎍ then changes back to right driveaway, finally through the "toll gate".

Autonomous Driving Performances Analysis. Autonomous driving performances are evaluated referring to the degree of human intervention (45%), frequency of antics (35%) and control smoothness as well as comfort of passengers (totally accounting for 20%). According to Fig. 15, when the obstacle detection runs on raspberry pi 3, the autonomous driving performances are acceptable and very close to the situation when running on our vehicle ECU.

What's more, when using grid size 25 × 25, 30 × 30 and cell size 1° × 30, the system performs best, no matter running on ECU or raspberry pi 3. We can also see that the Cartesian Model causes less antics than the Polar Model but the control smoothness is worse. That is because the Polar Model holds more details of the point clouds than Cartesian Model especially when the obstacles are nearby.

In WRC (World Robot Conference) 2017 (Fig. 3), Beijing, we use the ECU mentioned above to finish the detection and planning computations for our autonomous vehicle, smoothly tracking to complete the entire journey.

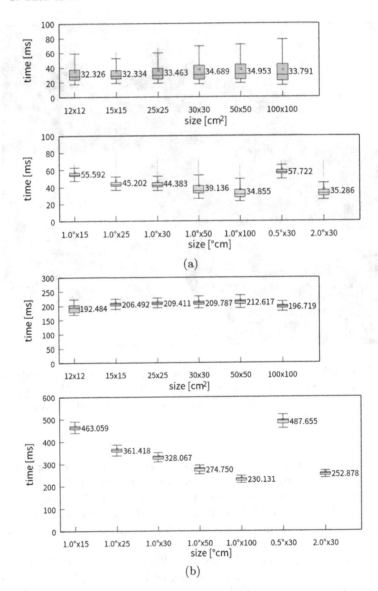

Fig. 14. Online obstacle detection time both on our vehicle ECU and Raspberry pi 3. *(a)* is on our vehicle ECU and *(b)* on raspberry pi 3; *blues* are for Cartesian Model and *greens* for polar model. (Color figure online)

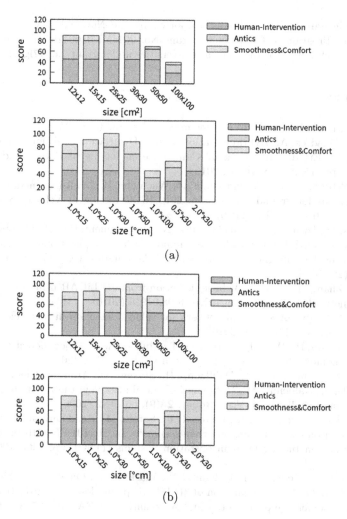

Fig. 15. Online obstacle detection performance both on our vehicle ECU and Raspberry pi 3. *(a)* is on our vehicle ECU and *(b)* on raspberry pi 3.

5   Conclusion

In this paper, we put forward a computationally efficient solution for LiDAR-based obstacle detection. Two projection models, Cartesian Model and Polar Model are proposed, providing the basis for high-performance computations of grid-based statistical features. Each scan is processed and moreover, 2 more nearest historical detection results are fused, giving more accurate obstacles information for path planning. A considerable amount of experimental work is carried out on our autonomous vehicle using our approach. The autonomous driving performances are still desirable even on a restrict-computation raspberry pi 3.

Acknowledgment. This work was supported by the National Key Research and Development Program of China under grant No. 2017YFB1001703 and the Fundamental Research Funds for the Central Universities under grant No. 17lgjc40.

References

1. Douillard, B., Underwood, J., Melkumyan, N., Singh, S., Vasudevan, S., Brunner, C., Quadros, A.: Hybrid elevation maps: 3D surface models for segmentation. In: 2010 IEEE/RSJ International Conference on Intelligent Robots and Systems (IROS), pp. 1532–1538. IEEE, 2010
2. Himmelsbach, M., Hundelshausen, F.V., Wuensche, H.-J.: Fast segmentation of 3D point clouds for ground vehicles. In: 2010 IEEE Intelligent Vehicles Symposium (IV), pp. 560–565. IEEE (2010)
3. Zermas, D., Izzat, I., Papanikolopoulos, N.: Fast segmentation of 3D point clouds: a paradigm on LiDAR data for autonomous vehicle applications. In: 2017 IEEE International Conference on Robotics and Automation (ICRA), pp. 5067–5073. IEEE (2017)
4. Li, B., Zhang, T., Xia, T.: Vehicle detection from 3D LiDAR using fully convolutional network. arXiv preprint arXiv:1608.07916 (2016)
5. Li, B.: 3D fully convolutional network for vehicle detection in point cloud. arXiv preprint arXiv:1611.08069 (2016)
6. Chen, X., Ma, H., Wan, J., Li, B., Xia, T.: Multi-view 3D object detection network for autonomous driving. arXiv preprint arXiv:1611.07759 (2016)
7. Thrun, S., Montemerlo, M., Dahlkamp, H., Stavens, D., Aron, A., Diebel, J., Fong, P., Gale, J., Halpenny, M., Hoffmann, G., et al.: Stanley: the robot that won the darpa grand challenge. J. Field Robot. **23**(9), 661–692 (2006)
8. Fernández, C., Izquierdo, R., Llorca, D.F., Sotelo, M.: Road curb and lanes detection for autonomous driving on urban scenarios. In: 2014 IEEE 17th International Conference on Intelligent Transportation Systems (ITSC), pp. 1964–1969. IEEE (2014)
9. Douillard, B., Underwood, J., Kuntz, N., Vlaskine, V., Quadros, A., Morton, P., Frenkel, A.: On the segmentation of 3D LiDAR point clouds. In: 2011 IEEE International Conference on Robotics and Automation (ICRA), pp. 2798–2805. IEEE (2011)
10. Himmelsbach, M., Mueller, A., Lüttel, T., Wünsche, H.-J.: LiDAR-based 3D object perception. In: Proceedings of 1st International Workshop on Cognition for Technical Systems, vol. 1 (2008)
11. Besl, P.J., McKay, N.D., et al.: A method for registration of 3-D shapes. IEEE Trans. Pattern Anal. Mach. Intell. **14**(2), 239–256 (1992)

Scheduling

On the Soft Real-Time Scheduling of Parallel Tasks on Multiprocessors

Xu Jiang[1] , Xiang Long[1](✉), Tao Yang[2], and Qingxu Deng[2]

[1] Beihang University, Beijing, China
long@buaa.edu.cn
[2] Northeastern University, Shenyang, China

Abstract. Recently, parallel task models have received more attentions as the prevalence of multiprocessors. The general purpose by using such parallel programming models is to guarantee bounded response time with minimal resource. Unfortunately, most previous work focus on hard real time problem while could not providing such performance guarantees. In this paper, we address the soft real-time scheduling problem under a general DAG (Directed Acyclic Graph) task model and present conditions where each parallel application with arbitrary deadline can achieve a bounded response time by using federated scheduling algorithm. To the best of our knowledge, this is the first time to consider the soft real-time scheduling under general DAG task model on multiprocessors.

Keywords: Soft real-time · Parallel · Scheduling

1 Introduction

As the growing prevalence of multiprocessors, parallel programming model has been paid much attention in real-time systems such as openMP and MPI, to exploit the intra-task parallelism such that rapidly increasing requirements and more cruel real-time constraints could be satisfied.

To fully utilize the computation capacity of multiprocessors is not for free, existing scheduling and analysis techniques for sequential real-time tasks are hard to migrate to the parallel workload setting. Parallel task models introduce new challenge to real-time scheduling due to the intro-parallelism and precedence constraints. New scheduling and analysis techniques are required to deploy parallel real-time tasks on multi-cores. A parallel real-time task is usually modeled as a Directed Acyclic Graph (DAG). Recently, several scheduling algorithms and analysis technicals of parallel applications under DAG model has been proposed, presented with schedulability test conditions in hard real-time environment, such as global EDF scheduling [12] and federated scheduling [20]. Many real-time applications implemented under such parallel programming models have soft real-time (SRT) constraints. Examples include wireless communication, video processing and image recognition. In these applications, providing

© Springer Nature Singapore Pte Ltd. 2018
Y. Bi et al. (Eds.): ESTC 2017, CCIS 857, pp. 65–77, 2018.
https://doi.org/10.1007/978-981-13-1026-3_5

soft real-time performance guarantees is important. However, achieving this performance requirement by using such hard real time analysis technicals is cruel as it may overkill many settings and furthermore results in significant utilization loss. Unfortunately, in most prior work on this topic, including all of the just-cited work, scheduling decisions are made on a basic HRT requirements, so none of these results can provide performance guarantees such as response time bounds. Thus, in this paper, our focus is to provide ensure bounded response times in supporting parallel task systems by applying SRT scheduling analysis techniques.

Response time bounds have been studied extensively in the context of global real-time scheduling algorithms such as GEDF [10]. It has been shown that a variety of such algorithms can ensure bounded response times in ordinary real-time sporadic task systems (i.e., without intra-task parallelism) with no utilization loss on multiprocessors. Motivated by these results, we consider whether it is possible to specify reasonable conditions under which bounded response times can be achieve by using some real-time scheduling techniques, for sporadic parallel task systems that are not HRT in nature. As we mentioned before, several scheduling algorithms have been proposed to schedule DAG tasks in recent years, among which *federated scheduling* [20] is a promising approach with both good real-time performance and high flexibility. In federated scheduling, DAG tasks are classified into *heavy* tasks (density > 1) and *light* tasks (density ≤ 1). Each heavy task exclusively executes on a subset of dedicated processors. Light tasks are treated as traditional sequential real-time tasks and share the remaining processors.

In this paper we consider parallel tasks under DAG model with arbitrary deadlines. Particularly, we addresses soft real-time requirements of DAG tasks by using the framework of federated scheduling. That is, we schedule heavy tasks and light tasks separately and try to determine the resource allocation problem for each task with latency requirement rather that satisfy their hard real-time constraints. The change of applying federated scheduling on such systems is that a heavy task with arbitrary deadline may penitentially generate jobs while previous released jobs have not been finished. For more detailed, our analysis is by the following steps:

First, we study the problem of determine the conditions that can provide bounded response time of an individual heavy task with arbitrary deadline executing on a given number of processors. The step is done by the analysis to the upper bound of workload during the time window between the release time and finishing time of a DAG job, while considering the interfering workload introduced by other jobs which may potentially execute simultaneity. Then we analyze the minimum total amount of work that could be done in this window by EDF scheduling. By combine these two results we can finally have the resource allocation requirement of each heavy task such that the response time requirement of each individual task could be satisfy.

Second, all light tasks are considered executing without intra-task parallelism, such that each light task can be treated the same as traditional sporadic sequential task. These tasks can be scheduled together on a sharing subset of processors. Thus by applying the tardiness analysis technicals on traditional sporadic sequential tasks, we can obtain the resource allocation method to make the latency requirement of all light tasks satisfied.

Finally, we propose federated scheduling algorithms to assign processors to each heavy task, and the remaining processors to light tasks based on the above results.

This paper is organized as follows:

- In Sect. 2, we explain the terminology that is used in the rest of paper and introduce the basic notion of response time and federated scheduling.
- In Sect. 3, we introduce technology to analyze the workload that may fall in the time interval between the release time and finishing time of a job. We also provide algorithms to calculate the response time of a heavy task on a given number of processors.
- In Sect. 4, we apply the classic results of calculating the tardiness bound of traditional sporadic sequential tasks under global EDF scheduling on light parallel tasks.
- At last, in Sect. 5, similar with federated scheduling, we propose algorithms to assign processors to heavy tasks and light tasks separately, such that the performance requirements of all tasks could be satisfy.

2   Preliminary

2.1   Task Model

We consider a task set τ consists of n sporadic tasks $\{\tau_1, \tau_2, ..., \tau_n\}$, executed on a multiprocessor platform of m identical processors with unit speed. Each task is with a period T_i and a relative deadline D_i. We say a task τ_i is constrained-deadline if it satisfies $D_i \leq T_i$, in contrast, an arbitrary-deadline task τ_i does not constrain the relation between D_i and T_i. In this paper we consider both of these two types.

Each task is represented by a directed acyclic graph (DAG). A vertex v in the DAG has a worst-case execution time c_i^j. Edges represent dependencies among vertices. A directed edge from vertex v_i^j to v_i^k means that v_i^k can only be executed after v_i^j is finished. In this case, v_i^j is a *predecessor* of v_i^k, and v_i^k is a *successor* of v_i^j. We say a vertex is *eligible* at some time point if all its predecessors in the current release have been finished and thus it can immediately execute if there are available processors. We assume each DAG has a unique head vertex (with no predecessor) and a unique tail vertex (with no successor). This assumption does not limit the expressiveness of our model since one can always add a dummy head/tail vertex to a DAG with multiple entry/exit points.

We use C_i to denote the total worst-case execution time of all vertices of DAG task τ_i. A chain in a DAG task is a sequence of vertices $\{v_i^k, v_i^{k+1}, ...v_i^{k+n}\}$, where v_i^k is a predecessor of v_i^{k+1}. We use L_i to denote the sum of c_i^j of each vertex v_i^j along the longest chain (also called the critical path) of τ_i. The *utilization* U_i of

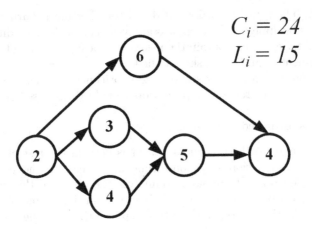

$C_i = 24$
$L_i = 15$

Fig. 1. A DAG task example.

a DAG task τ_i is $\frac{C_i}{T_i}$, and its *density* is $\frac{C_i}{D_i}$. A DAG task is called a *heavy* task if it density is larger than 1, and a *light* task otherwise.

Figure 1 shows a DAG task with 6 vertices. We can compute $C_i = 16$ and $L_i = 9$ (the longest path is $\{v_i^1, v_i^4, v_i^5, v_i^6\}$). This is a heavy task since the density is $\frac{16}{12} > 1$.

2.2 Tardiness and Response Time

A sporadic task τ_i generates a potentially infinite sequence of jobs with successive job-arrivals separated by at least T_i time units. We use J_i^h to denote the $h - th$ job of τ_i. The release time of a DAG job J_i^h is defined by r_i^h such that its deadline d_i^h can be calculated by $r_i^h + D_i$, while the finishing time is denoted by f_i^h.

In soft real time scheduling, the tardiness tar_i^h is defined by $tar_i^h = f_i^h - d_i^h$ which can measure the performance of a DAG task in a soft real time system. Similar, he response time R_i^h of a DAG job τ_i is calculated by

$$R_i^h = f_i^h - r_i^h$$

The response time bound is defined by the maximum response time among all jobs of a task

$$R_i^{up} = \max\{R_i^h\}$$

In hard real-time system, a sufficient condition for a DAG task set that is schedulable is that $R_i^{up} \leq D_i$ satisfies for each task τ_i. For soft real-time system, it is obvious that the tardiness is bounded while R_i^{up} is bounded.

2.3 Federated Scheduling

In the environment of hard real-time system, federated scheduling is a promising approach with both good real-time performance and high flexibility to schedule parallel real-time tasks on multi-cores where each heavy task exclusively executes on a subset of dedicated processors and light tasks are treated as traditional sequential real-time tasks and share the remaining processors.

Federated scheduling not only can schedule a large portion of DAG task systems that is not schedulable by other approaches, but also provides the best quantitative worst-case performance guarantee [20]. On the other hand, federated scheduling allows flexible workload specification as the underlying analysis techniques only require information about the critical path length and total workload of the DAG, and thus can be easily extended to more expressive models, such as DAG with conditional branching. In federated scheduling [20] of constraint deadline tasks, the workload of each job generated by a heavy task must be finished before its relative deadline, i.e., $R_i^h \leq D_i$, as $D_i \leq T_i$ thus it is safe to assume that only one job is ready to executed at a time instant, then the response time of a heavy task τ_i can be bounded using the classical result for non-recurrent DAG tasks by Graham [11]:

$$R_i \leq L_i + \frac{C_i - L_i}{m_i} \tag{1}$$

where m_i is the number of dedicated processors granted to this heavy task. Therefore, by setting $R_i = D_i$, we can calculate the minimal amount of processing capacity required by this task to meet its deadline $\frac{C_i - L_i}{D_i - L_i}$, and the number of processors assigned to a heavy task τ_i is the minimal integer no smaller than $\left\lceil \frac{C_i - L_i}{D_i - L_i} \right\rceil$. The light tasks are treated as sequential sporadic tasks, and are scheduled on the remaining processors by traditional multiprocessor scheduling algorithms, such as global EDF [2] and partitioned EDF [3].

However, for tasks with arbitrary deadlines where D_i may be greater than T_i, a task may release a DAG job prior to the completion of its previously-released DAG job. Thus the interfering workload of other jobs must be considered while calculating the response time of a DAG job. In [5], it provide algorithms for processor allocation such that each heavy task can guarantee its deadline.

Among the above technicals, the basic assumption is that no jobs will continue execute after its deadline (such case will be treated as a failure in hard real time systems). In this paper we do not make such assumption and aim to obtain the conditions that each task can guarantee a bounded response time. It can be observed that two necessary condition must be satisfied for a heavy task executed on m processors with bounded response time:

$$\frac{C_i}{T_i} \leq m \quad and \quad L_i \leq T_i$$

Otherwise, the finishing time of a DAG job may be delayed unlimited.

In the rest of the paper, we first analyze the number of processors that a heavy task is needed to guarantee a bounded response time. Then we show that all light tasks can also guarantee bounded response time on a given number of processors. At last, all tasks have their response time bounded.

3   Heavy Tasks

In this section, we seek to determine the number of processors that must be allocated to the exclusive use of each high density task such that its response time is bounded. For great detail, we will first analyze the upper bound workload which interferes the execution of a DAG job J_i^h during a problem window. Then we will analyze the lower bound of workload which can be done by EDF in this window. And finally we can determine that whether the upper bound of workload can be finished during the problem window.

3.1   Upper Bound Workload

To analyze the upper bound of workload, we first define the problem window of a DAG job J_i^h.

Definition 1. *The problem window of a DAG job J_i^h executed on m processors is defined by the time interval of $[r_i^h, r_i^h + R_i^h]$, where R_i^h is its response time.*

As we consider soft real time scheduling here, and a job may continue execute after its real deadline, for convenience, in the rest of the paper, we do not distinguish tasks with different types of deadline, i.e., $D_i \leq T_i$ and $D_i > T_i$, by defining a synthetic deadline of each task. The synthetic deadline d_i of τ_i is simply set to be equal to T_i. Note that deadline d_i is only used to determine the priority of jobs that execute simultaneity rather than the schedulability.

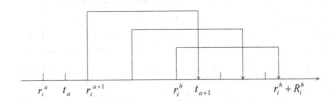

Fig. 2. Workload analysis.

As shown in Fig. 2, Without loss of generality, we assume that $R_i^h > T_i$. If $R_i^h \leq T_i$, no jobs execute simultaneity and the problem can be simply solved by Eq. (1).

We consider the case that any other job J_i^k has response time $R_i^k \leq R_i^h$, with ties broken arbitrary. During the problem window, EDF is only executing jobs with deadline no later than d_i^h. Let t_a denote a time instant that $r_i^h - t_a = R_i^h$ and r_i^a denote the release time of the first DAG job just before t_a. Then we have

$$r_i^a + R_i^a \leq r_i^a + R_i^h$$

$$\Rightarrow r_i^a + R_i^a \leq r_i^h$$

As we explain before, during the problem window, EDF only execute jobs with deadline no later than d_i^h, thus there can only be at most $\lfloor \frac{R_i^h}{T_i} \rfloor - 1$ other jobs have their workload fall in the problem window.

Let r_i^{a+1} denotes the release time of the first job after t_a and t_{a+1} denotes the time instant of $r_i^{a+1} + R_i^h$. It may be noticed that if there are actually $\lfloor \frac{R_i^h}{T_i} \rfloor - 1$ other jobs have their workload falls in the problem window, then it must satisfies

$$r_i^{a+1} + R_i^h < d_i^h$$

then we have

$$r_i^{a+1} + R_i^{a+1} < t_{a+1}$$

Thus the total amount of work of J_i^{a+1} that falls in the problem window is upper bounded by the capacity of the number of processors that assigned to task τ_i during the interval of $[r_i^h, t_{a+1}]$, which is at most

$$m(R_i^h \mod T_i) \tag{2}$$

On the other hand, the total workload of job J_i^{a+1} is at most C_i, together with Eq. (2) the total amount of workload of J_i^{a+1} that falls in the problem window is upper bounded by

$$\min\{m(R_i^h \mod T_i), C_i\} \tag{3}$$

Until now, we have the upper bound of the total amount of workload of other jobs falls in the problem window is

$$C_i(\max\{\lfloor \frac{R_i^h}{T_i} \rfloor - 1, 0\}) + \min\{m(R_i^h \mod T_i), C_i\}$$

Add up with the workload of J_i^h itself, we have obtain the upper bound workload that has to be finished in the problem window is

$$C_i \lfloor \frac{R_i^h}{T_i} \rfloor + \min\{m(R_i^h \mod T_i), C_i\} \tag{4}$$

In the next section, we determine the lower bound of workload that EDF can done in the problem window, together with Eq. (4), we can obtain the condition that R_i^h is bounded.

3.2   Lower Bound of Workload

In this section, we analyze the minimum work can be done by EDF in the problem window of job J_i^h.

We first construct a path $\pi = \{v_i^1, v_i^2, ..., v_i^{z-1}, v_i^z\}$ of job J_i^h recursively: let v_i^z be the latest finished vertex in the job of J_i^h and v_i^{z-1} be the latest finished vertex among all predecessors of v_i^z, continue this way until no predecessors can be found. The key observation is that all processors must be busy between the finishing time of v_i^k and the starting time of v_i^{k+1} for $\forall k : 1 \leq k \leq z - 1$. If not, according to EDF, v_i^{k+1} must be started earlier as all its predecessors are finished and there are still processors idle. Let l denote the length of path π, then we have the minimum work that can be done by EDF in the problem window is

$$m \times R_i^h - (m-1)l$$

As L_i is the length of the longest chain of task τ_i, such that $l \leq L_i$, then we have the lower bound of workload that can be done by EDF in the problem window of J_i^h is

$$m \times R_i^h - (m-1)L_i \tag{5}$$

From Eqs. (4) and (5), we now have both the upper bound of the workload need to be finished and lower bound of the work can be done in the problem window of a job J_i^h, then we can conclude the following theorem:

Theorem 1. *Given a heavy DAG task τ_i with arbitrary deadline executed on m processors by EDF, the upper bound R_i^{up} of the response time of τ_i can be derived by fixed-point interaction as follows:*

$$R_i^{up} \leftarrow \frac{(m-1)L_i + C_i \lfloor \frac{R_i^{up}}{T_i} \rfloor + \min\{m(R_i^{up} \mod T_i), C_i\}}{m} \tag{6}$$

Proof. Theorem 1 is obtained by combine Eqs. (4), (5) and polynomial transformation.

The pseudo-code of the interaction in Theorem 1 is shown in Algorithm 1. At the beginning R_i^{up} is initialized to be L_i and the algorithm stops until no more R_i^{up} can be updated.

Algorithm 1. The fixed-point interaction.

1: $R_i^{up} \leftarrow L_i$
2: **repeat**
3: calculate the upper bound of workload $W(R_i^{up})$ according to Eq. (4)
4:
$$R_i^{up}(new) = \frac{(m-1)L_i + W(R_i^{up})}{m}$$

5: **if** $R_i^{up}(new) > R_i^{up}$ **then**
6:
$$R_i^{up} \leftarrow R_i^{up}(new)$$

7: **else**
8:    **return** R_i^{up}
9: **end if**
10: **end repeat**

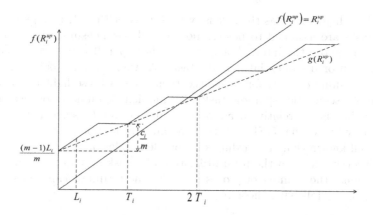

Fig. 3. The demonstration of fixed-point interaction.

Theorem 2. *A heavy task τ_i can achieve bounded response time on m processors if $\frac{C_i}{T_i} < m$.*

Proof. To prove Theorem 2, it is sufficient to prove that the interaction in Algorithm 1 is convergence. Let $f(R_i^{up})$ denote the RHS in Eq. (6), the curve of $f(R_i^{up})$ is shown in Fig. 3, it can be observed that $f(R_i^{up})$ can be represented as a graduating function of R_i^{up}, then we can use a curve of $g(R_i^{up})$ to approximate $f(R_i^{up})$ which is

$$g(R_i^{up}) = \frac{(m-1)L_i}{m} + \frac{C_i}{m \times T_i} R_i^{up}$$

The problem now changes into whether there exists a point where $g(R_i^{up})$ is no greater than R_i^{up}. And we know the sufficient condition is

$$\frac{C_i}{m \times T_i} < 1 \Leftrightarrow \frac{C_i}{T_i} < m$$

From Theorem 2, we know that if the total number of processors that assigned to a heavy task is strictly greater than its utilization, then it can execute with a bounded response time. Especially, despite an arbitrary small utilization, we can consider that a single DAG task is soft optimal under EDF scheduling (soft optimal indicates that the tardiness of a task is bounded with no utilization loss). That is, if soft real-time performance is needed in a system, at the extreme case, we only need to assign each heavy task m processors where $m > C_i/T_i$, while for other cases where better performance is requested, Algorithm 1 can be used to provide such performance guarantees.

4 Light Tasks

After we obtain the number of processors that is needed for heavy tasks to achieve bounded response time, now we need to consider to assign processors to the remaining light tasks.

For these light tasks, as their density is no greater than 1, i.e., $\frac{C_i}{D_i} \leq 1$, jobs of such tasks are assumed to possess no internal parallelism during run time, thus we can ignore the internal structure of these parallel tasks and treat the same as traditional sequential sporadic tasks. As we mentioned before, we set a synthetic deadline $d_i = T_i$ for each task, then each of these light tasks can be model into a sequential sporadic task with implicit deadline whose worst-case execution time is C_i, relative deadline is d_i and period T_i, such that it can be scheduled by traditional GEDF on the remaining processors.

It is well known that the tardiness is bounded under preemptive global EDF on multiprocessors when the total utilization of a task system is not restricted and may equal the number of processors [10]. The tardiness can be calculated according to the following theorem.

Theorem 3. *(From* [10]*) The tardiness of every task τ_i of a sporadic task system τ, where $\sum U_i \leq m$, is at most*

$$\frac{\sum_{\tau_k \in \varepsilon_{max}} (m-1)C_k - C_{min}}{m - \sum_{\tau_k \in \chi_{max}} (m-1)U_k} + C_i \tag{7}$$

under EDF on m processors.

In the above theorem, $\varepsilon_{max}(k)$ denote a subset of k tasks of τ with maximum worst-case execution time. $\chi_{max}(k)$ denote a subset of k tasks of τ with maximum utilization. C_{min} denotes the minimum worst-case execution time among all tasks in τ.

Further more, by the Corollary 1 in [10], each task can obtain tighter tardiness if more processors are provided and guarantee better soft real-time performance.

5   Processor Allocation

Until now, we can obtain the response times for both heavy and light tasks. Now we can turn our attention to the final processor allocation strategy. During the processor allocation, each heavy task is assigned to its dedicate processors, and all light tasks are assigned to the remaining sharing processors based on the performance request, i.e., the tardiness of each task. The pscedo-code of processor allocation is shown in Algorithm 2.

By applying Algorithm 2 to systems with soft real-time requirements, we can have all parallel tasks in such system satisfy their latency requirement thus providing guaranteed performance.

Algorithm 2. The processor allocation.

1: **for** each heavy task τ_i **do**
2:   **repeat**
3:

$$m_i \leftarrow \lceil \frac{C_i}{T_i} \rceil$$

4:     calculate R_i^{up} according to Algorithm 1
5:     **if** the request response time is satisfied **then**
6:         **break repeat**
7:     **else**
8:         **if** no processor remaining **then**
9:             **return failure**
10:        **else**
11:            $m_i \leftarrow m_i + 1$
12:        **end if**
13:    **end if**
14:    **end repeat**
15: **end for**
16: assign the remaining processors to all light tasks
17: **if** the request tardiness is not satisfied according to Corollary 1 in [10] **then**
18:     **return failure**
19: **end if**

---

6 Related Work

Early work on real-time scheduling of parallel tasks assume restricted constraints on task structures [1,13–16,22,23,25,30]. For example, a Gang EDF scheduling algorithm was proposed in [13] for moldable parallel tasks. The parallel synchronous task model was studied in [1,14,15,22,25,30]. Real-time scheduling algorithms for DAG tasks can be classified into three paradigms: (i) decomposition-based scheduling [12,27–29], (ii) global scheduling (without decomposition) [7,9,24], and (iii) federated scheduling [4–6,20].

The decomposition-based scheduling algorithms transform each DAG into several sequential sporadic sub-tasks and schedule them by traditional multiprocessor scheduling algorithms. In [29], a capacity augmentation bound of 4 was proved for global EDF. A schedulability test in [27] was provided to achieve a lower capacity augmentation bound in most cases, while in other cases above 4. In [28], a capacity augmentation bound of $\frac{3+\sqrt{5}}{2}$ was proved for some special task sets. In [12], a decomposition strategy exploring the structure features of the DAG was proposed, which has capacity augmentation bound between 2 and 4, depending on the DAG structure.

For global scheduling (without decomposition), a resource augmentation bound of 2 was proved in [8] for a single DAG. In [9,19], a resource augmentation bound of $2 - 1/m$ and a capacity augmentation bound of $4 - 2/m$ were proved under global EDF. A pseudo-polynomial time sufficient schedulability test was presented in [9], which later was generalized and dominated by [7] for constrained deadline DAGs. [19] proved the capacity augmentation bound $\frac{3+\sqrt{5}}{2}$ for EDF and 3.732 for RM. In [26] a schedulability test for arbitrary deadline DAG was derived based on response-time analysis.

For federated scheduling, [20] proposed an algorithm for DAGs with implicit deadline which has a capacity augmentation bound of 2. Later, federated scheduling was generalized to constrained-deadline DAGs [4], arbitrary-deadline DAGs [5] as well as DAGs with conditional branching [6].

For soft real-time scheduling, it has been shown global scheduling algorithms and several of its variants can ensure bounded deadline tardiness in sporadic task systems with no utilization loss on multiprocessors [10,17]. Under parallel task model, Cong. etc., has investigate the soft real time scheudling of parallel tasks with fork-join task model [21].

7   Conclusions

In this paper, we propose technicals to solve the resource allocation problem for soft real-time systems under DAG task model by using federated scheduling algorithm. We show that a heavy task can achieve bounded response time if the number of its assigned dedicate processors is strictly greater than its utilization. We also provide algorithms to determine whether a DAG task set can achieve soft real-time requirement on a given platform.

In the next step, we will investigate the tardiness bound of tasks under DAG model when using general global EDF scheduling. We will also integrate our approach with the work-stealing strategy [18] to support hight resource utilization with both hard real-time and soft real-time tasks at the same time.

References

1. Andersson, B., de Niz, D.: Analyzing global-EDF for multiprocessor scheduling of parallel tasks. In: Baldoni, R., Flocchini, P., Binoy, R. (eds.) OPODIS 2012. LNCS, vol. 7702, pp. 16–30. Springer, Heidelberg (2012). https://doi.org/10.1007/978-3-642-35476-2_2
2. Baruah, S.: Techniques for multiprocessor global schedulability analysis. In: RTSS (2007)
3. Baruah, S., Fisher, N.: The partitioned multiprocessor scheduling of sporadic task systems. In: RTSS (2005)
4. Baruah, S.: The federated scheduling of constrained-deadline sporadic DAG task systems. In: DATE (2015)
5. Baruah, S.: Federated scheduling of sporadic DAG task systems. In: IPDPS (2015)
6. Baruah, S.: The federated scheduling of systems of conditional sporadic DAG tasks. In: EMSOFT (2015)
7. Baruah, S.: Improved multiprocessor global schedulability analysis of sporadic DAG task systems. In: ECRTS (2014)
8. Baruah, S., Bonifaci, V., Marchetti-Spaccamela, A., Stougie, L., Wiese, A.: A generalized parallel task model for recurrent real-time processes. In: RTSS (2012)
9. Bonifaci, V., Marchetti-Spaccamela, A., Stiller, S., Wiese, A.: Feasibility analysis in the sporadic DAG task model. In: ECRTS (2013)

10. Devi, U.C., Anderson, J.H.: Tardiness bounds under global EDF scheduling on a multiprocessor. In: IEEE International Real-Time Systems Symposium, RTSS 2005, pp. 330–341 (2008). 12 pages
11. Graham, R.L.: Bounds on multiprocessing timing anomalies. SIAM J. Appl. Math. **17**, 416–429 (1969)
12. Jiang, X., Long, X., Guan, N., Wan, H.: On the decomposition-based global EDF scheduling of parallel real-time tasks. In: RTSS (2016)
13. Kato, S., Ishikawa, Y.: Gang EDF scheduling of parallel task systems. In: RTSS (2009)
14. Kim, J., Kim, H., Lakshmanan, K., Rajkumar, R.R.: Parallel scheduling for cyber-physical systems: analysis and case study on a self-driving car. In: ICCPS (2013)
15. Lakshmanan, K., Kato, S., Rajkumar, R.: Scheduling parallel real-time tasks on multi-core processors. In: RTSS (2010)
16. Lee, W.Y., Heejo, L.: Optimal scheduling for real-time parallel tasks. IEICE Trans. Inf. Syst. **89**, 1962–1966 (2006)
17. Leontyev, H., Anderson, J.H.: Tardiness bounds for FIFO scheduling on multiprocessors. In: Euromicro Conference on Real-Time Systems, ECRTS 2007, p. 71 (2007)
18. Li, J., Dinh, S., Kieselbach, K., Agrawal, K., Gill, C., Lu, C.: Randomized work stealing for large scale soft real-time systems. In: RTSS (2016)
19. Li, J., Agrawal, K., Lu, C., Gill, C.: Outstanding paper award: analysis of global EDF for parallel tasks. In: ECRTS (2013)
20. Li, J., Chen, J.J., Agrawal, K., Lu, C., Gill, C., Saifullah, A.: Analysis of federated and global scheduling for parallel real-time tasks. In: ECRTS (2014)
21. Liu, C., Anderson, J.H.: Supporting soft real-time DAG-based systems on multiprocessors with no utilization loss, vol. 41, no. 3, pp. 3–13 (2010)
22. Maia, C., Bertogna, M., Nogueira, L., Pinho, L.M.: Response-time analysis of synchronous parallel tasks in multiprocessor systems. In: RTNS (2014)
23. Manimaran, G., Murthy, C.S.R., Ramamritham, K.: A new approach for scheduling of parallelizable tasks in real-time multiprocessor systems. Real Time Syst. **15**, 39–60 (1998)
24. Melani, A., Bertogna, M., Bonifaci, V., Marchetti-Spaccamela, A., Buttazzo, G.C.: Response-time analysis of conditional DAG tasks in multiprocessor systems. In: ECRTS (2015)
25. Nelissen, G., Berten, V., Goossens, J., Milojevic, D.: Techniques optimizing the number of processors to schedule multi-threaded tasks. In: ECRTS (2012)
26. Parri, A., Biondi, A., Marinoni, M.: Response time analysis for G-EDF and G-DM scheduling of sporadic DAG-tasks with arbitrary deadline. In: RTNS (2015)
27. Qamhieh, M., Fauberteau, F., George, L., Midonnet, S.: Global EDF scheduling of directed acyclic graphs on multiprocessor systems. In: RTNS (2013)
28. Qamhieh, M., George, L., Midonnet, S.: A stretching algorithm for parallel real-time DAG tasks on multiprocessor systems. In: RTNS (2014)
29. Saifullah, A., Ferry, D., Li, J., Agrawal, K., Lu, C., Gill, C.D.: Parallel real-time scheduling of DAGs. IEEE Trans. Parallel Distrib. Syst. **25**, 3242–3252 (2014)
30. Saifullah, A., Li, J., Agrawal, K., Lu, C., Gill, C.: Multi-core real-time scheduling for generalized parallel task models. Real Time Syst. **49**, 404–435 (2013)

Cyber Physical System

Other Physical Systems

Research on Formal Design and Verification of Operating Systems

Zhenjiang Qian[1]([✉]), Yongjun Liu[1], Yong Jin[1], Xiaoshuang Xing[1],
Mingxin Zhang[1], Shengrong Gong[1], Wei Liu[2], Weiyong Yang[2],
Jack Tan[3], and Lifeng Zhang[4]

[1] Changshu Institute of Technology, Suzhou 215500, China
qianzj@cslg.edu.cn
[2] NARI Group Corporation, Nanjing 211000, China
[3] University of Wisconsin, Eau Claire, WI 54701, USA
[4] Kyushu Institute of Technology, Fukuoka 804-8550, Japan

Abstract. The security of operating system is the foundation of information system. There is no recognized answer about how to guarantee the OS security. The accepted and reliable approach is to validate the design and implementation of OS with formal methods of mathematical logic reasoning. In this paper, we propose to use the "lightweight" formal method to describe and design the system. Through the formalization of OS functionality model and security requirements, we can get the description of system functionality design and security requirements on the same domain. We use logical reasoning to verify whether the system functionality design meets the security requirements. If the verification cannot pass, indicating that there are problems in the system functionality design, then we improve the design and implementation, and verify the re-designed functionality again. The verification result shows that the proposed method is feasible.

Keywords: Operating system · System security · Formal design
Formal verification

1 Introduction

Information security of computer systems is an extremely important task in the field of information technology. Advances in information security technology promotes the progress of information, but also hinders development in many areas. Academics and industry have taken strenuous works, but the security of information systems is still full of uncertainties. None of the security products can guarantee complete security to achieve the desired goals. The main reason is that the operating system (OS) cannot provide the ideal security services and assurance.

The OS security includes two levels. One is the security service level provided by the OS, such as the common usability, anonymity, pseudo-anonymity and non-observability, etc. Second is the OS own security level, including integrity, effectiveness (non-bypass), verifiability and confidentiality. Integrity embodies in maintaining the principle of event handling, the response behavior, the state of the relevant objects

© Springer Nature Singapore Pte Ltd. 2018
Y. Bi et al. (Eds.): ESTC 2017, CCIS 857, pp. 81–88, 2018.
https://doi.org/10.1007/978-981-13-1026-3_6

and control strategies consistent with the expected design. In order to protect the security of the OS, the system should guarantee that the OS codes are not modified, and the core data is not tampered. So far, there is no recognized answer about how to guarantee the OS security.

The accepted and reliable approach is to validate the design and implementation of OS with formal methods of mathematical logic reasoning. Formal methods can ensure the correctness of the software programs to the greatest extent. In the actual application process, due to the abstraction levels of verification, the complexity and scale of the programs, and difference between the logic of programming and verification, etc., developers often try to avoid to use formal methods. For the abstraction levels of verification, we can focus on whether the high-level security policies are implemented in accordance with the expected, and also consider the verification of the underlying hardware models and protocols. For different levels of abstraction, the methods described are not the same. For the complexity of the programs, it is determined by the complexity of the problems to be solved. For example, the simple applications in the user layer can be described by a strict logic system and efficiently validated by reasoning. In some problems, we need to use a combination of a variety of logical systems in the verification process with human intervention and interaction. For the scale of the programs, it often has great influence on the complexity of formal design and verification. The complexity of verification shows the trend of exponential growth with the increase of the scale of the programs. Meanwhile, the formal methods often use various logic systems, such as first order logic (FOL), higher-order logic (HOL), temporal logic (TL), separation logic, etc., and these logics are different with programming methods of system implementation. The programmers are unfamiliar with these logics, and it also affects the promotion of formal methods.

This paper attempts to use the "lightweight" [1] formal method to describe and design the system, and the logic system used has strong expressiveness ability, and is easy to use. In this paper, we propose a formal technique and method which is easy to model, describe and demonstrate the design and implementation of the OS.

In the remainder of this paper, we discuss the related work in Sect. 2. The method of formal design and verification of OS is illustrated in Sect. 3. We conclude the paper and talk about our future direction in Sect. 4.

2 Related Work

In the domain of security OS, there are two main kinds of works. One is OS security enhancements, to increase security features for the existing OS. The other, from various aspects of the system design, implementation and verification, uses formal methods to ensure the security of OS.

In the term of OS security enhancements, SELinux [2] is a typical representative. From the nineties of last century, many research institutions have done a lot of works, including Kirin, Red Flag Linux, Ansheng OS [3, 4], etc.

In the formal work, OS formal verification work can be traced back to the seventies of last century. In 1978, UCLA developed the UCLA Secure Unix project for the PDP-11 machine [5]. UCLA gave a secure kernel prototype of the UNIX user interface, and demonstrated the consistency of some of the abstract levels. UCLA did not prove that all kernel levels are consistent with implementation.

Provably Secure Operating System (PSOS) was designed by SRI International [6] in 1973–1981 and its purpose was to provide a generic OS that was provable of security. PSOS proposed a multi-level hierarchical abstraction method, and the abstract description of hardware and software architecture are type-safe. PSOS only provided some simple examples to illustrate that the implementation and the specification were consistent.

Kernel for Isolated Tasks (KIT) was a small OS kernel, and Bevier described KIT's automated formal verification method in the dissertation [7] in 1987. KIT had little functionality, and could not be used as a normal OS.

The VFiasco project [8] held at the Technical University of Dresden aimed at the formal verification of a small L4-compatible operating-system microkernel Fiasco. As a solution, a subset of C++ was improved. The project used PVS [9] for modeling and verification. Due to the flaw of the early design, the verification result was unsatisfactory.

The Robin project started in 2006 as a collaborating between Technical University of Dresden, Radboud University Nijmegen, and industrial partners. The project is supposed to develop a minimal trusted-computing base "microhypervisor" for virtualizing multiple instances of conventional operating systems in a secure way. Tews reviewed the project in [10]. The Robin project exploited the Intel Virtualization Technology to virtualize legacy operating systems. The hypervisor was implemented in a subset of C++. For verification a simplified x86 hardware model as well as semantics of a C++ subset was specified in PVS.

The L4.verified project was initiated by the Australian National ICT Laboratory (NICTA) in 2004–2006. The project focused on formal verification of the ARM architecture of the L4 microkernel. The system correctness was proved using Isabelle/HOL [11] interactive proof tool. Heiser introduced the validation work in the report [12]. The goal of validation was to use Isabelle/HOL to demonstrate that the final execution was consistent with the expected definition of the abstract model. The project suggested that the kernel validation must demonstrate the consistency of the three abstraction layers: the implementation layer of the C language, the specification layer of system running, and the abstract kernel model layer. The project also used the access control model to demonstrate some of the security properties of the system. NICTA was committed to using the formal method to improve the reliability and integrity of the system, and improve the efficiency of real-time system [13].

The Verisoft project, which began in 2003, is a large-scale project of computer system design and verification, and aimed to achieve complete verification of the entire computer system from the underlying hardware to the upper application layer. Verisoft proposed the concept of pervasive formal verification [14]. In 2007, its successor project Verisoft XT further proposed that formal design and verification not only focus on the correctness of the compiler, or the correctness of the machine instruction model, and also the overall design of the system [15, 16].

From the beginning of the 1990s to the present, Shao led the Flint project team [17] to do a lot of work in formal verification. Flint proposed a new programming language VeriML [18], and λHOL^{ind} logic that was on the basis of λHOL logic and incorporated the inductive definition of the data type, providing rich formal description capability and type security. Flint proposed to combine the authentication logics of different modules of OS to form a complete verification system and ensure the scalability of the verification model [19]. Meanwhile, Flint also studied the verification methods for parallel programs [20], as well as the hierarchical abstraction methods to validate various functional modules in the OS [21].

3   Formal Design and Verification of OS

This chapter illustrate the proposed formal design and verification method of OS. The architecture of overall formal work is shown in Fig. 1.

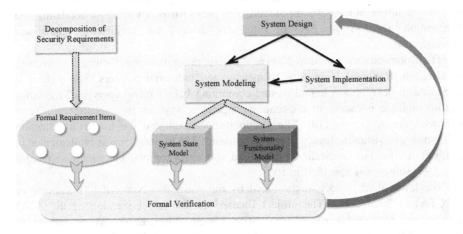

Fig. 1. The architecture of overall formal work.

3.1   Decomposition of Security Requirements

OS's own security is the basis of security of computer information system security. OS is a service system that provides resource management services, communication services, and security services for user processes. The security of user processes is guaranteed by their own design and implementation, as well as OS security services. OS's own security is guaranteed by the security attributes of OS function modules and security mechanisms of hardware.

Generally speaking of security, it is difficult to determine the specific items. For example, we can define the scope of security requirements for confidentiality, completeness, usability, anonymity, etc., but cannot determine their specific requirements. We need to decompose the security requirements. For example, we decompose the confidentiality into specific contents, such as user authentication, access control; and we can split user authentication into encryption, signature, and security password protocols. So we can decompose each security requirement into a tree, where the leaf nodes are specific and definite requirement items.

We follow the following principles for decomposition of the security requirements: decomposition from abstract requirements to specific ones, and from general requirements to explicit ones; transformation from requirements to implementation methods and functionality, and from functionality requirements to operational functionality.

3.2   System State Modeling

The functional requirements of the OS are generally described in natural language, while the functionality design is ultimately described in formal language. Similarly, the security of the OS was originally described in non-formal language. The consistency analysis between formal description and formal description is a difficult problem.

In order to accurately analyze the consistency between OS functional requirements and functionality design, as well as the overall properties of OS, we formalizes the service functionality and security of the OS by establishing the state model.

OS is a service system, composed of file system, memory management system, process management system, and equipment management system modules. Each service process is responsible for one type of service. And each service process consists of a set of data objects and a set of codes. When the service process receives a service request, it decides to modify the data objects according to the current system status. The effect of the service is reflected in the change of the values of the set of data objects. For example, the progress of creating a process is that the process management service looks for an idle item in its own process control block array, where it writes some data about the process to be created, and the effect of the creation process is reflected in the change of the process control block array and the corresponding process queue. For another example, the service request handling for reading data from a file is to calculate the parameters of the disk block to be read according to the current set of directory items and file nodes of the file system, and read the disk block data into data object in cache. Finally the data is copied to the user process space. The core function is the modification of the cache data and the user process space data.

According to the above analysis, the system state model of OS is a 5-tuple: $(S, \Sigma, \delta, s_0, \Gamma)$. S is the system state set, which is composed of all possible working objects of the system and represented as Cartesian products of several sets. Σ is an input alphabet that represents a collection of various atomic events that may occur during system operation. δ is the state transition function, and its mapping relation with definition domain is $S \times 2^{\Sigma \setminus \phi} \rightarrow S$, in which the second parameter is nonempty subset of Σ. s_0 is the initial state. Γ is the set of terminating states.

3.3   Formal Functionality Model and Formal Description of Security Requirements

Based on the OS state model, we describe the functionality of OS system behavior in logical language and logical formulas to form a verifiable OS formal functional model. In order to ensure the security of the system, we use logical reasoning to prove that these system behavior will not have impact on system security. We define the OS domain on the basis of the state vector of the OS, and use it as the domain of the logic system. With the OS domain, we establish the mapping for the logical system, and describe the system behavior with the logical formulas to verify that the system functionality design meets the security requirements.

Through the decomposition of security requirements, we can get specific security requirements. But these requirements are not described in the formal form, and cannot be verified by logical reasoning. Therefore, we describe each security requirement item on the basis of the OS formalization function model and the OS domain, and further form the security requirements expressed by the logical formulas.

OS Domain. Suppose that the maintained objects are abstractly represented as X_1, X_2, ..., X_t, which can have the same or different domains of values, and denote $S = X_1$ $X_2 \times ... \times X_t$. We represent a system call as a function f, which maps $(x_1, x_2, ..., x_t) \in$ S into $(x_1', x_2', ... x_t') \in$ S, i.e., $f(x_1, x_2, ..., x_t) = (x_1', x_2', ... x_t') \in$ S. Suppose that the entire OS has n system calls, i.e., $f_1, f_2, ..., f_n$, and denote $F = \{f_1, f_2, ..., f_n\}$. We use P to denote a set of propositions on OS domain M for expressing the logical relationship among elements, functions, elements, and functions of S. Then OS domain M is defined as $M = (S, F, P)$.

Logical Language. The purpose of our establishment of the OS domain is to map a first-order language L to the OS domain M, in which each element of L corresponds to an element in S, and each m-ary function symbol in L corresponds to a m-ary function in S, And each n-element predicate P in L corresponds to an n-order relation on S. So L is used to represent and analyze the properties of the OS's system functionality.

Representation of Security Requirements in Logic Language. We describe the decomposed security requirements as a set of propositions on M, such as $p_1, p_2, ..., p_m$. Through the mapping from M to L, we can express this set of propositions as a set of logical formulas in L. Thus, we can describe the security requirements of the OS as a set of logical formulas about the system states, such as $p_1(s), p_2(s), ..., p_m(s)$. And we describe a state of the OS as a model of L, in which the change of the state vector corresponds to the argument assignment in L.

3.4   Formal Verification of Design Security

Through the formalization of OS functionality model and security requirements, we can get the description of system functionality design and security requirements on the same domain. Based on this, we use logical reasoning to verify whether the system functionality design meets the security requirements. If the verification cannot pass, indicating that there are problems in the system functionality design, then we improve the design and implementation, and verify the re-designed functionality again.

We represent the OS system functionality as the self-mapping on state vectors, and describe the security requirements of the system as logic formulas in the first-order language L with the domain M. The running progress of OS is essentially the transformation of state vectors. Suppose that the initial state of the system is s_0. After a series of system operations, such as $f_1, f_2, ..., f_n$, the transition of states is $s_1, s_2, ..., s_n$. Obviously we can initialize the OS to a safe state, i.e., s_0 is safe. So our proof is that for any of the systems operations, denoted with f_k, it maps the state s_i to $f_k(s_i)$, and p is the predicate proposition of the security requirement. Then if the proposition

"$p(s_i) \rightarrow p(f_k(s_i))$" is always established, the system can always remain in a safe state. The correctness validation of formal design can be translated into the proof of the above proposition.

4   Conclusion

In this paper, we propose to use the "lightweight" formal method to describe and design the system. We decompose the security requirements into specific and definite requirement items. With the logic language and formal description, we construct the operating system state model and describe the requirement items formally. Based on the state model and formal description of system requirements, we use logical reasoning to verify whether the system functionality design meets the security requirements. If the verification cannot pass, indicating that there are problems in the system functionality design, then we improve the design and implementation, and verify the redesigned functionality again. The verification result shows that the proposed method is feasible.

The formal design and verification of the OS is still a difficult task, consuming a lot of labor and time. How to adopt modular proof method for improving the efficiency of verification, and efficient verification reuse are our future research efforts.

Acknowledgment. This work is supported by the Natural Science Foundation of China under grant No. 61402057, the Natural Science Foundation of Jiangsu Province in China under grant No. BK20140418, the Qing Lan Project of Jiangsu Province in China under grant No. 2017, and Science and Technology Project of State Grid Corporation in China (Research on Key Techniques of Trusted Root and Trust Chain Construction in Power Cloud Platform).

References

1. Jackson, D.: Alloy: a lightweight object modelling notation. ACM Trans. Software Eng. Methodol. **11**(2), 256–290 (2002)
2. Bill, M.: SELinux: NSA's Open Source Security Enhanced Linux. O'Reilly Media, Sebastopol (2004)
3. Qing, X., Zhu, J.: Covet channel analysis on ANSHENG secure operating system. J. Software **15**(9), 1385–1392 (2004)
4. Qing, X.: Covert channel analysis in secure operating systems with high security levels. J. Software **15**(12), 1837–1849 (2004)
5. Walker, B.J., Kemmerer, R.A., Popek, G.J.: Specification and verification of the UCLA Unix security kernel. Commun. ACM **23**(2), 118–131 (1980)
6. SRI International. http://www.sri.com. Accessed 31 Oct 2017
7. Bevier, W.R.: A verified operating system kernel. Ph.D. thesis. University of Texas at Austin (1987)
8. Hohmuth, M., Tews, H., Stephens, S.G.: Applying source-code verification to a microkernel: the VFiasco project. In: 10th Workshop on ACM SIGOPS European Workshop, pp. 165–169. ACM, New York (2002)

9. Owre, S., Rushby, J.M., Shankar, N.: PVS: a prototype verification system. In: Kapur, D. (ed.) CADE 1992. LNCS, vol. 607, pp. 748–752. Springer, Heidelberg (1992). https://doi.org/10.1007/3-540-55602-8_217

10. Tews, H.: Microhypervisor Verification: Possible Approaches and Relevant Properties. In: Nluug Voorjaarsconferentie 2007, pp. 96–109. Nluug Voorjaarsconferentie, Nijmegen (2007)

11. Blanchette, J.C., Bulwahn, L., Nipkow, T.: Automatic proof and disproof in Isabelle/HOL. In: Tinelli, C., Sofronie-Stokkermans, V. (eds.) FroCoS 2011. LNCS (LNAI), vol. 6989, pp. 12–27. Springer, Heidelberg (2011). https://doi.org/10.1007/978-3-642-24364-6_2

12. Heiser, G., Elphinstone, K.: L4 microkernels: the lessons from 20 years of research and deployment. ACM Trans. Comput. Syst. 34(1), 1–29 (2016)

13. Klein, G., Andronick, J., Elphinstone, K., Murray, T., Sewell, T., Kolanski, R., Heiser, G.: Comprehensive formal verification of an OS microkernel. ACM Trans. Comput. Syst. 32(1), 1–70 (2014)

14. Alkassar, E., Hillebrand, Mark A., Leinenbach, D., Schirmer, Norbert W., Starostin, A.: The verisoft approach to systems verification. In: Shankar, N., Woodcock, J. (eds.) VSTTE 2008. LNCS, vol. 5295, pp. 209–224. Springer, Heidelberg (2008). https://doi.org/10.1007/978-3-540-87873-5_18

15. Alkassar, E., Cohen, E., Hillebrand, M., Kovalev, M., Paul, W.J.: Verifying shadow page table algorithms. In: 2010 Conference on Formal Methods in Computer-Aided Design, pp. 267–270. IEEE, Switzerland (2010)

16. Alkassar, E., Cohen, E., Hillebrand, M., Pentchev, H.: Modular specification and verification of interprocess communication. In: 2010 Conference on Formal Methods in Computer-Aided Design, pp. 167–174. IEEE, Switzerland (2010)

17. Flint Team. http://flint.cs.yale.edu/ Accessed 31 Oct 2017

18. Stampoulis, A.: VeriML: a dependently-typed, user-extensible, and language-centric approach to proof assistant. Ph.D. thesis. Yale University (2012)

19. Gu, R., Shao, Z., Chen, H., Wu, X., Kim, J., Sjöberg, V., Costanzo, D.: CertiKOS: an extensible architecture for building certified concurrent OS kernels. In: 2016 USENIX Symposium on Operating Systems Design and Implementation, pp. 653–669. USENIX Association, Savannah (2016)

20. Chen, H., Wu, X., Shao, Z., Lockerman, J., Gu, R.: Toward compositional verification of interruptible os kernels and device drivers. In: 2016 ACM SIGPLAN Conference on Programming Language Design and Implementation, pp. 431–447. ACM, Santa Barbara (2016)

21. Costanzo, D., Shao, Z., Gu, R.: End-to-end verification of information-flow security for C and Assembly Programs. In: 2016 ACM SIGPLAN Conference on Programming Language Design and Implementation, pp. 648–664. ACM, Santa Barbara (2016)

A Spatial-Temporal Model for Locating Electric Vehicle Charging Stations

Dong Ji, Yingnan Zhao, Xinyang Dong, Mingyang Zhao, Lei Yang, Mingsong Lv, and Gang Chen[✉]

School of Computer and Engineering, Northeastern University, Shenyang, Liaoning, China
chengang@cse.neu.edu.cn

Abstract. A perfect charging station network plays a key role in Electric Vehicle (EV) adoption. In order to find optimal cost to construct the network and maximize satisfaction of usage consideration, we proposes a data driven framework for solving the problem of locating the charging station. Spatial-temporal models are built to analyze the EV usage behavior in the urban area. The features such as charging demand, high energy consumption area, and highly traveled paths are captured. We evaluate the proposed models on a real-world EV dataset. The results clearly demonstrate the efficiency and accuracy of our models on locating EV charging stations.

Keywords: Spatial-temporal · Electric vehicle · Charging station

1 Introduction

Electric vehicles (EV), plug-in hybrid electric vehicles (PHEVs) use electricity as primary fuel to run. They are promoted to the most commercially viable green alternatives to combustion vehicles. However, due to the imperfect of charging station networks, EV users cannot be able to rely on public charging to fulfill their needs which will prevent widespread adoption of EV. Therefore, constructing effective charging stations has been a crucial task for government, manufacture and stack holders to promoting and popularizing of electric vehicles. In additionally, due to the features of EV charging, traditional station planning method may be not suitable for EV charging station. The EV usage patterns will be different to the patterns of Internal combustion engine (ICE) vehicles, planning charging stations also requires the understanding of how EVs to be dispatched and routed to ensure their range and charging requirements. EV charging has three typical features:

Supported by the Fundamental Research Funds for the Central Universities (Grant No: N161604002), partially sponsored by National Natural Science Foundation of China (Grant No. 61532007).

- EV batteries require more time to recharge compared to refueling an ICE vehicle, EV users' charging behaviors have the regular pattern, e.g. destination charging, which happens when an EV arrives at its destination;
- Range limited is one of the most critical drawbacks of the current EV technology, e.g. BMW i3 batteries can just support 200 km range [1], drivers care about the available range, energy consumption of the passed trip;
- EV moving rules as another factor should be considered, hot routes and spots reflect the car flow directions and activity areas.

In order to optimized plan of charging stations based on the above features, firstly, each costumers' regular patterns will be dug out. Secondly, from the view of decision maker, summary results should also be came up with based on the first step results. In this paper, we propose a spatial-temporal model for locating electric vehicle charging stations. The contributions are as follows:

- We proposed charging demand model, in which the destination charging demand can be captured by analyzing the parking area and duration.
- We proposed energy consumption model to locate and estimate the highly energy consumption areas by using statistical analysis method in each grid cells on map.
- We proposed hot path model to find the routes that highly traveled by using the cluster method.
- We evaluated our method using EVs real data in Beijing. The results demonstrate the usefulness of our method and the analysis results are consistent with the actual situation.

The rest of the paper is organized as follows: Sect. 2 presents an overview of related work, followed by preliminaries in Sect. 3. The spatial-temporal analysis model is presented in Sect. 4. Section 5 presents the evaluation results. Section 6 discusses the work and gives an outlook for future work.

2 Literature Review

The problem of charging station placement in a city has been investigated by many researchers. In order to help decision makers to efficiently decide the locations and size of charging stations, various mathematical models have been developed. Lam et al. [2] analyzed optimal charging stations placement problem to get maximum coverage at minimum cost and the convenience of drivers. They proved the problem is NP-hard and proposed four solution methods to tackle the problem. Ge et al. [3] proposed a methodology for charging locations based on grid partitioning and genetic algorithm. He et al. [4] proposed balance density of electric vehicles charging points makes the density to meet the standard of queuing time and the cost constraint by the enforcement of guidance. Li et al. [5] formulated a multi-period location problem as a mixed integer linear program and solved by a heuristic based on genetic algorithm.

The above methods are mathematical modeling method by capturing topological dynamics of networks and travel law of the emerging EV markets.

Some researchers also build the data mining model to be token as an indicator of the deployment of charging infrastructure. Chen et al. [6] modeled a mixed integer programming problem to optimally site a constrained number of charging stations based on the parking information from over 30,000 personal-trip records collected by household travel survey in Seattle, Washington, United States. Cai et al. [7] used 11,880 trace data of taxis in Beijing to dig out the travel patterns. Their results proved that locating the charging stations by using the travel patterns can help to improve electrification rate and reduce consumption of gasoline. A data-driven optimization-based approach for charging infrastructure planning was presented using extensive vehicle activity data [8]. Han et al. [9] determined the location and scale of the charging station through real trajectory data of general taxis and real battery performance data of EV taxis to generate a more realistic solution.

This paper focuses on mining the EV users' behaviors to recommend the locations of charing station. Firstly, the EV parked places are as an indicator to have desired to charge, which can be equipped with chargers; secondly, average energy consumption in each area are calculated to find the high energy consumption regions, and we can build high-power charging stations in these regions to prolong the EV driving range; thirdly, traffic flow and the hot path can be as some places that people want to go, charging station should be installed in this place where more people can easily get charging service.

3 Preliminaries

In this section, we first clarify some terms used in this paper and briefly describe the architecture of our work.

Data Introduction: The data is 291 EVs driving and charging data in Beijing, China from May 1st in 2015 to May 1st in 2016. The dataset is about 181 GB, 157 million items, 66 attributes which is captured roughly every 10 s. It includes the time-stamped location (longitude and latitude), vehicle speed, charging/discharging status, gears position (Table 1) and some information related to EV battery (Table 2), such as State of Charge (SOC). The data size and attributes provide a lot of information and we can use it to verify our model.

Table 1. A sample set of vehicle trajectory data.

Time	Longitude	Latitude	Speed	Gear position
2015/5/5 6:37:30	116.557325	39.916019	33.5	D
2015/5/5 6:37:40	116.558724	39.916042	53.5	D
2015/5/5 6:37:50	116.561982	39.916179	47.9	D

Grid Based Map: To extract road network with vehicular trajectories and reduce computational complexity, we partition city areas into an $I \times J$ grid map based on the universal transverse mercator (UTM) coordinate system which

Table 2. A sample set of vehicle battery data.

Time	Current	Voltage	Temperature	SOC
2015/5/5 6:37:30	6.4	352.1	23	60.4
2015/5/5 6:37:40	11.5	349.7	23	60.4
2015/5/5 6:37:50	51.5	345.5	23	61.2

is transfered from longitude and latitude. The below Fig. 1 shows the flow of converting trajectories into grid based map data.

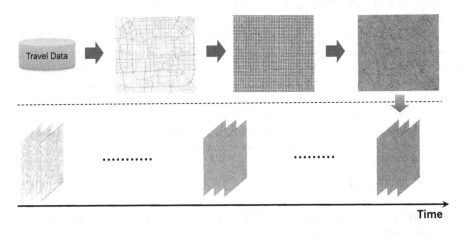

Fig. 1. Converting trajectories into grid based map data.

Parking Event: EV users' parking events are one of the main factors of influence on the density and quantity of a public charging network. In this paper, parking event will be detected when the gear position is "P" (Park), vehicle speed equals to 0, excluding the charging events. But due to the time of recharging EVs is much more time-consuming than refueling a conventional gasoline vehicle, we define that a EV will not have the possibility of charging if the dwelling time is less than 30 min, e.g. waiting for traffic lights.

Trip Event: Based on the parking event detection, each vehicle's trajectory could be divided into several trips. Each trip has some attributions after data preprocessing, such as trip distance, time-stamped traversed grid cell, energy consumption, and locations that from origin to destination.

Charging Event: Charging event means that the EV is recharged by a charger at the charging station or recharged while driving with a regenerative brake system. Based on the charging events analysis, we can find where have already built the charging stations, then our recommended locations for charging stations can be adjusted. The recovery energy while driving can also be used to get more precise analysis and prediction results of energy consumption in different areas. The below Fig. 2 illustrates the parking event, trip event and charge event.

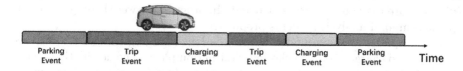

Fig. 2. Parking event, Trip event and Charging event.

***Travel Trajectory*:** Due to the sampling nature of location-acquisition technologies where the trajectory data are sampled at discrete timestamps. The trajectory is a sequence of spatial points that the vehicle follows through space as a function of time $Tr = \langle (x_0, y_0, t_0), (x_1, y_1, t_1), ..., (x_k, y_k, t_k) \rangle$, each point consists of latitude, longitude, and a time stamp. The sequence of grid cells traversed by trajectory defined in this paper is $Trgrid = \langle (g_0, t_0), (g_0, t_1), ..., (g_k, t_k) \rangle$.

4 Spatial-Temporal Analysis of EVs

In this section, we provide a complete description of the data driven model followed by a description of each component used to capture the EVs behaviors. The below Fig. 3 shows the framework of the proposed method. First, the data are mapped into grid based map and preprocessed to get the spatial-temporal distribution of parking event, EV trip event and charging event. Second, charging demand model, energy consumption model, and hot route model are built, which define the time and the place that EVs should get recharged. Third, we use the results from different models to give the recommend locations of charging station in urban area.

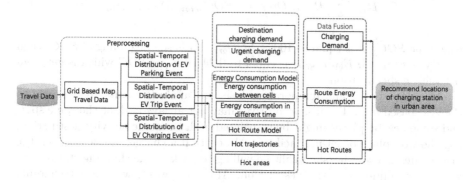

Fig. 3. Framework of the EV charging station location method.

4.1 Charging Demand Model

The proposed charging demand model is based on three aspects: (i) when EVs need to be recharged, (ii) where are the most frequent associated locations and (iii) what are the values of these demand? In order to answer these questions, a spatial-temporal analysis model is proposed.

In the spatial analysis model, due to the long charging time of EV, drivers are willing to charge their vehicles in a destination place. The destination places mainly include: home, workplace, and other places (e.g. leisure time place) where drivers go frequently and where are best locations for building charging station. To implement this model, the first step is to extract the parking events, charging events are used to exclude the locations where have charging facilities. The second step is to mine these preprocessing locations by identifying geographic zones. Distance-based clustering method is deployed to reduce the systematic noise and error in the data, because even the vehicle parks at a fixed location, a GPS device in vehicle would record a cluster of positions around the true position point due to the random deviations, which causes false appearance that slow moving and random travel directions of vehicle. So with the help of spatial clustering method, the GPS data could be filtered first to substitute the point clusters with their centroids.

In the temporal analysis model, we acknowledge the duration of parking as an indicator of demand for charging the vehicle. The probability that a vehicle i recharged in one place j during the whole day is calculated as Eq. (1) which is the same as [10]:

$$P_j^i = T_j^i / T^i \tag{1}$$

where T_j^i is the vehicle i recharged time in place j, T^i is the vehicle i total parking time. In this paper, we assume that each vehicle battery will be fully charged during its stay in charging station. So the total EV i charging demand value D_j in place j during the whole day is given by Eq. (2)

$$D_j = \sum_{i=1}^{M} P_j^i \cdot (SOC_{full} - SOC_{original}) \cdot E_{kwh/soc} \tag{2}$$

where the SOC_{full} is equal to 100%, $SOC_{original}$ is the beginning of SOC when the EV is charged. $E_{kWh/SOC}$ is equal to 0.24 kWh per SOC which is get from the vehicle specification.

After the spatial and temporal analysis, the analysis results are assigned to the grid based map. Because as a driver may not always park at the same spot, and some nearby places might be associated with the same activity destination, e.g. the workplace or leisure facilities. Moreover if a charger is not far from the driver's destination, he/she might be willing to park at the charging station and walk a few minutes to the destination. After this work, we can get charging demand of each day in each grid cell, and can also get the monthly or yearly demand by summing the daily results.

4.2   Energy Consumption Model

The charging demand not only depends on the current battery SOC, but also on the future energy consumption which means the decrease rate of SOC. Due to range anxiety, the drivers will probably charge their vehicles if consuming a lot of energy in the past road. Hence, it is important to understand the characteristics of energy consumption of EV as a function of time. More than that, based on each driver's consumption results, we can infer the high energy-consumption areas which means EVs will consume more energy to pass these areas, and drivers will be more likely to have the "range anxiety" which is the phenomenon that EV drivers continually concern of becoming stranded with a limited range vehicle.

Energy consumption value is related to the terrain, road condition, outside temperature, and driving styles, etc. In order to capture the energy consumption, each individual vehicle is modeled in three dimensions which is a function of location, time and energy consumption of each grid cell. The average energy consumption of the traversed grid cells in a trip can be calculated as Eq. (3), the grid cells average consumption in each unit time is Eq. (4):

$$E^{trip(n)} = \frac{SOC_{end}^{trip(n)} - SOC_{start}^{trip(n)}}{N_{traversed}^{trip(n)}} \cdot E_{kwh/soc} \tag{3}$$

$$E_j^t = \frac{1}{N_j^t} \sum_{n_j^t=1}^{N_j^t} E^{trip(n_j^t)} \tag{4}$$

where $SOC_{start}^{trip(n)}$, $SOC_{end}^{trip(n)}$ represents start and end SOC from origin to destination; $N_{traversed}^{trip(n)}$ means the number of traversed grid cells, N_j^t is the number of trip event passed the grid cell j in unit of time t. After getting each individual energy consumption data, we calculate the expectation of all the drivers data, and get each grid cell energy consumption in different time.

4.3   Hot Routes Model

The daily routines of the road users determine the routes to work, to shopping facilities as well as to the activities of leisure time. These repeating behaviors typically recur at commuters and the individual transport, it reveals people's movement rule or behavior pattern. Hot routes are general paths in the road network which contains heavy traffic. In this paper, hot route model is used to dig out the information of users' movement rule. The hot routes have three attributes: Direction (the start and end point of hot route); Length (the geographic distance from the start to the end point); Weight (the popularity of the hot route). Based on the previous statements, the hot-routes are represented by a sequence of grid cells. Our method is based on the [11] method with some improvements. The following parts show the method to find the hot routes in the grid based map.

Types of Trajectories in Grid Map. We map the vehicles trajectories Tr to the grid map. Each grid cell may have three types of trajectories traversed. The start points of the trajectories are in the grid cell g, $Trgrid_{start}(g)$ denotes the set of these trajectories; $Trgrid_{end}(g)$ denotes the set of trajectories that the end points of trajectories are in this grid cell g; $Trgrid_{pass}(g)$ denotes the set of trajectories that traverse grid g. Then the traffic of grid $Traf(g)$ equals to $|Trgrid_{start}(g) + Trgrid_{end}(g) + Trgrid_{pass}(g)|$.

Density Reachable. Based on the reference [11] concept called density-reachable which has directly and indirectly density-reachable. We transfer this concepts to trajectory model to detect the hot route based on the grid map, and redefine the definitions. *Directly Density reachable* in grid based map means that $|Trgrid(g_1) \cap Trgrid(g_2)| \geq \lambda$. λ is the minimum traffic threshold, the grid cell g_1 and g_2 are adjacent. *Route Density reachable* means that for a grid cell chain $L = (g_1, g_2, ..., g_n)$, g_i is Directly Density reachable to g_{i+1}. For every ϵ consecutive grid cells $L_i = (g_i, g_{i+1}, ..., g_{i+\epsilon})$ in the chain L, $|Trgrid(i) \cap Trgrid(i+1) \cap ... \cap Trgrid(i+\epsilon)| \geq \lambda$.

Hot Routes Detection. The hot routes should satisfy the following conditions:

(i) When the number of trajectories from the region g reaches a certain threshold, whatever the number of trajectories which comes from adjacent areas entering the grid cell g it is, we can consider it as hot-route;

(ii) If each quantity that the adjacent area of entering the g does not meet condition (i), but the sum is up to the threshold, g could also be the start of a hot-route. g' is the adjacent area of g, and it cannot be directly density up to g;

(iii) If it can't meet the conditions of (i) and (ii), The sum of the trajectory quantities of entering the g and leaving g reach to the threshold. g could also be the start of a hot-route. g' is the adjacent area of g, and it can't be directly density up to g.

Based on these definitions, first step to detect the hot routes is that traversing all grid cells to get all the hot areas. Then, we start to perform cluster searching in all hot areas. We can see whether the grid cells within the sliding window are Directly Density reachable. If so we can add it to clustering, and if not, terminating the execution of clustering.

5   Evaluation

5.1   Experimental Setup

In this section, we run experiments on the real dataset from Beijing (the capital of China) to evaluate our approach. Each location will be matched into each grid cell and the grid cell's area is $100\,m \times 100\,m$. In such a way, the whole city

(5th ring area in Beijing) is partitioned into 300×300 cells in total. We use application programming interface of Gaode Map [12] and Baidu Map [13] to get the point of interests (e.g. hospital, recreational, business parks and colleges etc.) and real estate records.

In order to show our analysis results, we build an interactive interface of platform, Fig. 4 shows our platform. Different analysis model can be opened by clicking the options at the bar column. Then the results will be shown on the map, and detail information at the left. With the help of the platform, people can easily get a comprehensive view of the results.

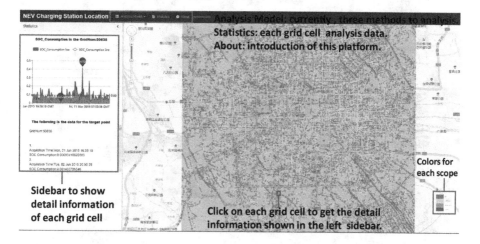

Fig. 4. Hot route results in Beijing.

To get better results, we check different parameters to our model, and based on our data and experiments, we partition the time into hours in energy consumption model, so the base unit of time t is hour. The minimum traffic threshold λ in this paper is 200 and when the number of trajectories from the region g reaches 1000, we called it hot route.

5.2 Recommended Locations

Locations Based on Charging Demand Model. According to the requirements from the decision makers, the locations of parking events can be adjusted based on the distance-based clustering method. Figure 5 illustrates the feature of park event spots. Each circle's number shows the times that parking in those areas. It can be observed that most parking events are outside the 1st ring road. Because ancient building takes up a lot of space inside the 1st ring road areas. Land price is high, workplaces or leisure time place will be not built in these areas. We can also see that most events happened inside the 4th ring of Beijing, like red and purple labels, and eastern areas have more events than other places. Because business and entertainment activities areas are mainly inside the 4th ring, especially, eastern areas is the economic heart of the capital where headquarters of hundreds of companies from around the world are located in.

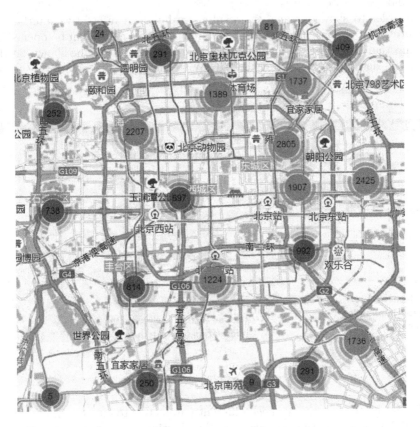

Fig. 5. Parking spots results in Beijing. (Color figure online)

In regarding to the station scale, there are two design schemes, one is to build a large-scale charging station with many chargers, and the other is that many small-scale charging station are scattered across the different areas. Figure 6 shows a density map which shows the different charging demand degree of each cell in the whole year. From this figure, we can find two phenomenas, the one is that most of the cells in one area have high charging demand, these connected high demand areas (the red areas) can be considered to build a large scale charging station, like the red regions in the east; the other is that the demand value of some cells are very high but the adjacent cells are sparse, these places we can consider to build small-scale charging stations. According to the results, the charging demand of a grid cell in the whole year ranges from 0 kWh to 204.51 kWh, the average demand in a cell is 19.62 kWh, the total energy demand is 1455895.99 kWh.

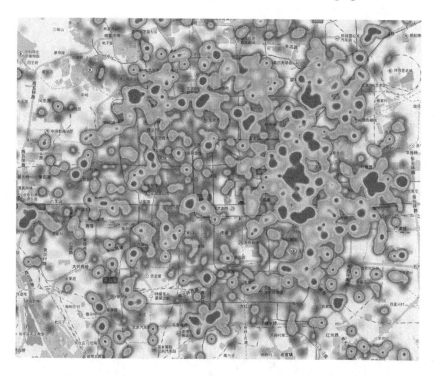

Fig. 6. The locations that need to charge in Beijing. (Color figure online)

Locations Based on Energy Consumption Model. We identify energy consumption for each time period, Fig. 7 shows energy consumption variational process in the whole day. Each sub-figure represents 4 h average data. 8 to 12 o'clock and 16 to 20 o'clock have more consumption data than other time interval due to the rush hours. At the same time, the highest value of energy consumption happens in the morning and evening peak hours.

According to the detail results, the consumption value is from 10 to 20 Wh in the most of time. The average value of energy consumption of the grid cells is 15.38 Wh and the median value is 15.48 Wh. We can see that in the east areas of Beijing, the consumption is higher than other places. Then these high-energy consumption places can be considered to build high-power fast-charging stations for EVs. It can improve EVs trafficability in these areas.

Locations Based on Hot Route Model. The red lines highlight the feature of frequent trajectories which is shown on the Fig. 8. Different gradation of red color shows the different degree of heavily traveled. From the figure, most of hot routes are located in the ring roads and two streets that linked the eastern and western areas, e.g. the most famous thoroughfare Chang'an street. We also find that the start and the end of the hot routes (e.g. traffic hubs, train stations, central business district and 798 art district) are the same regions that park

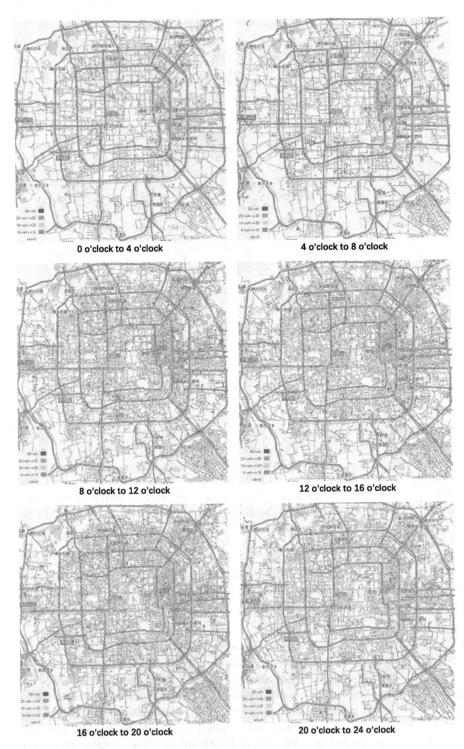

Fig. 7. Energy consumption of each grid cell in a city.

event located in by comparing hot route model with charging demand model results, which can further confirm locations of charging stations.

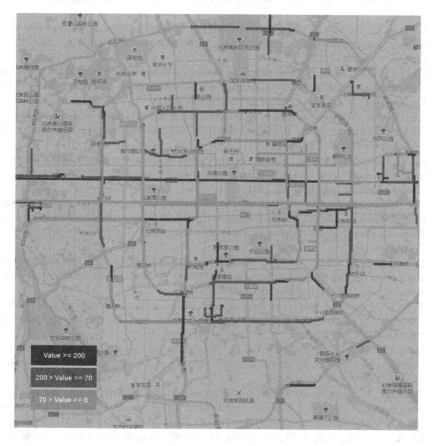

Fig. 8. Hot route results in Beijing. (Color figure online)

6   Conclusion

This paper proposes a charging station planning framework for an urban area. We provide three models to siting the charging stations by considering the spatial and temporal distribution of EV drivers' behaviors which are able to accurately capture the EV charging areas, demand and increase charging convenience of EV users. Although we only examine the models in Beijing city, the methodological framework also can be used to other cities with similar dataset, moreover, these understandings can be not only used in the siting the charging station but also urban planning, traffic management, advertising and other decision support fields. In future work, we will further model the locations of charging station combining with the spatial-temporal analysis results, and heuristics methods can be developed to solve such problems.

References

1. BMW i3. https://www.bmw.com/en/bmw-models/bmw-i3.html. Accessed 28 Mar 2018
2. Lam, A.Y., Leung, Y.W., Chu, X.: Electric vehicle charging station placement: formulation, complexity, and solutions. IEEE Trans. Smart Grid **5**(6), 2846–2856 (2014)
3. Ge, S., Feng, L., Liu, H.: The planning of electric vehicle charging station based on grid partition method. In: 2011 International Conference on Electrical and Control Engineering (ICECE), pp. 2726–2730. IEEE (2011)
4. He, B., Hou, Y.: Research on estimation method of the balance density of electric vehicles charging points. In: IEEE International Conference on Energy Internet (ICEI), pp. 273–278. IEEE (2017)
5. Li, S., Huang, Y., Mason, S.J.: A multi-period optimization model for the deployment of public electric vehicle charging stations on network. Transp. Res. Part C Emerg. Technol. **65**, 128–143 (2016)
6. Chen, T.D., Kockelman, K.M., Khan, M.: The electric vehicle charging station location problem: a parking-based assignment method for Seattle. In: Transportation Research Board 92nd Annual Meeting, Washington, D.C., vol. 340, pp. 13–1254 (2013)
7. Cai, H., Jia, X., Chiu, A.S., Hu, X., Xu, M.: Siting public electric vehicle charging stations in Beijing using big-data informed travel patterns of the taxi fleet. Transp. Res. Part D Transp. Environ. **33**, 39–46 (2014)
8. Yang, J., Dong, J., Hu, L.: A data-driven optimization-based approach for siting and sizing of electric taxi charging stations. Transp. Res. Part C Emerg. Technol. **77**, 462–477 (2017)
9. Han, D., Ahn, Y., Park, S., Yeo, H.: Trajectory-interception based method for electric vehicle taxi charging station problem with real taxi data. Int. J. Sustainable Transp. **10**(8), 671–682 (2016)
10. Cavadas, J., de Almeida Correia, G.H., Gouveia, J.: A MIP model for locating slow-charging stations for electric vehicles in urban areas accounting for driver tours. Transp. Res. Part E Logistics Transp. Rev. **75**, 188–201 (2015)
11. Li, X., Han, J., Lee, J.-G., Gonzalez, H.: Traffic density-based discovery of hot routes in road networks. In: Papadias, D., Zhang, D., Kollios, G. (eds.) SSTD 2007. LNCS, vol. 4605, pp. 441–459. Springer, Heidelberg (2007). https://doi.org/10.1007/978-3-540-73540-3_25
12. Gaode Map API. http://lbs.amap.com/. Accessed 28 Mar 2018
13. Baidu Map API. http://lbsyun.baidu.com/. Accessed 28 Mar 2018

COSRDL: An Event-Driven Control-Oriented System Requirement Modeling Method

Weidong Ma[✉], Yang Deng, Lixing Xu, Wenfeng Lin, and Zhi Liu

Computer Science Laboratory, Institute of Electronic Engineering,
China Academy of Engineering Physics, Mianyang 621999, China
bobmars@163.com, bingo_dy@163.com, butterfly@163.com,
linwenfeng_job@163.com, liuzhi0816@126.com
http://www.caep.ac.cn

Abstract. This paper develops a requirement modeling language called CosRDL for modeling and analyzing of the time series embedded control systems. The system consists of a series of parallel active task that is composed of the functions for different control behaviors, which is largely applied in the development of embedded control systems. CosRDL can specify the features event-driven behaviors, and each event in CosRDL can contain such as input/output and communication of active objects. The active object is a concept model that expresses a computing or control processing. It contains a set of operation, an event queue and task priority. A requirement model and system model of the CosRDL is proposed for analyzing event-driven control systems. The requirement model of CosRDL is built by directed acyclic graph (DAG) to describe the system behavior. The system model of CosRDL is built by uFusion framework. The uFusion was designed to implement the event-driven system architecture. Meanwhile, a case study is presented to illustrate our approach to requirement modeling in the development of event-driven control systems.

Keywords: Requirement modeling language · Control system
Event-driven framework · System model

1 Introduction

Control systems are widely used in many areas including automation, missile, aeronautics etc. The control system generally is a timed sensitive property so that most of them are real-time systems. The control system is stimulated by possibly asynchronous events, which means that they continuously wait for the occurrence of some external or internal event such as a time tick, an arrival of a

W. Ma—The work in this paper has been supported mainly by major project of fund of China Academy of Engineering Physics (Grant No. 060608-2017).

data packet, an execution command, or a particular signal. After recognizing the event, the control system react by performing the appropriate computation that may include manipulating the hardware or generating soft events that trigger other internal software components. Once the event handling is complete, the software goes back to waiting for the next event.

Clearly, we need a kind of programming framework that can respond to a multitude of possible events, any of which can arrive at unpredictable times and in an unpredictable sequence. The developers of modern GUI systems, and many embedded applications, including the control system, have adopted a common program structure that elegantly solves the problem of dealing with many asynchronous events in a timely manner. This program structure is generally called event-driven programming.

The control system response to an event depends as much on the event type as on the application context in which the event arrives. State machines provide very strong support for handling the context. The most ways of associating events are defined event-handler functions that are ultimately based on the prevalent event-action paradigm, in which event types are mapped to the code that is supposed to be executed in response.

In control system, the I/O requirement and device control are mainly functional that can be modeled by event-driven. The requirement capture and analysis for event system is a tedious job because of lots of complex states and event operations in the system. In the traditional software engineering, the requirement engineers have to spend plenty of time to understand and analyze system requirement manually to find whether there is inconsistency or ambiguity in the system requirement.

A lot of control systems are safety critical that have to be spent great efforts in designing and developing embedded software. During the software life cycle, the defects may be introduced in all phases, from requirement analysis to software maintenance. There are few approaches and tool to support inspecting the requirement documents, and we have to spend much time on requirement analysis and software design, but cannot avoid the defects arising from ambiguities, contradictions and omissions in requirement analysis phase.

In this paper we submit an event-driven framework called uFusion and a control-oriented system requirement describe language called CosRDL. The CosRDL is a method to modeling the real-time control system, which deal with a series of response with event triggered during software running life according to outer environment.

2   Related Works

In this section we briefly provide some background information on Event-Driven Framework and Requirement Modeling of Embedded System.

2.1   Event-Driven Framework

The traditional event-driven architecture is immensely popular in event-driven graphical user interface frameworks since 1990 s, such as MFC, Tcl/Tk, X-Windows, Sun-View, Java/AWT/Swing, Action Script, Qt, .NET, and so on. The event-driven architecture permits more flexible patterns of control than any sequential system that an event-driven scheme uses the CPU more efficiently and tends to consume less stack space, which are all very desirable characteristics for embedded systems. A single queue event-driven system is clearly divided into the event-driven infrastructure and the application (see Fig. 1). The event-driven infrastructure consists of an event loop, an event dispatcher, and an event queue. The application consists of event-handler functions that all share common data.

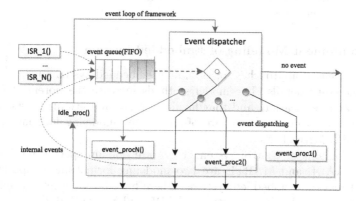

Fig. 1. The principle of event-driven framework executed with a single queue. When the system is running, the dispatcher must be able to check for events continuously and frequently. This shows that the event-handler functions must execute quickly, and the event-handler function must be no error and to avoid any blocking code or simply long-running code. Some error in event-handler function can be to halt the entire application.

In the domain of embedded system there are some event-driven frameworks such as Contiki, OXF and QF etc.

Contiki is a lightweight, open source and multi-tasking operating system written in C language that supports tiny, low-cost, battery-operated and wireless sensor networks [1]. Contiki is developed by Swedish Institute of Computer Science by Adam Dunkels and it is highly portable operating system built around an event-driven kernel. A typical Contiki configuration is 2 kbytes of RAM and 40 kbytes of ROM. A process of Contiki is defined by an event handler function and an optional poll handler function.

The Contiki kernel is a lightweight event scheduler that sends the events to running processes and calling the processes polling handlers. The execution of a process can only be triggered by dispatched events or a polling mechanism. Contiki kernel provides two kinds of events: synchronous events and asynchronous events that the synchronous events are sent out immediately to target processes, and scheduled while asynchronous events are in queued and dispatched later [2]. Contiki's protothreads, have been used in many different embedded systems.

The Object Executive Framework (OXF) is designed by IBM to support Rhapsody. The main extensions of Rhapsody statecharts are hierarchy, concurrency and object-oriented communications and actions. Rhapsody allows C, C++ and Java code as all the models we deal with.

Quantum Framework (QF) is using the active objects to implement the event driven platform [3]. QF is event driven framework from Quantum Leaps that is used to implement event driven programming and UML state chart in embedded system and developed in C or C++. The active object denotes an autonomous object engaging other active objects asynchronously via events. The UML further proposes the UML variant of statecharts with which to model the behavior of event-driven active objects.

2.2   Requirement Modeling of Embedded System

Using model-based approaches for designing embedded systems helps abstract away unnecessary details. The model methods increase the potential for easy validation and verification, and that facilitate reuse and evolution. As to build the model of embedded system, we often use the modeling language such as UML, SysML, MARTE etc. [4,5].

In the domains of control system, there are domain specific methods and languages. AADL and MARTE are two modeling formalisms supporting the analysis of real-time embedded systems. There have been continuous efforts to establish a strong relationship between AADL and MARTE [6,7].

To address hybrid real-time and embedded systems, the paper [8] proposes to extend statecharts [9] using both MARTE and the theory of hybrid automata that called the extension hybrid MARTE statecharts. It provides an improvement over the hybrid automata. The formal syntax and semantics of hybrid MARTE statecharts are given based on labeled transition systems and live transition systems.

Giotto is a periodic-driven modeling language [10]. The tasks defined in a mode of Giotto are performed in parallel, and omit this feature and leaves it to the implementation language. The SPARDL (spacecraft requirement description language) is developed as a requirement modeling language for modeling and analyzing periodic control systems [11–14]. SPARDL can specify the features such as periodic driven behaviors, procedure invocations, timed guard, and mode transition, and provides the basic modeling element mode that represents the observable state in the control system.

The PTA-OZ combines the specification language Object-Z with the probabilistic processes PTA [15]. It can provide descriptions for both static and dynamic semantics of embedded software models. PTA-OZ is defined as a probabilistic timed automation that combined with Object-Z. The paper [16] presents a method to evaluate throughput and response time of systems described in MARTE models. A MARTE model includes a use case diagram, a deployment diagram and a set of activity diagrams. It can be transformed the MARTE model into a network of timed automata [17] in UPPAAL and use UPPAAL to find the possible best throughput and response time of a system, and the best solution in the worst cases for both of them.

The paper [18] presents the complex UML/MARTE design space exploration methodology, an approach based on a novel combination of Model Driven Engineering (MDE), Electronic System Level (ESL) and design exploration technologies. From that UML/MARTE based model, the automated generation framework proposed produces an executable, configurable and fast performance model which includes functional code of the application components. The paper also presents the performance model generation framework, including the enhancements with regard the previous simulation and estimation technology, and the exploration technology.

2.3 HCSP Modeling of Embedded System

Hybrid Communicating Sequential Process (HCSP) is a formal language for describing hybrid systems, which extends CSP by introducing differential equations for modeling continuous evolutions and interrupts for modeling the arbitrary interaction between continuous evolutions and discrete jumps. The syntax of HCSP can be described as follows [19,20]:

$$P ::= \text{skip} \mid x := e \mid \text{wait } d \mid ch?x \mid ch!e \mid P; Q \mid B \to P \mid P \sqcap Q \mid P^*$$
$$\mid \ []_{i \in I} io_i \to P_i \mid \langle F(\dot{\mathbf{s}}, \mathbf{s}) = 0 \& B \rangle \mid \langle F(\dot{\mathbf{s}}, \mathbf{s}) = 0 \& B \rangle \unrhd []_{i \in I}(io_i \to Q_i) \quad (1)$$
$$S ::= P \mid S \| S$$

where $x, \mathbf{s}$ for variables and vectors of variables, respectively, B and e are boolean and arithmetic expressions, d is a non-negative real constant, ch is the channel name, io_i stands for a communication event, i.e., either $ch_i?x$ or $ch_i!e$, P, Q, Q_i are sequential process terms, and S stands for an HCSP process term. Given an HCSP process S, we define $Var(S)$ for the set of variables in S, and $\Sigma(S)$ the set of channels occurring in S, respectively. The informal meanings of the individual constructors are as follows:

- skip, $x := e$, wait d, $ch?x$, $ch!e$, $P; Q$, $P \sqcap Q$, and $[]_{i \in I} io_i \to P_i$ are defined as usual. $B \to P$ behaves as P if B is true, otherwise terminates.
- For repetition P^*, P executes for an arbitrary finite number of times.
- $\langle F(\dot{\mathbf{s}}, \mathbf{s}) = 0 \& B \rangle$ is the continuous evolution statement. It forces the vector $\mathbf{s}$ of real variables to obey the differential equations F as long as B, which defines the domain of $\mathbf{s}$, holds, and terminates when B turns false.
- $S_1 \| S_2$ behaves as if S_1 and S_2 run independently except that all communications along the common channels connecting S_1 and S_2 are to be synchronized. S_1 and S_2 in parallel can neither share variables, nor input or output channels.

Thus HCSP is expressive enough for describing distributed components and the inter-actions between them, also the modeling of embedded system.

3   Framework of Event-Driven System

3.1   Framework of uFusion

In this section we introduce the concepts associated with event-driven, real-time application frameworks that called uFusion. The uFusion is an event-driven framework that structured according to the Hollywood principle, which means an event-driven application is not in control while waiting for an event. Only once the event arrives, the event-driven module that named active object is called to process the event and then it quickly relinquishes the control again. Therefore, an event-driven program to wait for many events in parallel, so the system remains responsive to all events that need to handle. The inversion of control gives the event-driven infrastructure all the defining characteristics of a framework.

The uFusion framework is structured according to inversion of control that makes a framework different from a toolkit. A toolkit is essentially a set of predefined functions that we must write the main body of the application and call the various functions from the toolkit. When we use a framework, we reuse the main body and provide the application code that it calls, so all control resides in the framework. The uFusion based on event-driven architectures recognizes that the events are controlling the application, not the other way around. The uFusion Framework is showed in Fig. 2.

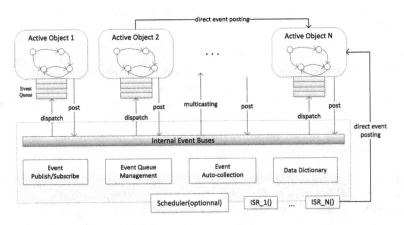

Fig. 2. The uFusion framework of control system includes several active objects that execute as a thread or photothread. Each active object received and dispatched the events.

The difference of the uFusion, Contiki, OXF and QF showed in Table 1.

Table 1. The compare results of four frameworks. The HSM is hierarchy state machines.

Feature	Contiki	OXF	QF	uFusion
Asynchronize	Yes	Yes	Yes	Yes
Synchronize	Yes	No	No	No
Directness	Yes	Yes	Yes	Yes
indirectness	No	No	Yes	Yes
Normal	Yes	Yes	Yes	Yes
Urgency	No	No	Yes	Yes
Point to point	Yes	Yes	Yes	Yes
Multicast	No	No	Yes	Yes
Broadcast	Yes	No	No	Yes
Allocate	User manage	Static	Static/Dynamic	Static/Dynamic
Garbage collection	-	-	Yes	Yes
Model	Protothreads	HSM	HSM	Protothreads/HSM
Collaboration	2 levels	-	64 levels	64 levels
Preemptive	-	OS Need	Single stack/OS need	Single stack/OS need
Trace	-	-	Yes	Yes

3.2 Development of uFusion

We design a graphics mode of uFusion to develop an embedded system that showed in Fig. 3. The designer develops the system according to the follow steps.

Firstly, the designers need to analyze the system requirements, inputs and outputs. Then we disassemble it to an event list. Secondly, it must ensure that the events are agglomerated to some active objects, and defined the event-handler. Once every active object was defined, we can produce the framework codes that can be run with the uFusion.

The FActive is a data structure that define an active object:

```
struct _FActive {
    Fsm super;
    FF_EQUEUE_TYPE  eQueue;
    FF_OS_TASK_PARAM param;
    F_UINT8 ucPrio;
    FActiveVtbl const * vtbl;
};
```

The struct _Fsm is define as:

```
typedef struct _Fsm {
    struct FBaseVtbl* FsmVtbl;
    union FsmAttrA state;
    union FsmAttrB temp;
}Fsm;
```

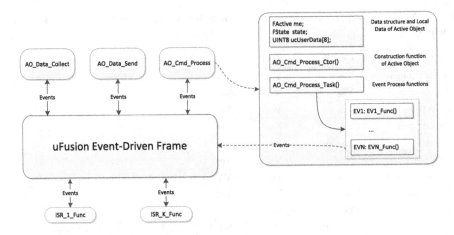

Fig. 3. The Design mode of uFusion framework. The FActive defines an active object that include structure Fsm, FF_EQUEUE_TYPE, FF_OS_TASK_PARAM and FActiveVtbl. The struct _Fsm is define as struct FBaseVtbl, union FsmAttrA, and union FsmAttrB. And we can define a specific active object as a structure that includes the FActive super and other data elements.

And we can define a specific active object as:

```
typedef struct {
    FActive   super;
    FTimeEvt timeEvt;
    F_UINT8 ucSENDData[AO1_SIZE];
}AO_DATA_SEND;
```

The AO_Cmd_Process_Ctor() is the initialization function of the active object named AO_Cmd_Process. AO_Cmd_Process_Task() is the event process function that defined some event handler.

4   Approach of CosRDL

4.1   Approach of CosRDL-Based Development

In most corporations, the system engineers write requirement by natural language with document software like Word, Tex. The requirement documents of natural language have no clearly semantic information and formal syntax structure. Our approach is to translate the original requirement document into semi-structure requirement by mining technics for the software own characteristics shown in Fig. 4. The idea is just to add some domain key words that written by control domain terms identified by data dictionary, so that the semi-structure requirement document keeps everything unchanged.

For the system and hardware requirement, we described it by AADL (architecture analysis and design language). Moreover, we propose a modeling language

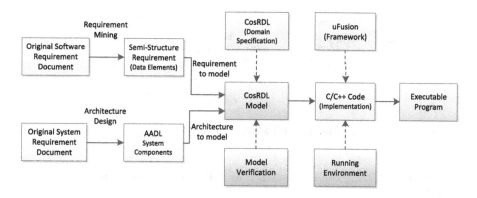

Fig. 4. Approach of CosRDL-based model development.

called CosRDL as the system target. The CosRDL shows a kind of graphics view to engineers to communicate each other at different levels, and it transform form CosRDL to C/C++ language transparent by modeling tools. CosRDL has supported formal semantics which can facilitate to formal analysis and verification.

4.2 The Requirement Model of CosRDL

In this section we discuss the requirement model of CosRDL that is defined in the follow:

Definition 1. *The requirement model of CosRDL is a hierarchical modeling that defined in a tuple that includes five objects, the action set, the outer environment object, and the function σ, s, and S:*

$$CosRDL_{req} ::= (Acts, Envs, \sigma, s, S) \qquad (2)$$

The $Acts = \{a_1, a_2, ..., a_n\}$ is a node set of all operations for the control device, including the computing units and actuators, which relays on the time and parameters of outer environment. The can be considered as a state, an operation or a computing unit. The $Envs = \{e_1, e_2, ..., e_m\}$ defines an array state parameters such position, speed, accelerator and the inner states. $s \in Acts$ is an initial node, and the $s \subseteq Acts$ is a final node set.

The σ mapps the environment parameters and trigger time to an operation or a group of operations :

$$b = \sigma(a, e, t), where \ a, b \in Acts, e \in Envs, t \in R \qquad (3)$$

$t \in R$ is a trigger time variable.

Every node $v \in Acts$, if v has more than 2 input from other mode, we define two operation $\otimes$ and $+$. The operation $\otimes$ means that all input is triggered, thus the node is activated. The operation $+$ means that if one input is triggered, then the node is activated.

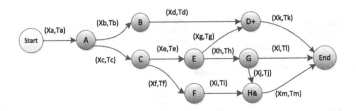

Fig. 5. DAG Model of $CosRDL_{req}$.

So the $CosRDL_{req}$ can be expressed as a directed acyclic graph (DAG) such as Fig. 5.

The DAG is a finite directed graph with no directed cycles, and it consists of finitely many vertices and edges, with each edge directed from one vertex to another, such that there is no way to start at any vertex v and follow a consistently-directed sequence of edges that eventually loops back to v again. Equivalently, a DAG is a directed graph that has a topological ordering, a sequence of the vertices such that every edge is directed from earlier to later in the sequence.

In the requirement CosRDL model, a sequence of the vertex that is expressed an operation or a group of operations can be executed by partially ordered relation. The edges are expressed a trigger condition, which includes environment parameters and time.

4.3 Syntax of CosRDL

Definition 2. *CosRDL is a formal language for describing a special hybrid control systems, which introduces the event set and the channels (to execute actions) for modeling the control system. The syntax of CosRDL can be described as follows:*

$$P ::= x := y \mid P; Q \mid P^* \mid P(e,t) \to Q \mid ch?x \to P(e,t) \mid P(e,t) \to ch!x \quad (4)$$

Where x, y for variables, and the variables t is global clock timer for non-negative real number. The vectors e is the state vector of the system for describing the state and the environment.

ch is the channel name, the equation of $ch?x \to P(e,t)$ indicates that the data x come from the channel ch, and affected the state value of vectors $P(e,t)$. $P(e,t) \to ch!x$ means that the action node P send variable x to channel ch in the state value of vectors e, t.

The equation of $P(e,t) \to Q$ indicates that the system state P turn to the system state Q when the condition (e,t) is satisfied.

The operation nodes are defined by syntactic elements. It support to model the architecture of a control-orient system at Backus-Naur Form to specify the system behaviors in detail as:

$$P \rightarrow \{decls \quad stmts\}$$
$$decls \rightarrow decls \mid type \quad id \mid \varepsilon$$
$$type \rightarrow type[\text{num}] \mid \text{basic}$$
$$stmts \rightarrow stmts \quad stmt \mid \varepsilon$$
$$stmt \rightarrow loc = bool$$
$$\mid \text{if}(bool) \quad stmt \quad \text{else} \quad stmt$$
$$\mid \text{while}(bool) \quad stmt$$
$$\mid \text{break}$$
$$\mid P$$
$$loc \rightarrow loc[bool] \mid \text{id}$$

$$(5)$$

The syntactic of *bool* is an expression that defined as:

$$bool \rightarrow bool \| join \mid join$$
$$join \rightarrow join \&\& equality \mid equality$$
$$equality \rightarrow equality == rel \mid equality! = rel \mid rel$$
$$rel \rightarrow expr < expr \mid expr > expr$$
$$\mid expr >= expr \mid expr > expr$$
$$expr \rightarrow expr + term \mid expr - term \mid term$$
$$term \rightarrow term * unary \mid term \mid term/unary \mid unary$$
$$unary \rightarrow !unary \mid -unary \mid factor$$
$$factor \rightarrow (bool) \mid loc \mid \text{num} \mid \text{real} \mid \text{true} \mid \text{false}$$

$$(6)$$

4.4   The System Model of CosRDL

Definition 3. *The system model of CosRDL is a hierarchical modeling language that defined in a sequence of active objects, a related data dictionary, the global events set, schedule policy, global clocker and schedule frameworks:*

$$CosRDL_{system} ::= (ActObj, Evts, DataDict, uFrm, t) \qquad (7)$$

ActObj defines a set of active objects. *Evts* defines a set of global event that used by the *ActObj*. *uFrm* is the uFusion component.

DataDict defines the set of data dictionary that mainly consist of the global variables used by the system and *ActObj*. Table 2 shows an example of the data dictionary that defines three variables.

The first item is an integer variable named nHeight1 whose default value is zero and defined the value range. The second one is used as a read-only variable that denotes the acceleration of the control system, which is an input from the sensor of acceleration. The last one uSW1 is a write-only variable that is used to drive 8 bits relay.

Table 2. An example of the data dictionary.

Name	Type	Bits	Read/Write	Dim	Range	Default value	Unit
nHeight1	Int32	32	R/W	0	-	0	meter
fGZ1	Float32	32	R	0	-	0.0	m/s2
uSW1	UInt8	8	W	0	0–255	0	-

Definition 4. *The active object is defined to be a tuple as follows:*

$$ActObj ::= (Acts, EvtQueue, pri) \tag{8}$$

Acts is a set of the event process operations. EvtQueue is an event queue. The pri is a priority of the active object.

So the *ActObj* is event process model which can be showed in Fig. 3. The event process function can be modeled in simulink/stateflow, activity diagram, Pseudocode, or C/C++ codes.

4.5   The Strategy of Translation Requirement Model to System Model of CosRDL

The requirement model of CosRDL describes the functional behavior of the embedded system and the relation between the system with outer environment. The system model of CosRDL describes the software architecture, module interaction and interoperation of active objects, including the event process function of every active object. We need a good strategy for translating the requirement model into system model. The key process of the translation is how to produce the active object effectively and define the events and event process functions.

It may be seen that the suggested procedure is designed the active object according to the longest paths of the DAG graph that no branch path.

5   Case Study

This section introduces a case study that indicate how to use CosRDL and uFusion. We build a simplified CosRDL model of electronics system of the missile showed in Fig. 6. The Fig. 7 indicates the system model CosRDL-based that translated from Fig. 6.

The operations of the model are divided into three phase: powered phase, free flight phase and reentry phase. Every phase has to execute some operations or compute some algorithms by embedded computer that based on the event come from environment or inner timer.

Traditionally, we developed the embedded program manually to cost a lot of time. If the requirements change frequently, we have to modify code every time. As presented earlier, the approach of CosRDL is a model-driven development,

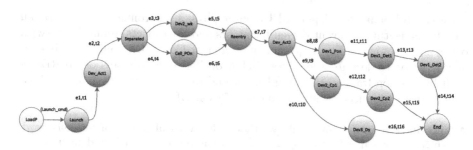

Fig. 6. A simplified requirement model CosRDL-based of electronics system

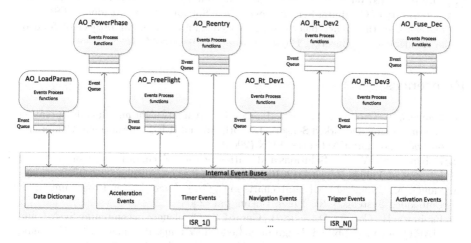

Fig. 7. A CosRDL-based system model for a control system

thus we developed the embedded software with CosRDL and uFusion framework. If the requirements were changed, we modified the requirement model based on CosRDL and automatically translate it into the system model that bind with uFusion.

In this case we designed eight active objects to implement the embedded program based the uFusion framework, including the load parameter, power phase, free flight, reentry trigger, three devices active object and the fuse decision active object. It must handle acceleration Events, Timer Events, Navigation Events, Trigger Events and Activation Events etc. Every event was defined and post and dispatch by specific active object.

6 Conclusions

The model-driven development approach that based on CosRDL is to solve the modeling, reuse and analyzing for the embedded control systems. These system consists of a series of parallel active objects, and the objects can be executed for some control behaviors depended by outer physics environment. CosRDL can specify the features of event-driven behaviors and the objects communicate with other active objects. The requirement model of CosRDL is built by directed acyclic graph to describe the system behavior. The system model of CosRDL is built by uFusion framework to implement and reuse in system design. The final codes can be produced by system model of CosRDL.

Acknowledgements. First of all, we thank all the collaborators of the joint work presented in this paper for their great contribution. Some works of the domain model of embedded system are proposal by prof. Geguang Pu and Weika Miu who work in East China Normal University. Other researches of the formal modeling and hybrid CSP are depended on prof. Naijun Zhan and Shuling Wang, who work in the State Key Laboratory of Computer Science, Institute of Software, China Academy of Science.

The work in this paper has been supported mainly by major project of fund of China Academy of Engineering Physics (Grant No. 060608-2017)

References

1. Dunkels, A., Gronvall, B., Voigt, T.: Contiki - A lightweight and flexible operating system for tiny networked Sensors. In: 29th Annual IEEE International Conference on Local Computer Networks, LCN (2004)
2. Kalyoncu, S.: Wireless Solutions and Authentication Mechanisms for Contiki Based Internet of Things Network (2016). https://core.ac.uk/-display/36300735
3. Samek, M.: Practical UML Statecharts in C/C++: Event-Driven Programming for Embedded Systems. CRC Press, Burlington (2008)
4. Espinoza, H., Cancila, D., Selic, B., Gérard, S.: Challenges in combining SysML and MARTE for model-based design of embedded systems. In: Paige, R.F., Hartman, A., Rensink, A. (eds.) ECMDA-FA 2009. LNCS, vol. 5562, pp. 98–113. Springer, Heidelberg (2009). https://doi.org/10.1007/978-3-642-02674-4_8
5. Khan, A.M., Mallet, F., Rashid, M.: Combining SysML and Marte/CCSL to model complex electronic systems. In: 2016 International Conference on Information Systems Engineering, pp. 12–17 (2016)
6. Architecture analysis and design language (AADL) (2014). http://www.aadl.info/
7. Mallet, F., Andre, C., DeAntoni, J.: Executing AADL models with UML/MARTE. In: 2009 14th IEEE International Conference on Engineering of Complex Computer Systems, pp. 371–376 (2009)
8. Liu, J., Liu, Z., He, J., Mallet, F., Ding, Z.: Hybrid MARTE statecharts. Front. Comput. Sci. **7**(1), 95–108 (2013)
9. The mathworks: Stateflow and stateflow coder, users guide (2014). http://www.mathworks.com/help/releases/R13sp2/pdf_doc/stateflow/sf_ug.pdf
10. Henzinger, T.A., Horowitz, B., Kirsch, C.M.: Giotto: a time-triggered language for embedded programming. Technical report, Department of Electronic Engineering and Computer Science, University of California, Berkeley, Berkeley, CA, USA (2001)
11. Wang, Z., Li, J., Zhao, Y., Qi, Y., Pu, G., He, J., Gu, B.: SPARDL: a requirement modeling language for periodic control system. In: Margaria, T., Steffen, B. (eds.) ISoLA 2010. LNCS, vol. 6415, pp. 594–608. Springer, Heidelberg (2010). https://doi.org/10.1007/978-3-642-16558-0_48

12. Wang, Z., Pu, G., Li, J., Chen, Y.: A novel requirement analysis approach for periodic control systems. Front. Comput. Sci. **7**(2), 214–235 (2013)
13. Yang, M., Wang, Z., Geguang, P., Qin, S., et al.: The stochastic semantics and verification for periodic control systems. Sci. China Inf. Sci. **55**(12), 2675–2693 (2012)
14. Gu, B., Dong, Y., Wang, Z.: Formal modeling approach for aerospace embedded software. J. Softw. **26**(2), 321–331 (2015). http://www.jos.org.cn/1000-9825/4784. htm (in Chinese)
15. Xu, H., Zhang, Y., Gu, J.: A formal modeling methods for embedded software architecture. Acta Electronica Sin. **42**(8), 1515–1521 (2014)
16. Yan, G., Zhu, X.-Y., Yan, R., Li, G.: Formal throughput and response time analysis of MARTE models. In: Merz, S., Pang, J. (eds.) ICFEM 2014. LNCS, vol. 8829, pp. 430–445. Springer, Cham (2014). https://doi.org/10.1007/978-3-319-11737-9_28
17. Alur, R., Dill, D.L.: A theory of timed automata. Theoret. Comput. Sci. **126**(2), 183–235 (1994)
18. Herrera, F., Posadas, H., Penil, P., Villar, E., Ferrero, F., Valencia, R., Palermo, G.: The COMPLEX methodology for UML/MARTE modeling and design space exploration of embedded systems. J. Syst. Archit. **60**(1), 55–78 (2014)
19. He, J.: From CSP to hybrid systems. In: A Classical Mind, Essays in Honour of C.A.R. Hoare, pp. 171–189. Prentice Hall International Ltd. (1994)
20. Chaochen, Z., Ji, W., Ravn, A.P.: A formal description of hybrid systems. In: Alur, R., Henzinger, T.A., Sontag, E.D. (eds.) HS 1995. LNCS, vol. 1066, pp. 511–530. Springer, Heidelberg (1996). https://doi.org/10.1007/BFb0020972

Formal Collision Avoidance Analysis for Rigorous Building of Autonomous Marine Vehicles

Rongjie Yan[1], Xiangtong Yao[2], Junjie Yang[2], and Kai Huang[2(✉)]

[1] State Key Laboratory of Computer Science, ISCAS, Beijing, China
yrj@ios.ac.cn
[2] School of Data and Computer Science, Sun Yat-sen University, Guangzhou, China
{yaoxt3,yangjj27}@mail2.sysu.edu.cn, huangk36@mail.sysu.edu.cn

Abstract. The prosperity of autonomous vehicles puts forward the even higher and stricter requirement for safe navigation. Collision avoidance is an essential ingredient to ensure safety for these vehicles. Instead of designing an optimization algorithm to avoid collision, we investigate the fundamental rules of collision avoidance for autonomous marine vessels. In the investigation, to analyze the completeness and consistency of the rules, we enumerate all the encountering scenarios and present the through analysis from various perspectives. To check the effectiveness of the rules, we also construct a formal model for autonomous vessels in navigation. Primary experimental results have demonstrated that applying current rules is not sufficient to avoid collision. More precise standards or facilitated strategies are necessary to guarantee safety for the navigation of autonomous marine vessels.

1 Introduction

Collision avoidance is an important topic in avionic, ground, marine transportations, especially for autonomous areas. The prosperity of the research for unmanned surface vehicles in both academic and industrial groups, puts forward more challenges for the design of correct collision avoidance strategies. In the community of marine vehicles, existing solutions mainly employ fuzzy logic [7], artificial intelligence based techniques [9] such as planning [2], evolutionary algorithms, or ant colony algorithms [11] to draw collision avoidance strategies. These decision makings follow the standards such as 1972 International rules for collision avoidance (COLREGS) for marine vehicles. Though various efforts have been attempted to analyze the correctness of the algorithms, there are few works on verifying the correctness and completeness of the underlying standards, which is fundamental. The lack of formalization of the rules may lead to various understanding, and thus very different decisions from different viewpoints.

This work has been partly funded by the National Key Basic Research (973) Program of China under Grant No. 2014CB340701, and the National Science Foundation of China under Grant No. U1435220 and 61370156.

© Springer Nature Singapore Pte Ltd. 2018
Y. Bi et al. (Eds.): ESTC 2017, CCIS 857, pp. 118–127, 2018.
https://doi.org/10.1007/978-981-13-1026-3_9

In this paper, we investigate the rules on collision avoidance in COLREGS for autonomous surface vessels. To formally analyze the effectiveness of the rules in various encountering cases, we also model the behavior of an autonomous marine vessel in navigation, without considering environment and weather conditions.

The contributions of the paper are as follows. First, we have studied the completeness of the rules for collision avoidance. Due to the ambiguity of the description, it is hard to provide a formalization for precise collision avoidance with respect to various encountering scenarios. We enumerate the encountering scenarios for two vessels with a potential collision risk, and present the expected action from their own perspective, instead of assuming one is the home and the other is the target. Second, we present a formal model for an autonomous surface vessel, to check the effectiveness of the rules for collision avoidance. In the model, we mainly consider its behavior in collision avoidance, without any optimization strategies. Some primary experimental results have already revealed that applying the rules alone without other facilities cannot avoid collision, when multiple vessels are involved in the encountering situation.

The organization of the paper is as follows. Section 2 reviews the related work in the literature. Section 3 recaps the basic concepts on marine vessels and the formalization. We present the formalization in Sect. 4. Section 5 demonstrates the verification results. Section 6 concludes.

2   Related Work

Being a critical research topic, collision avoidance for various vehicles has been investigated by many researchers. In the community of collision avoidance for marine vessels, many works have attempted to design autonomous navigation systems to avoid collision [6,8,11]. For example, Perera et al. adopt a fuzzy logic based design making process according to the rules of COLREGS [6]. An ant colony algorithm is employed for collision avoidance route planning [11]. The work in [9] has summarized artificial intelligence based techniques for collision avoidance, such as evolutionary algorithms, fuzzy logic, expert systems and neural networks, and combination of these techniques. Experimental evaluations have been carried on intelligent guidance for ship autonomous navigation and collision avoidance [5]. There are also some works adopting mathematical models for the design of a safe ship trajectory. Sutulo et al. have simulated the design by formal models based on manoeuvring theory [10]. Lu et al. have verified collision avoidance behaviors for unmanned surface vessels using probabilistic model checking [4]. However, except for having been interpreted with fuzzy logic [7], few work has focused on the rigorous analysis of the rules for collision avoidance in COLREGS. Different from these works, we attempt to formally analyze the rules and check its effectiveness without any navigation optimizations.

3   Preliminaries

We mainly investigate collision avoidance cases for marine surface vessels. First, the related terms for a marine vessel and the corresponding rules for collision avoidance are explained. Then the concept for marine vessel behavior modelling is recapped.

3.1   Basic Concepts on Marine Vessels

The structure and the corresponding terms of a marine vessel are illustrated in Fig. 1. The left and right sides of a vessel are called port and starboard sides, respectively. Every vessel is equipped with two sidelights for navigation in night. During navigation, position, velocity and orientation are important features of a vessel (for simplicity, we ignore other features such as type and size).

When an autonomous vessel encounters the other, a vessel regards itself as the home and the other as the target. According to the rules of COLREGS, the vessel coming from the starboard side has higher priority in the encountering situation, and is called *Stand on* vessel. And the vessel coming from the port side has lower priority and is called *Give way* vessel. Passing on the port side of a vessel is recommended in an encountering situation.

Three types of encountering scenario exist, i.e., `head-on`, `crossing` and `overtaking`. To differentiate various cases and clarify the corresponding actions, we adopt the division introduced in [11] that the surrounding of a home is divided into five regions, as shown in Fig. 2(a). The informal description for collision avoidance rules in COLREGS[1] can be summarized as follows.

1. `head-on`: two vessels are meeting on reciprocal or nearly reciprocal courses, both sidelights are visible by night. That is, a target appears in E area, w.r.t the home. Each shall alter its course to starboard.
2. `overtaking`: a vessel shall be deemed to be overtaking when another is approaching from a direction more than 22.5° abaft her beam. That is, a home is approaching the target in its C area. If the home is on the starboard quarter of the target, the home should alter its course to starboard, otherwise to port.

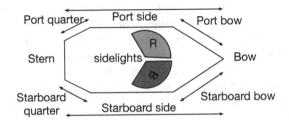

Fig. 1. Terms on the parts of a marine vessel

---

[1] http://www.otenmaritime.com/international-collision-regulations/.

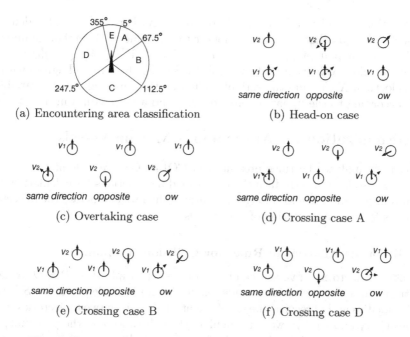

(a) Encountering area classification

(b) Head-on case

(c) Overtaking case

(d) Crossing case A

(e) Crossing case B

(f) Crossing case D

Fig. 2. Enumeration of encountering scenarios between two vessels

3. **crossing**: only one sidelight of the other is visible. That is, a target is approaching from A, B or D area of a home. The (give way) vessel that has the other on her own starboard side shall keep out of the way. For the vessel from B region, a left turn can be taken to avoid collision [11]. If a starboard alteration is simply not practicable, it may be better to slow down.

3.2 Timed Automata

We introduce timed automata (TA) [1] to model the behavior of an autonomous vessel, which can describe the state transformation with respect to certain conditions, such as timing, event-triggered constraints.

Let X be a set of clocks, $\boldsymbol{V}$ be a set of bounded integer variables. We use $C(X, \boldsymbol{V})$ and $U(X, \boldsymbol{V})$, respectively, to denote the set of linear constraints and the set of updates over clocks and integer variables, where updates on clocks are restricted to resetting clock variables to zero.

A TA is a tuple $A = (L, X, \boldsymbol{V}, E, Inv, l_0)$, where L is a set of locations, $E \subseteq L \times C(X, \boldsymbol{V}) \times U(X, \boldsymbol{V}) \times L$ is a set of edges, $Inv : L \rightarrow C(X, \boldsymbol{V})$ assigns invariants to locations, and l_0 is the initial location. A network of n timed automata (NTA) is a tuple of timed automata $A_1 || \cdots || A_n$ over X and $\boldsymbol{V}$. A clock valuation γ for a set X is a mapping from X to $\mathbb{R}^+$, where $\mathbb{R}^+$ is the set of non-negative real numbers. A variable valuation u is a function from $\boldsymbol{V}$ to $\mathbb{Z}$, where $\mathbb{Z}$ is the set of integers. A pair of valuation (γ, u) satisfies a constraint ϕ over X and $\boldsymbol{V}$, denoted by $(\gamma, u) \models \phi$, if and only if ϕ evaluates to *true* with the valuations γ and u. Let $\gamma_0(x) = 0$ for all $x \in X$. For $\delta \in \mathbb{R}^+$, $\gamma + \delta$ denotes the clock valuation that maps every clock x to the value $\gamma(x) + \delta$. For an update $\eta(Y, \boldsymbol{V'})$ over a pair of (γ, u), where $Y \subseteq X$ and $\boldsymbol{V'} \subseteq \boldsymbol{V}$, $(\gamma, u)[\eta(Y, \boldsymbol{V'})]$ denotes the clock valuation that maps all clocks in Y to zero and agrees with γ for all clocks in $X \setminus Y$, and the variable valuation that maps all integer variables in $\boldsymbol{V'}$ according to the update expression in η and agrees with u in $\boldsymbol{V} \setminus \boldsymbol{V'}$.

4   Formalization for Autonomous Marine Vessels

To formally analyze the rules presented in COLREGS, we present the syntax of marine vessels, and introduce the corresponding functions for calculating the risk of collision and the encountering scenarios. Then we enumerate the expected behaviors for the encountering of two vessels.

4.1   Rigorous Analysis of Rules for Collision Avoidance

The set of trajectories of vessels can be defined as the tuple $\mathcal{V} = \langle P, S, O \rangle$, where P is the set of locations which include longitude and latitude positions, S is the set of velocities and O records the set of orientations. Given two trajectories from two vessels v_1 and $v_2 \in \mathcal{V}$, we can calculate their distance and the possibility of collision, to take action in advance. The function to judge the collision is denoted by $\mathcal{R} : \mathcal{V} \times \mathcal{V} \mapsto \mathbb{B}$, where $\mathbb{B} = \{true, false\}$.

In the case of collision risk, we need to further determine the relative position of involved vessels to take the corresponding action, whose function can be defined as $\mathcal{P} : \mathcal{V} \times \mathcal{V} \mapsto D$, where $D = \{A, B, C_p, C_s, D, E\}$ is the set of relative positions. In the function, the first parameter is from the home, and the second is from the target. Informally speaking, it presents the relative position of the target with respect to the home. For the ease of formalization, area C is divided into two subareas with $C = C_p \cup C_s$ and the regions of C_p and C_s are $(180°, 247.5°]$ and $(112.5°, 180°]$, respectively.

Additional to the function for judging relative position, we further introduce the function for orientation comparison: $\mathcal{O} : \mathcal{V} \times \mathcal{V} \mapsto T$, where $T = \mathbb{B} \cup \{un\}$, to specify same (true), opposite (false) and otherwise (ow) direction, corresponding to the cases in **overtaking**, **head-on**, and **crossing** scenario.

The actions a vessel can take include altering the course to port (AP), to starboard (AS), slowing down (SD), or unchange (UC), which are denoted by $\mathcal{A} = \{AP, AS, UC, SD\}$. Then the action function can be described as $\alpha : \mathcal{V} \times \mathcal{V} \mapsto \mathcal{A} \times \mathcal{A}$. The actions mentioned in the rules of COLREGS mainly involves the first three.

An action can be taken when there exists some potential collision. For autonomous vessels, each of them may consider itself as the home and react according to its own perspective on the scenario. Consequently, conflicts may exist between the actions of multiple autonomous vessels. We first analyze the completeness of the rules. Then the actions for the same set of vessels from different viewpoints will be listed to check the consistency of the rules. For the orientation function, we have $\mathcal{O}(v_1, v_2) = \mathcal{O}(v_2, v_1)$. However, $\mathcal{P}(v_1, v_2) \neq \mathcal{P}(v_2, v_1)$, thus $\alpha(v_1, v_2)$ and $\alpha(v_2, v_1)$ may differ. Therefore, we enumerate all the cases to check the existence of conflicts. In Table 1, we use $\mathcal{P}$ to denote $\mathcal{P}(v_1, v_2)$ and $\mathcal{P}'$ for $\mathcal{P}(v_2, v_1)$. For the ease of comparison of actions, the pair is organized as (v_1, v_2), and the action for $\mathcal{P}'$ is denoted by α'.

Table 1. Classification for various encounter scenarios

No.	$\mathcal{O}$		$\mathcal{P}$				$\mathcal{P}'$	
		Area	Scenario	$\alpha(v_1, v_2)$		Area	Scenario	$\alpha'(v_1, v_2)$
1	true	E	-			E	-	
2	false		head-on	(AS,AS)			head-on	(AS,AS)
3	un		-				-	
4	true	C	being overtaken	(UC, AP)∨ (UC, AS)	A∨ E∨ D	overtaking	(UC, AP)∨ (UC, AS)
5	false		no risk		C		no risk	
6	un		being overtaken	(UC, AP)∨ (UC, AS)	A∨B∨ D	crossing	(AS,UC)∨ (UC,AS)
			no risk		C		no risk	
7	true	A	overtaking	(AP,UC)	C_p	being overtaken	(AP,UC)
8	false		no risk		A		no risk	
9	un		crossing	(AS,UC)	A∨D	crossing	(UC, AS)∨ (AS,UC)
			no risk		B		no risk	
10	true	B	no risk		D		no risk	
11	false		no risk		B		no risk	
12	un		crossing	(UC,AP)	A∨D	crossing	(UC, AS)∨ (AS,UC)
			no risk		B∨C		no risk	
13	true	D	no risk		B		no risk	
14	false		no risk		D		no risk	
15	un		crossing	(UC,AS)	A∨B	crossing	(UC,AS)∨(AP,UC)
			no risk		C∨D		no risk	

In Table 1, the columns for $\mathcal{P}$ follows the rules described in COLREGS. The columns for $\mathcal{P}'$ show the view when v_2 regards itself as the home and present the subsequent actions. "-" is to denote the undefined scenario in COLREGS.

If v_2 appears in area E of v_1 (as shown in Fig. 2(b)), only vessels in opposite orientations are considered in the rules of COLREGS. Other directions are not defined in this scenario, even though one may appear in area E. In fact, the case for the same directions can be regarded as the **overtaking** case.

When v_2 appears in area C of v_1 (as shown in Fig. 2(c)), if two vessels are navigating with the same direction, v_2 is overtaking v_1 and should react accordingly. If their directions are opposite, the risk does not exist. If the direction of v_2 is not the same as or opposite to that of v_1, we use the included angle from the directions of two vessels to infer the encountering case. That is, if the included angle is smaller than 22.5°, it is the **overtaking** case and v_2 is required to steer. Otherwise, no action will be taken. Then, we shift the view to v_2. If v_1 and v_2 have the same direction, v_2 may appear in area A, E or D of v_1. Because of the same direction, v_2 is overtaking v_1 and it should steer. If the directions of two vessels are opposite, there is no risk. If the included angle between the directions of v_1 and v_2 is smaller than 22.5°, v_1 may appear in area A, B, or D in **crossing** scenario. Area E is excluded for their included angle is not zero. If the included angle is greater than 22.5°, v_1 may be in area C, without any potential collision risk.

When v_2 appears in area A of v_1 (as shown in Fig. 2(d)), if the directions of two vessels are the same, v_1 is overtaking v_2. It should alter to port, which is not clearly stated in the rule. When we shift the view to v_2, v_1 is in the area of C_p and it should alter to port. The case of opposite directions for two vessels contains no risk. If the directions of the two vessels are not the same or opposite, it may be a crossing. More precisely, when the included angle of the two vessels is in the range of $(180°, 355°)$, v_2 is crossing v_1. In the view of v_2, v_1 appears in area A or D in the `crossing` scenario. If the included angle is beyond the scope, there exists no collision risk in the view of v_1. In the view of v_2, v_1 is in area B of v_2, without any collision risk.

When v_2 appears in area B of v_1 (as shown in Fig. 2(e)), no collision exists for the cases of same or opposite direction. And the condition for potential collision is similar to that of area A. When we shift to the view of v_2, v_1 appears in area A or D for the `crossing` case. In the other case, v_1 appears in area B or C of v_2, without any collision risk.

When v_2 appears in area D of v_1 (as shown in Fig. 2(f)), if the included angle of two vessels is in the range of $(5°, 180°)$, there is a potential collision risk, where v_1 appears in area A or B of v_2. When v_1 appears in the area C or D of v_2, there exists no risk.

For autonomous vessels, there may not exist a centre controller. Therefore, one can react with respect to its own perspective, but is unable to force others to act accordingly. Consider Case 6 in Table 1, from the viewpoint of v_1, it may expect that v_2 alters to port. However, in the same situation, v_2 may steer to starboard, which is not consistent.

For the case of potential collision risk coming from multiple vessels, the rule in COLREGS requires that all alter to starboard, which is consistent.

4.2 Vessel Behavior Formalization

During navigation, an autonomous vessel keeps on collecting surrounding environment information and detecting potential collision. Meanwhile, it also broadcasts its location, velocity and orientation information. Once a potential collision exists, it will react according to the scenario and the rules of COLREGS. Multiple autonomous vessels may encounter together. Therefore, a vessel may have to avoid collision with various vessels at the same time. Once the risks disappear, it will restore the previous orientation. As actions are constrained by timing constraints, we employ timed automata to model the behavior of a vessel, as shown in Fig. 3.

In Fig. 3, there are three locations, where `Init`, `Safe` and `Risking` represent the initial, navigation without potential collision and reacting to the risk phrase, respectively. The one marked with "c" is introduced for the ease of modelling, where two actions to and from that location belong to an atomic behavior, without time elapse and action interleaving.

We introduce two clocks in the model, one for updating position, the other for recording the duration of collision avoidance. Additional to the clock variables, position, velocity, orientation variables are also used to record the trajectory

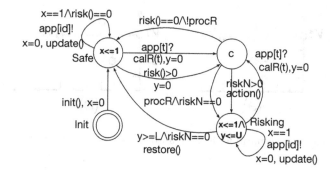

Fig. 3. The timed automaton for vessel behavior description

information. Meanwhile, we use two variables (riskN and procR) to record the number of risks a vessel is encountering, and the status whether it is in the process of dealing with the risks. Channel app is used to broadcast the current position of a vessel, and aware the location of others. The following functions are applied in the modelling.

- update() to update the position of a vessel every time unit,
- calR(t)($\mathcal{R}$) to calculate the existence of a risk with vessel t,
- risk() to detect the risks found by other vessels,
- action()(α) to calculate the action for collision avoidance,
- restore() to make the vessel return to the initial route.

To exclude continuous steering during collision avoidance between two vessels, we assume that the two react once to the same risk if the risk does not come from new vessels. Once a potential collision is detected, the time bound (lower bound L and upper bound U) for avoiding the risk can be calculated. The vessel can return to its previous route when the risk disappears. During the reacting process, a vessel may detect the potential risk coming from different vessels. Therefore, we use riskN to count the number of vessels in the risk.

In the cases of multiple vessels, we assume that they communicate by their broadcast with location, speed and orientation information. And the model will be a network of timed automata.

5 Verification

Based on the behavior of the autonomous marine vessel and the analysis of the rules in COLREGS, we have constructed the model for collision prediction and avoidance in UPPAAL [3]. Due to the limitation of the tool in angle computing and the cost of verification, we consider four directions (north, south, east, west) of navigation, and constrain the scope of navigation to be finite.

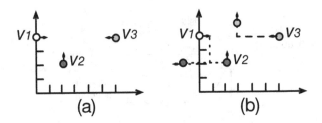

Fig. 4. The collision scenario with three autonomous vessels (Color figure online)

The properties we mainly investigate are as follows:

1. existence of deadlock;
2. existence of collision, i.e., two vessels appear in the same location at the same time.

For the scenario with two vessels, the model does not contain deadlock or potential collision risk. However, in the case of three vessels, there exist collision risks. We present the scenario in Fig. 4. The initial locations and directions of the three vessels are shown in Fig. 4(a), where the speeds of the vessels are the same. The trajectories of navigation (in dash lines) and the final status of the vessels are shown in Fig. 4(b), where the vessels in red (v_2) and in white (v_1) meet together at the same time. Initially, there exists a potential collision risk for v_1 and v_2. As v_2 is in area B of v_1, it alters to port. At the same time, v_1 detects the risk. As it is in area D of v_2, it alters to starboard. When v_3 (in gray) are approaching v_1, v_1 and v_3 detect the potential risk. Because v_1 have detected two risks, it alters to starboard. And v_3 alters to starboard. However, v_2 and v_3 have no any collision risk yet. Because v_1 and v_2 are in the process of collision avoidance, v_2 does not take any further action to avoid the risk, which results in the collision.

The cause of this collision comes from the encountering of multiple vessel, where one may ignore the effect of the new action to the previous potential risk.

6   Conclusion

In this paper, we have mainly investigated the rules of collision avoidance in COLREGS for marine vehicles. The rules assign two encountered vessels with various roles and expect that they can act accordingly. However, the assumption may not be appropriate for autonomous vessels which contain little manual intervention. The enumeration of the encountering scenarios described in the rules for two vessels has revealed the potential conflict reaction. Further formal analysis has also demonstrated that applying the rules without other facilities cannot avoid collision when facing multiple vessels. More precise standards for autonomous marine vessels are expected to enhance the efficiency of collision avoidance and ensure safe navigation.

References

1. Alur, R., Dill, D.L.: A theory of timed automata. Theor. Comput. Sci. **126**(2), 183–235 (1994)
2. Anderson, S.J., Karumanchi, S.B., Iagnemma, K.: Constraint-based planning and control for safe, semi-autonomous operation of vehicles. In: 2012 IEEE Intelligent Vehicles Symposium (IV), pp. 383–388. IEEE (2012)
3. Behrmann, G., David, A., Larsen, K.G.: A tutorial on UPPAAL. In: Bernardo, M., Corradini, F. (eds.) SFM-RT 2004. LNCS, vol. 3185, pp. 200–236. Springer, Heidelberg (2004). https://doi.org/10.1007/978-3-540-30080-9_7
4. Yu, L., Niu, H., Savvaris, A., Tsourdos, A.: Verifying collision avoidance behaviours for unmanned surface vehicles using probabilistic model checking. IFAC-PapersOnLine **49**(23), 127–132 (2016)
5. Perera, L.P., Ferrari, V., Santos, F.P., Hinostroza, M.A., Soares, C.G.: Experimental evaluations on ship autonomous navigation and collision avoidance by intelligent guidance. IEEE J. Ocean. Eng. **40**(2), 374–387 (2015)
6. Perera, L.P., Carvalho, J.P., Soares, C.G.: Autonomous guidance and navigation based on the COLREGS rules and regulations of collision avoidance. In: Proceedings of the International Workshop Advanced Ship Design for Pollution Prevention, pp. 205–216 (2009)
7. Pietrzykowski, Z., Malujda, R.: Applicability of fuzzy logic to the COLREG rules interpretation. Zeszyty Naukowe/Akademia Morska w Szczecinie, pp. 109–114 (2012)
8. Praczyk, T.: Neural anti-collision system for autonomous surface vehicle. Neurocomputing **149**, 559–572 (2015)
9. Statheros, T., Howells, G., Maier, K.M.D.: Autonomous ship collision avoidance navigation concepts, technologies and techniques. J. Navig. **61**(1), 129–142 (2008)
10. Sutulo, S., Moreira, L., Soares, C.G.: Mathematical models for ship path prediction in manoeuvring simulation systems. Ocean Eng. **29**(1), 1–19 (2002)
11. Tsou, M.-C., Hsueh, C.-K.: The study of ship collision avoidance route planning by ant colony algorithm. J. Mar. Sci. Technol. **18**(5), 746–756 (2010)

High Performance Embedded Computing

Optimization of Convolution Neural Network Algorithm Based on FPGA

Feixue Tang, Weichao Zhang$^{(\boxtimes)}$, Xiaogang Tian$^{(\boxtimes)}$,
Xiaoye Fan, and Xixin Cao

Peking University, Beijing 10087, China
{zhangweichao, txg4794}@pku.edu.cn

Abstract. The traditional CNN algorithm requires a great deal of computation and is difficult to be optimized. The computation of throughput on the hardware platform does not match the memory bandwidth very well. The existing scheme doesn't take full advantage of logical resources, and also doesn't make full use of memory bandwidth. Neither of them can get the best performance. In this paper, we use the commonly used im2col method in the software implementation and convert convolution operation into matrix multiplication. Therefore, it improves the calculation speed effectively. In the hardware implementation aspect, we propose a nested loop optimization structure. Firstly, the correlation of the parameters is analyzed, multiplication times are reduced and the multiplication of the inner loop is replaced by an addition operation. Hence, the maximum operating frequency and power consumption are improved remarkably. Secondly, the input data and the convolution kernel are multi-level partitioning optimization. The multi-layer input data is grouped by 2k, and the data of each layer is optimized by L group. At the same time, the convolution kernel is also grouped by 2k and the convolution kernel with the parallel data synchronization operation optimization. So the structure has a significant improvement in the degree of parallelism. The external bandwidth and the internal bandwidth can be improved significantly in the condition of the same total computation.

Keywords: CNN · Cyclic parameters · Correlation · Nested cyclic partitioning
FPGA

1 Introduction

Convolutional Neural Network (CNN) is a deep learning algorithm derived from artificial neural networks. It has been widely used in the field of computer vision such as image classification [1] and recognition [2], as it can imitate the behavior of the biological visual nerve so that it can obtain a high accuracy in recognition. Recently, with the rapid growth of modern applications based on deep learning algorithms has further improved research and implementation. In particular, a variety of deep CNN accelerators based on FPGA platform are proposed, which has high performance, reconfiguration and fast development cycles. Although the current FPGA accelerator has shown a better performance than the general-purpose processor, the accelerator

© Springer Nature Singapore Pte Ltd. 2018
Y. Bi et al. (Eds.): ESTC 2017, CCIS 857, pp. 131–140, 2018.
https://doi.org/10.1007/978-981-13-1026-3_10

design space has not been well explored. A serious problem is that the computational throughput of the FPGA platform does not match the memory bandwidth well [3]. As a result, existing programs either fail to make full use of logical resources, or do not take full advantage of memory bandwidth. They all cannot get the best performance. At the same time, applications of deep learning increase the complexity and scalability to make this problem more serious. In this paper, the commonly used im2col method is used in the software implementation, and the convolution operation is transformed into matrix multiplication to improve the computational speed. In the hardware implementation, a nested loop optimization structure is proposed. Through analyzing and separating the correlation of the parameters. It has been significantly improved in the degree of parallelism, the external bandwidth and bandwidth have been further optimized.

2   Software Implementation

2.1   Introduction of Algorithm

The traditional CNN calculation method requires a great deal of computation and is difficult to optimize. It has a lot of layers of for-loop in the software programming. Multi-layer for-loop nesting makes the complexity of the algorithm become too high, and is difficult to optimize at all levels. It will very slow in speed when the data is too large. There are a variety of software optimization options. In order to make full use of these optimizations, we use the commonly used im2col method to convert the convolution operation into matrix multiplication to calculate in the software implementation.

Im2col's basic idea is to convert multidimensional data into a two-dimensional matrix. It's an operation that convert the convolution operation into a matrix multiplication. We can get the matrix multiplication and then reverse back to the original multi-dimensional form. As matrix multiplication has many ways to be optimized in the software. Therefore, this method can increase the speed of the convolution algorithm. The process pf im2col is showed in Fig. 1.

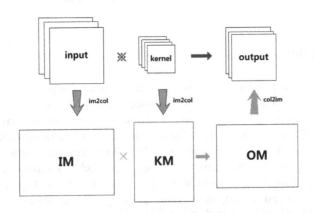

Fig. 1.   The process of im2col

Figures 2 and 3 show how to convert the input data and the convolution kernel into a matrix. For the input data, we will take the convolution kernel size as a unit and convert each small convolution piece to a row. If there are multiple channels of input, the column which the small piece of the corresponding location transforms merges into a big column. In turn, we will get a matrix which size is (ic × kw × kh) × (oh × ow). For the convolution kernel, there are ic convolution kernel corresponding to each output. To make ic convolution kernels tile into one row. And they form successively a kernel matrix which size is oc × (ic × kw × kh).

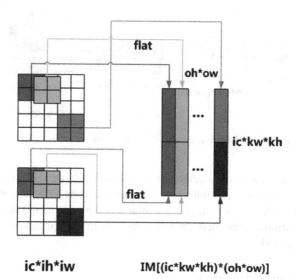

Fig. 2. The input data transforms a matrix

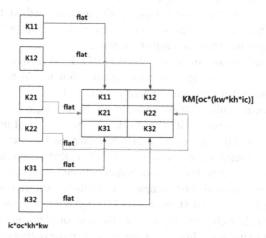

Fig. 3. Convolution kernels transform a matrix

After these two transformations, the convolution process of the input matrix and the convolution kernel can be transformed into the multiplication operation of the kernel matrix and the input matrix. The kernel matrix and the input matrix are multiplied by a matrix to obtain an output matrix which size is oc × (ow × oh).

Finally, the output matrix transforms into an output form of network through col2im method, as shown in Fig. 4. Each row of the output matrix corresponds to an output, and the one-dimensional columns are transformed into a two-dimensional form of oh × ow.

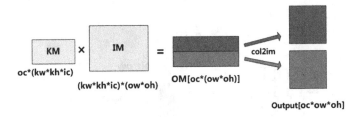

Fig. 4. Calculation process and output matrix restoration

As there are a variety of acceleration methods (such as GPUs) for the matrix operations on the software. A number of methods are used to accelerate in the most important matrix multiplication stages. Therefore, it achieves a significant increase in convolution operations. Even there are large amounts of data, it can also complete the calculation task quickly.

2.2 Achievements and Analysis

Since the usual convolution inputs are 1024 × 150 × 150 approximately, our experiments achieved on this order of magnitude of data. We also achieved the traditional convolution calculation method, and compared with the new method. In order to reduce the impact of external uncertainties on each run time, we conducted five experiments and found an average run time as a statistical result.

Our experimental environment was linux14.04, Titan graphics. We used c++ language. The network structure was single convolution neural network. The input image and convolution kernels were randomly generated.

From the statistical results, two methods can get the result quickly when the number of input data channels is small. With the increase of the number of input channels, the running time of the traditional method is getting slower and slower. Finally, we need half an hour to get the results. However, when we use matrix optimization in the above method, although there are additional conversion data and transformation process, the running time has not changed. The comparison results are showed in Fig. 5.

In the new method, ic = 1000, iw = ih = 150, kw = kh = 5, sw = sh = 1. In the case of larger input data channel, the time of the convolution operation of the traditional method (Conv) increases linearly as the channel of the output data increases from 1 to 100, but the time of the new method (Mat) remains steady.

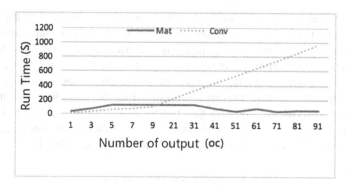

Fig. 5. Compare the new method(Mat) to the traditional method (Conv) on the convolution operation time

In im2col, we have replaced convolution with the method of matrix multiplication, the matrix multiplication parallel method can be used to realize. Therefore, even if the image data increase, it will only use more threads, the total time of the calculation will not vary greatly.

3   Hardware Implementation

3.1   Hardware Optimization

Although the current FPGA accelerator has showed a better performance than the general-purpose processor, the accelerator design space still has not been well explored. A serious problem is that the computational throughput of the FPGA platform does not match the memory bandwidth very well. The application of depth learning increases the complexity and scalability constantly to make this problem more serious.

We discuss the difference of many design methods. Work [6–8] implemented complete CNN application on FPGA, but they used different collateral measures. Work [6, 8] mainly used feature map to realize the parallelism of the internal convolution kernels. Work [5] chose to maximize the reuse of the data according to CNN's communication problems, so the requirements of the bandwidth reduced to a minimum. Work [7] used the parallelism between "inter-output" and "intra-output". Work [4] mainly used software to set up the CNN application, and complete the convolution filter with a hardware structure of systolic accelerator. This design saved a large amount of hardware resources. Our work uses the commonly used im2col method in the software implementation, and convert the convolution operation into matrix multiplication. In the hardware implementation, we propose a nested loop optimization structure. Eventually, we increase the speed and improve the bandwidth.

In the hardware implementation process, we found the cycle operation in each layer must carry out a multiplication operation and call the multiplier each time. Due to the multiplier call, hardware resource consumption and energy consumption will increase. At the same time, with the increase of the complexity of the multiplication, the computing frequency will also decline. After analysis, we know that the for-loop operation in the innermost layer is not related to the innermost loop variable. If a dimension that participates in an operation is irrelevant to the loop variable of this layer, we think that it is independent about the operand, otherwise it is relevant. If some dimension can be separated into the location of the layer loop, we think that the operand is separable. Taking the im2col operation of the convolution kernel as an example: after analysis, we consider that the parameters such as n, m, v, u are not related to the convolution kernel (krnl) and the convolution kernel converted matrix (KM) each time. The relevance and separability are shown in Table 1.

Table 1. Variable and relevance analysis

	krnl		KM	
n	Independent	Separable	Independent	Separable
m	Independent	Separable	Relevant	Separable
v	Independent	Separable	Relevant	Separable
u	Independent	Inseparable	Relevant	Inseparable

The nesting loop can be optimized as shown in Fig. 6 in the hardware implementation process. It makes multiplication of the innermost loop transform into an addition. After hardware compilation simulation, the highest frequency of this program increases.

```
for(n=0; n<oc; ++n){

  for(m=0; m<ic; ++m){

    for(v=0; v<kh; ++v){

      for(u=0; u<kw; ++u)

      {

      KM[n][(kh*m + v)*kw +u]=

      krnl[n][m][v][u];

}}}}
```

```
for(n=0; n<oc; ++n)

{    temp_n1= n*kh*kw*ic;

     temp_n2= n*oc;

     for(m=0; m<ic; ++m)

     {    temp_m1 = m*kh;

          temp_m2 = (temp_n2 + m)*kh;

          for(v=0; v<kh; ++v)

          {    temp_v1= ( temp_m1 + v) * kw;

               temp_v2= (temp_m2 + v) * kw;

               for(u=0; u<kw; ++u)

               { KM[n][temp_v1 + u]=krnl[n][m][v][u];

}}}}
```

Fig. 6. Nested loop optimization (left for optimization before right optimization)

In the hardware implementation process of the im2col method, the nesting loop of the hardware is realized by a counter or a state machine. The size of the counter is related to the size of the input image data. Compared with the previous single-layer input data, this method differs in the hardware implementation process. Firstly, it need to obtain the cache space to store the converted image data and convolution kernel data. Secondly, the results of the convolution are stored in the cache. Finally, the cache results are transformed into the output image data through data conversion. It can be seen that the size of the cache data space determines the effectiveness of the method in the im2col method. After analysis, we found two different results according to the size of the input data with limited hardware resources. In the case of small input data, it can be efficient and fast that using im2col method to calculate convolution operation and output results. However, in the case of large input data, large amounts of data will consume more hardware resources, even more than the maximum requirements of hardware resources and lead to a mismatch between throughput and computing speed.

We propose a CNN accelerator in order to achieve convolution fast and efficiently in the case of multiple channels and Kernel based on two limiting modules of the limitations of throughput calculation and communication. It is optimized from the perspective of the loop. It can achieve the internet optimization of the processing unit and the buffer through the realization of circular partitioning optimization. And it can also achieve the optimization of data throughput and off-chip access bandwidth.

When the number of iterations is large, the workload will increase and the parallelism will be weakened. The cycle partitioning algorithm can increase the parallelism and reduce the number of iterations. In the calculation process of CNN nesting loop, the partitioning optimization is showed in Fig. 7. Where ic, oh, ow, kh, kw, represents respectively the number of input images, the output image width, the height of the output image, the width of the convolution kernel and the height of the convolution kernel.

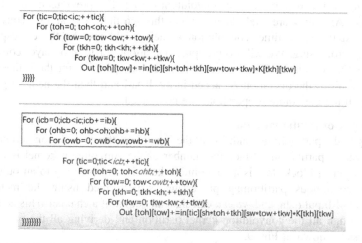

Fig. 7. Partitioning optimization (for the optimization before and after the optimization)

Partition of Input data

The optimization of the input image data is a kind of nested optimization. Firstly, the outer ic layer achieves partitioning traversal read. Secondly, the inner single layer achieves partitioning traversal optimization. Finally, the data of the size of the convolution kernel is processed in parallel. Figure 8 shows the frame diagram of the input image data optimization.

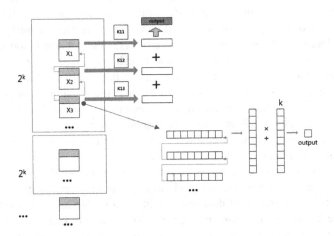

Fig. 8. The partitioning process of input data

Firstly, the input data of ic channels is divided into ic/2k group (2k means the number of the corresponding convolution kernels) and each group has 2k layers. 2k layer data are inputted in serial and are read out in parallel through the cache. Secondly, we select the L line of each Layer relative to each layer. We need only to read the previous m line for $m \times m (m < L)$ convolution kernel. The previous m line data can be obtained. Also they are read out in parallel through the cache and do convolution operation. At the same time, convolution kernel should also be the corresponding partitioning processing. We will do grouping operations for ic × oc layer convoluted core and each group is 2k. Finally, we do convolution operation for the L line data in turn. The result of the operation is cached in the RAM and then the next 2k group is read until all the convolution operations are completed.

Partition of Convolutional data

According to the partitioning condition of the input data, the convolution kernel is also synchronization partitioning. Since the number of the convolution kernel is ic × oc, each ic is a set of block (that is a convolution kernel corresponding to an output is a unit), the continuous partitioning processing is performed using the method in (1) partition of Input data, and we can calculate an output of a channel. This is done by looping through all the convolution kernel partition and deriving all the output data. The process is shown in Fig. 9.

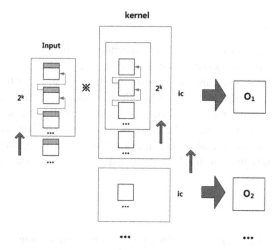

Fig. 9. The partitioning process convolutional kernel

3.2 Hardware Optimization Analysis

Compared with the direct reading in serial and doing convolution operation, the above method improves the parallelism of FPGA processing. It makes the calculation throughput and memory bandwidth be a good match and does a reasonable use of the calculation and logic unit. The input data is converted from the original single layer data into the synchronous input of 2^k layer data. Therefore, the degree of parallelism is improved. The degree of parallelism is increased by:

$$T_i = 2^k \times 2^k \times kw \times kh \times iw \times ih \tag{1}$$

Which kw and kh represents the length and width of the convolution kernel. iw and ih represents the length and width of the input image. However, the total amount of calculation has not changed and still remain in the order of magnitude T_{obw}:

$$T_{obw} = ic^2 \times oc \times kh \times kw \times iw \times ih \tag{2}$$

Which ic and oc represents the data channels number of input and output.

The calculation of inner bandwidth and external bandwidth is shown in Eqs. (3) and (4). As can be seen from the formula, as the degree of parallelism increases, the internal bandwidth will be significantly increased, while the external bandwidth will be reduced accordingly.

$$BW_{in} = \#ip \times f \times w_b \tag{3}$$

$$BW_{out} \approx \frac{T}{Parallel} \tag{4}$$

Which wb represents the bit wide, sc represents the total calculation.

4 Conclusion

In this paper, we implemented the CNN algorithm on hardware and software, and optimized some hardware performance issues. In the hardware, we optimized the calculation of throughput and memory bandwidth balance in order to make it can be effectively used, improved the degree of parallelism, increased the internal bandwidth and reduced the external bandwidth. However, there are still some shortcomings. For example, the cache requirement of the corresponding intermediate computing results will increase so that the choice of k and L is not unlimited increase. We can achieve the best processing results through the k value, L value and the amount of data cache.

References

1. Lecun, Y., Bottou, L., Bengio, Y., Haffner, P.: Gradient-based learning applied to document recognition. Proc. IEEE **86**(11), 2278–2324 (1998)
2. Ren, S., He, K., Girshik, R., Sun, J.: Faster R-CNN: towards real-time object detection with region proposal networks. IEEE Trans. Pattern Anal. Mach. Intell. **39**(6), 1137–1149 (2015)
3. Zhang, C., Li, P., Sun, G., Guan, Y., Xiao, B., Cong, J.: Optimizing FPGA-based accelerator design for deep convolutional neural networks. In: ACM/SIGDA International Symposium on Field-Programmable Gate Arrays, pp. 161–170. ACM (2015)
4. Farabet, C., Poulet, C., Han, J.Y., LeCun, Y.: CNP: An FPGA-based processor for convolutional networks. In: International Conference on Field Programmable Logic and Applications, pp. 32–37. IEEE (2009)
5. Peemen, M., Setio, A.A., Mesman, B., Corporaal, H.: Memory-centric accelerator design for convolutional neural networks. In: IEEE International Conference on Computer Design, pp. 13–19. IEEE (2013)
6. Sankaradas, M., Jakkula, V., Cadambi, S., Chakradhar, S., Durdanovic, I., Cosatto, E., Graf, H.P.: A massively parallel coprocessor for convolutional neural networks. In: IEEE International Conference on Application-Specific Systems, Architectures and Processors, pp. 53–60. IEEE (2009)
7. Chakradhar, S., Sankaradas, M., Jakkula, V., Cadambi, S.: A dynamically configurable coprocessor for convolutional neural networks. ACM SIGARCH Comput. Archit. News **38**(3), 247–257 (2010)
8. Cadambi, S., Majumdar, A., Becchi, M., Chakradhar, S., Graf, H.P.: A programmable parallel accelerator for learning and classification. In: International Conference on Parallel Architectures and Compilation Techniques, pp. 273–284. IEEE (2017)

Co-design and Implementation of Image Recognition Based on ARM and FPGA

Yuan Qu, Yixiang Chen[✉], and Wenjie Chen

School of Computer Science and Software Engineering,
MOE Research Center for Software/Hardware Co-Design Engineering,
East China Normal University, Shanghai 200062, China
yxchen@sei.ecnu.edu.cn

Abstract. With the development of the Internet of things, the image recognition system is widely required in many fields. It has very high requirement in real-time, but usually it has high complexity and large data. So the real-time, which improved by hardware acceleration, is the key of image recognition system. Traditional processors have the disadvantages of low flexibility and configurability for prototype of embedded system. The family of Xilinx Zynq7000 processors integrate dual-core ARM Cortext-A9 and low-power FPGA. It can improve the operating efficiency and dynamical configurability of developing image applications. It also can reduce the power consumption of image processing. In this paper, we present an ARM and FPGA Co-design architecture of image recognition system based on Zynq7000 processor. Then we validate this architecture by the leaf recognition system. This architecture is based on module designed at system-level and modeled at algorithm-level. After determining the algorithm option, we partite the ARM and FPGA of modules depending on algorithm simulation, and then implement them separately. Finally, ARM and FPGA modules are interconnected by interface or driver. When the joint debugging is completed, prototype development of the embedded application is finished. As the experiment shown, FPGA and ARM co-design is 1.84 times faster than the pure ARM.

Keywords: Co-design and implementation · ARM + FPGA
Image recognition

1 Introduction

The Image recognition system is widely required in many fields, such as, national and public safety, transportation, finance, industrial production, products detection, etc. Currently, most of the image recognition systems have the characteristics of large data, complicated algorithm and high real-time requirement. The main chips in the image processing field include ASIC (Application Specific Integrated Circuit), DSP (Digital Signal Processing), GPU (Graphics Processing Unit), general purpose processors (such as ARM), FPGA (Field Programmable Gate Array) and other chips. ASIC-based systems can reduce power consumption and improve computational performance, but because of its customization, it leads to poor flexibility and is not suitable for prototype

© Springer Nature Singapore Pte Ltd. 2018
Y. Bi et al. (Eds.): ESTC 2017, CCIS 857, pp. 141–153, 2018.
https://doi.org/10.1007/978-981-13-1026-3_11

development of embedded system. DSP has obvious advantages in image middle-processing (such as image preprocessing, feature extraction, etc.), but it is difficult to design and expand a complex multi-tasking image processing system [1]. GPU can reduce the computing complexity, and it is suitable for largescale parallel computing, but it will produce high power consumption. ARM applications have low developing cost, high developing efficiency, but when it's applied to image recognition system, it is very poor in real-time. FPGA has dynamic configurability, and it's flexible and low power consumption. But if we only use FPGA to develop embedded applications, it can't implement complex image processing algorithm in a short time. Xilinx Zynq7000 is based on Embedded Processing Platform (EPP) architecture, and it combines dual-core ARM Cortext-A9 processor and low-power FPGA to provide a flexible, configurable design platform for hardware and software co-design [5].

Nowadays, there are about 310000–420000 plant species that is known in the world. The recognition and classification of plants have great value for distinguishing plant species, exploring the genetic relationship among plants and clarifying the evolution of plant system. Plant classification also is directly related to the medical industry, food industry and other fields closely related to human survival. Uluturk [6] not only extract seven basic leaf morphological features after image preprocessing, but also extract other three features using half-leaf image. By this way, the recognition rate is up to 92.5%. Ameur [10] integrate the leaf and bark information for tree species recognition. As their experiments show, leaves can provide more classification information than bark. Liao [2] recognize leaves based on Altera's Nios II processors, and the decision-making module is implemented by FPGA for accelerating. Compared to pure ARM, ARM + FPGA co-design improves the speed of seven times.

In this paper, we take the leaves recognition system as the case to study the ARM and FPGA co-design and implementation of image recognition system. The system is designed and implemented on Zynq series processors. At first, the system is divided into four modules. Then, we model for each module using MATLAB tools and calculate the runtime of sub-module. For the sub-module whose runtime is the longest, we implement it on FPGA, but other modules are implemented on ARM. Finally, the data exchanges between PL (Programmable Logic) and PS (Processing System) are achieved by AXI (Advanced Extensible Interface) bus. The experimental results show that ARM + FPGA is 1.84 times faster than pure ARM.

2 Image Recognition Workflow

The image recognition system includes four parts: image acquisition, image reprocessing, feature extraction and classification. As shown in Fig. 1.

Fig. 1. Image recognition system workflow

For the above four parts, respectively, details are described as follows:

A. *Image Acquisition*

Image acquisition is the process of sampling and quantifying. It can be completed by camera on the Zynq board or external USB camera.

B. *Image Acquisition*

The purpose of the preprocessing is to remove the interferences during image acquisition. Preprocessing also can remove secondary information that is not necessary for feature extraction. The information of edge extraction directly decides the final recognition result. The edge information usually is extracted by edge operator. The Canny operator, the Laplace operator, the Sobel operator, etc., [4] commonly are used to extract edge information.

The banalization transforms the edge image into a binary image by the threshold method. The threshold can be determined by the fixed threshold or self-adjusting threshold. Self-adjusting threshold needs loop iteration, and it will produce large calculation for different images. The fixed threshold has less calculation, but it has quite different calculation results for different images.

C. *Feature Extraction*

Feature extraction is a key link of the image recognition system. Image characteristics, image stability and feature numbers must be considered. Different recognition objects have different features, so we extract different features depending on the object characteristics.

D. *Classification Decision*

Classification decision can determine the type of recognition object. Feature vectors of recognition object are input of this part, and then the trained classifier would classify the sample depending on a set of rules.

3 ARM and FPGA Co-design

The Xilinx Zynq7000 processors are heterogeneous multi-core system [3], which includes homogeneous dual-core ARM Cortex A9 processors and programmable FPGAs. In order to develop application on the Zynq SOC, Xilinx introduces Vivado design suite to support developing embedded applications based on system and IP core. Adopting ARM and FPGA co-design method, with Vivado tools, can take full advantage of merits of the heterogeneous multi-core processor, improve flexibility of embedded system, and broaden optimization space of the system.

Zynq7000 processors can be divided PS (processor system) part and PL (programmable logic) part. PS part includes dual-core ARM, DDR DRAM controller, Interconnect and other peripherals. PL part includes AXI Interconnect, AXI VDMA, and acceleration modules, etc.

PS interact with PS by AXI interface. AXI handshake protocol describes the way of data transmission between master and slave. When slave is ready for receiving data, it will send READY signal. When master is ready for transmitting, it will produce VALID signal. When VALID and READY signals are all valid. Master will continue to transmit next data. Zynq7000 supports three types of AXI bus, including AXI4, AXI-lite and AXI-Stream. AXI4 and AXI-lite interfaces include five different channels, read address channel, write address channel, read data channel, write data channel and write response channel. Every channel is an independent AXI handshake protocol. AXI-Stream is continuous stream interface. It doesn't have address option, so it supports unlimited data burst transmission. AXI-Stream doesn't have address, like FIFO, and needs AXI-VDMA converting memory-mapped with streaming. Read and write models are as shown in Figs. 2 and 3.

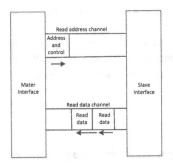

Fig. 2. Channel architectures of reads.

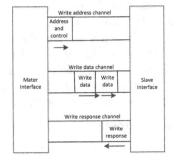

Fig. 3. Channel architectures of writes

AXI4 supports mass address transmission. AXI-lite is used to control or access some low-speed peripherals. AXI-Stream support data transmission at high speed. There are three AXI interfaces: AXI_ACP, AXI_HP, and AXI_GP. The throughput of AXI_HP and PL's DMA is 1200 MB/s, suitable for large data transmission. AXI_ACP can support PL that directly accesses the cache of PS. It can maintain consistency of cache. AXI_GP is general-purpose interface. AX7020 total has four AXI_GP ports, including 32 bit mater interfaces and 32 bit slave interfaces.

The architecture of ARM and FPGA co-design is as follows: at first, the ARM and FPGA co-design needs to be designed at the system level by Unified Modeling Language (UML) or System Modeling Language (SysML) [12]. And then the algorithm of each module should be determined based on system functional requirements, using C language, Matlab, SystemC, etc.... Then, in order to meet the system requirements, resource limits and system performance, we should divide ARM and FPGA of the system. For the FPGA parts, Vivado HLS can be used to design IP core, and it can convert C/C++ language to RTL implementation. The RTL level implementation can be exported to Vivado. We can design logical module in Vivado, and produce Bit stream by Vivado tool. So far FPGA hardware design has been completed. After the verification of hardware, PS part uses Vivado SDK development tools to generate boot file boot.bin. PS can access the PL by mmap, and the IP core of PL can be accessed by PS as an external device of Linux application. Linux application can be developed by QT designer. The architecture of ARM and FPGA co-design flowchart is shown in Fig. 4.

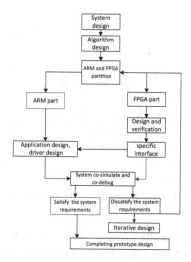

Fig. 4. Flow chart of ARM and FPGA co-design.

For the simple application, we can develop bare-metal applications through the SDK integrated by Vivado design suite. It can schedule the hardware co-processor through the software interface.

For the complex application, first, we should debug the software in the SDK, and then we need to develop software applications in the Linux platform. The ARM and FPGA application can interact by user pointer, driver or memory mapping. Finally, software and hardware parts can co-simulate and co-debug. If it can meet the system requirements, the prototype design has been completed. Otherwise, PS and PL should be divided again and system should be designed again.

4 Case Study

We take leaf recognition system as the study case to present ARM and FPGA co-design architecture of image recognition system. The purpose of leaf recognition system is to identify the type of leaves, which mainly includes four parts: image acquisition, image preprocessing, feature extraction and classification. Image acquisition camera captures the image. Image preprocessing optimizes the collected images for facilitating feature extraction, such as cutting, de-noising, segmentation, etc. Feature extraction can build mathematical model based on leaf characteristics to reduce the image information. The classification decision is based on the characteristics of the captured leaves, and the leaves are classified through a set of rules.

A. *System Modeling*

According to the description of leaf recognition system, the system mainly includes four modules: image acquisition module, preprocessing module, feature extraction module and classification decision module. We model for the leaf recognition system using SysML. The BDD diagram is shown in Fig. 5.

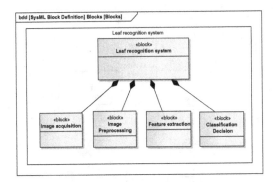

Fig. 5. BDD diagram of leaf recognition system.

The image acquisition module obtains the image to be processed, and the pre-processing module processes the image by grayscale, edge detection, banalization and edge extraction. The feature extraction module is based on the convex hull and the minimum circumscribed rectangle. According to the features of leaves, classifier can determine the type of leaves. System activity diagram is shown in Fig. 6.

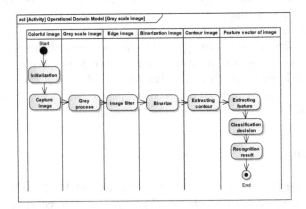

Fig. 6. Activity diagram of leaf recognition system.

B. *Algorithm Flow Chart*

After image acquisition, the computational capacity is reduced by gray scale processing. The image edge can be extracted by calculating convolution between Sobel operator and image. The Sobel operator [4] can smooth image noise, and provide more accurate edge direction information. It is calculated simpler and faster than other operators, so it's widely used in edge detection. This operator consists of two sets of 3×3 matrices, which are transversal and longitudinal. Then, calculating convolution between Sobel operator and image can obtain the brightness difference between the horizontal and the vertical. A represents the original image. Gx and Gy respectively represent image gray values detected by the lateral and longitudinal edges. As shown in Eq. (1) [4]:

$$G_x = \begin{bmatrix} -1 & 0 & +1 \\ -2 & 0 & +2 \\ -1 & 0 & +1 \end{bmatrix} * A \text{ and } G_y = \begin{bmatrix} +1 & +2 & +1 \\ 0 & 0 & 0 \\ -1 & -2 & -1 \end{bmatrix} * A \qquad (1)$$

Gray value at each pixel of the image can be calculated by Eq. (2) [4], which combines horizontal and vertical gray values of each pixel

$$G = \sqrt{G_x^2 + G_y^2} \qquad (2)$$

If the gradient G is greater than a certain threshold, and then the point (x, y) is the edge point. The gradient direction is calculated by Eq. 3 [4]:

$$\theta = \arctan\left(\frac{G_y}{G_x}\right) \qquad (3)$$

Fixed threshold is used to image banalization, which can reduce calculation. So we select fixed threshold for banalization. After testing, the threshold is set to 25. If the pixel is larger than 25, the pixel is set to 0. If the pixel is lower than 25, the pixel is set to 255. The largest of all the contours is the contour of the leaves which is extracted.

Most of the features are based on the leaf contour, so contour of the leaves should be extracted at first. Then we can select appropriate model to extract features based on characteristics of leaf.

Convex [3] can contain the least set of points in all points of the leaf, which is in two dimensional space. The related features of the convex hull includes the ratio of the convex hull to contour area of the leaf, the ratio of the convex hull to the perimeter of the leaf and the sunken numbers of the convex hull. Actually, the ratio of the convex hull to contour area of the leaf can distinct the single angle shape and many angles shape, the ratio of the convex hull to the perimeter of the leaf can distinct blade edge and smooth edge of the leaf. The sunken numbers of the convex hull can distinct the leaf owning many angles and the leaf owning single angle. Then, we can build minimum circumscribed rectangle based on the set of convex hulls.

The minimum circumscribed rectangle and related features [6] is two dimensional form of the minimum outer frame, which only retains the ratio of width and length of the contour, which has an obvious distinction on the elongated leaves.

The image moment of inertia [3] is a weighted overlay of the pixel values in the image. By means of the space moment of inertia and the center moment of inertia, we can define the normal moment of inertia, which is not affected by image scaling. Hu invariant moments are obtained based on the normal moment of inertia.

Convex hull can be extracted by Sklansky algorithm [3]. Then the ratio of convex hull to leaf contour area, the ratio of convex hull to leaf perimeter and the sunken number of convex hull can be calculated for classifying leaves. The minimum circumscribed rectangle only retains the ratio of width and length. So it can distinct

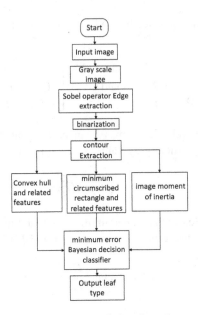

Fig. 7. Algorithm design flow chart.

elongated leaves obviously. The image moment of inertia is a weighted overlay of the pixel values in the image. Based on the extracted feature vectors of the recognition object, the type of leaves is judged by the trained minimum error Bayesian decision classifier.

We determine the algorithm of leaf recognition system by modeling algorithm using MATLAB. The algorithm design flow chart is shown in Fig. 7.

Algorithm design results are shown in Fig. 8, 9, 10 and 11. The training classifier defined Type3 for the Toona Sinensis.

Fig. 8. Original image.

Fig. 9. Gray-scale image.

Fig. 10. Banalization image.   **Fig. 11.** Output leaf type.

Table 1. Software running time of each module.

Image acquisition	Image preprocessing	Feature extraction	Classification decision
0.2679 s	1.0192 s	0.6472 s	0.3933 s

C. ARM and FPGA partition of leaf recognition system

Modeling by MATLAB can get the software running time of each module, as shown in Table 1:

As shown in Table 1, image preprocessing takes the longest time during leaf recognition. Therefore, preprocessing part can be transplanted to Vivado HLS. It can be accelerated by implementing on FPGA. Besides, Vivado HLS can optimize the loop by pipeline or optimize IO by memcpy or Array Partition. By this way, the system efficiency will be improved. So image preprocessing part can be divided to FPGA implementation. Other parts are divided to ARM implementation. The result of the ARM and FPGA partition of the leaf recognition system is shown in Fig. 12:

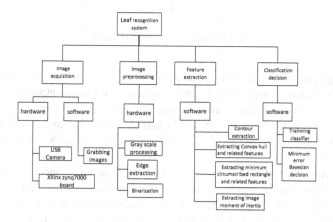

Fig. 12. ARM and FPGA partition of the leaf recognition system.

D. *Hardware Design of FPGA*

At first, image preprocessing is programed with C/C++ language by Vivado HLS. Then, the C/C++program will be translated to Verilog or VHDL languages, and produces IP core after system synthesis. The IP core is imported to Vivado, which is custom IP. Based on system requirement, we can design the block and configure clock and interruption. In this implementation, dual video camera is used to capture images. HDMI is used to video output. Custom IP is as two video device, which are mounted to ARM. The hardware block design is as Fig. 13. The hardware block can generate RTL code, and then generate bit stream. Of course, constraint file can generate after configuring pins and electric level.

For ZYNQ block, we should do PS-PL configuration, configuring three HP slave AXI interfaces, which are for input, output and custom IP. Besides, we should configure peripheral I/O pins based on system design, for example, Quad SPI Flash, Ethernet, USB, SD, UART, I2C and GPIO. DDR, clock and interrupt are needed to be configured, too.

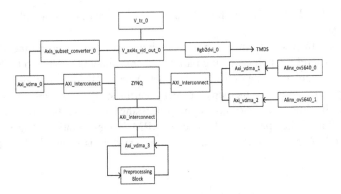

Fig. 13. Block Design of Hardware

For image capturing, axi_vdma_1 and axi_vdma_2 are buffers of capturing images and can convert data format from stream to m-map. For image output, axi_vdma_0 is the buffer of output and it can convert m-map to stream. Axis_subset_converter_0 can convert the data width from 32 bits to 24 bits. V_axi4s_vid_out_0 and v_tc_0 can convert AXI_Stream to RGB888. Rgb2dvi_0 can convert RGB888 to TMDS signal for driving HDMI monitor.

For custom IP, axi_vdma_3 can fetch the data from DDR and send it back after processing. After running synthesis, it can generating bit stream. Then the bit stream can export and launch to SDK. SDK would generate hardware platform, including custom IP driver, system.hdf and system.bit etc. So far, hardware design has been finished.

E. *Developing Application of ARM*

If the partition divides some simple control task to ARM, the ARM application can be developed by SDK and run the program on the bare-metal. Otherwise, the ARM application should run the Linux OS, and it can be developed by QT Creator.

ARM application will define two video devices by modifying driver and device tree and configuring Linux kernel, which are input and output of custom IP. Then, ioctl command can request buffer and it can be mapped to virtual address. So ARM application can interact data with hardware by mmcpy. For example, as follows, v4l2_dequeue_buffer can fetch a frame from dev_0 and copy it to dev_2. Then, we can fetch a frame from dev_3, which is preprocessed by FPGA.

```
b = v4l2_dequeue_buffer(&dev_0, dev_0.vid_buf);
memcpy(dev_2.vid_buf, dev_0.vid_buf, b −> v4l2_buff_length);
```

Finally, stream and device should be close and mmap should be released.

F. *System Integration*

This experiment selected ALINX AX7020 as the ARM and FPGA co-design platform. The AX7020 integrates Xilinx's Zynq-7000 XC7Z020-2CLG400I chip (referred to as Zynq7020). And it provides two high-speed DDR3 memory with 4Gbit capacity, 256Mbit flash memory, 2-channel 40-pin expansion port that connects the camera module and 1 HDMI interface that can transmit 1080P video images. This experiment selected camera with USB, and the resolution is 1080P.

In this paper, PetaLinux [5] would be transplanted to the ARM for achieving leaf recognition, which is suitable for embedded system as its openness. In this implementation, UCI Folio dataset [13] is used, which includes 32 different leaves. Every type has 20 pictures. The overall architecture of leaf recognition system is shown in Fig. 14. The architecture of system implementation is shown in Fig. 15.

Zynq7020 chip can be divided into PS (processor system) part and PL (programmable logic) part. For PS part, the calculation unit uses dual-core ARM Cortex A9 processor with 1 GHz frequency. And each processor is equipped with 32 KB

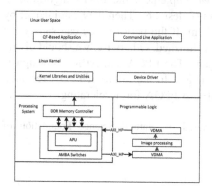

Fig. 14. Overall architecture of system

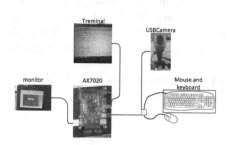

Fig. 15. Architecture of system implementation

Table 2. FPGA resource utilization of the image pre-processing module.

Name	BRAM_18 K	DSP48E	FF	LUT
FIFO	0	–	150	1144
Instance	3	17	2316	2342
Multiplexer	–	–	–	6
Register	–	–	11	–
Total	3	17	2477	3493
Available	280	220	106400	53200

instruction cache and dual-core processors share the secondary cache with 512 KB; For PL part, logic unit (Logic Cells) is 85 K, lookup table (LUTs) is 53200, the flip-flops is 106400, the multiplier is 550, and the block RAM is 4.9 Mb.

PL part is designed to IP core using Vivado HLS. Image preprocessing module on FPGA uses 0.0105 s. Table 2 shows the resource utilization of the image preprocessing module.

Image preprocessing part of the FPGA implementation is faster 97.1 times than the ARM implementation. The system runtime of ARM is 2.032 s, and the system runtime of ARM and FPGA is 1.104 s.

FPGA and ARM co-design is faster 1.84 times than pure ARM, and power consumption is reduced, too.

5   Conclusions

In this paper, we introduce the FPGA and ARM co-design architecture of image recognition system based on Xilinx zynq7000. First, we introduce the workflow of image recognition system. Then, the FPGA and ARM co-design architecture is introduced. Finally, we take the leaf recognition system as the case study to implement the co-design architecture. At first, we model for leaf recognition system using SysML. Then, we design implementation algorithm for each module of the system using MATLAB. Next, we design the partition of ARM and FPGA by analyzing implementation algorithm of each module. Next, we implement the FPGA algorithm in Vivado, and implement the ARM algorithm in QT designer. Then they can interact by mmap and driver. Finally, we will co-debug them. If the performance can satisfy the system requirements, prototype development has finished. Otherwise, we should divide the FPGA and ARM, and implement them again. The FPGA and ARM co-design is faster1.84 times than the pure ARM implementation. In the future, if FPGA resource allows, we can migrate more algorithm modules to FPGA for accelerating.

Acknowledgement. This work is partially sponsored by Natural Science Foundation of Shanghai (15ZR1410000).

References

1. Liu, H., Fu, Y.: Design of image processing system platform based on Zynq chip. Comput. Modernization **240**(8), 1–5 (2015)
2. Liao, Y.P., Zhou, H.G., Fan, G.R.: Accelerating recognition system of leaves on Nios II embedded platform. In: International Symposium on Computer Communication Control and Automation, pp. 334–337. IEEE (2010)
3. Lu, J., et al.: Embedded System Hardware and Software Co-Design Combat Guide Based on Xilinx Zynq. China Machine Press, Beijing (2013)
4. Zhang, J., et al.: A hardware accelerated OpenCV image processing methods. Image Multimedia (2015)
5. Li, L.: Based on Zynq-7000 video processing system framework design. Comput. Technol. Dev. (2016)
6. Uluturk, C., Ugur, A.: Recognition of leaves based on morphological features derived from two half-region. In: International Symposium on Innovations in Intelligent Systems and Applications, pp. 1–4. IEEE (2012). A brief guide to the systems modeling language
7. Drozdenko, B., et al.: High-level hardware-software co-design of an 802.11a transceiver system using Zynq SoC. In: Computer Communications Workshops, pp. 682–683. IEEE (2016)
8. Liao, Y.-P.: Accelerating recognition system of leaves on Nios II embedded platform. In: 2010 International Symposium on Computer, Communication, Control and Automation (2010)
9. Wang, Z., et al.: Based on ZYNQ dense optical flow method hardware and software co-processing. Comput. Eng. Appl. (2014)
10. Ameur, R.B., Valet, L., Coquin, D.: A fusion system for tree species recognition through leaves and barks. Computational Intelligence, pp. 1–8. IEEE (2017)
11. Zhou, Z.: Machine Learning. Tsinghua University Press, Beijing (2016)
12. Delligatti, L.: A Brief Guide to the Systems Modeling Language. China Machine Press, Beijing (2014)
13. http://dataju.cn/Dataju/web/datasetInstanceDetail/60

Embedded System and Applications

Power Quality Analysis Based on Time Series Similarity and Extreme Learning Machine

Meimei Li[1,2(✉)], Shouqing Jia[1], Shuqing Zhang[2], Zheng Gong[2], and Guaifu Li[1]

[1] Northeastern University, Qinhuangdao, Hebei, China
ysulmm@163.com
[2] Yanshan University, Qinhuangdao, Hebei, China

Abstract. Aiming at the problem of the existing fault monitoring method such as intensive computation, dependence on the length of data, and difficult of finding out the abnormal situation, a fast and effective method of recognizing power quality fault is proposed in this paper. Confidence intervals are first partitioned by a pre-judgment method based on time series similarity, and the failure characterization is simplified by measuring similarity between the recorded data and normal data template. Then, S-transform analysis and extreme learning machine were combined to identify the fault type. This method could reduce the amount of calculation and number of fault parameters effectively, finding out the monitored fault immediately. The results of simulation show that the method could realize the fault pre-judgment and analysis effectively with the feature of fast and accurate. Experiment analysis to ChengDe Steel Mills proved the feasibility and the superiority of this method.

Keywords: Metrology · Analysis of power quality · Similarity measure
S-transform · Extreme learning machine

1 Introduction

With the rapid development in today' society, the widespread application of various power electronic equipment and the increase in impacting, non-linear and fluctuating load, it is greatly important to study the effective detection and identified classification method to control the power quality disturbance [1–4].

The general step to traditional power quality diagnosis is collecting all kinds of characteristic signals, extracting feature quantity of signal, constructing discriminate function and recognizing patterns. Many ways, like parameter modeling - AR modeling and ARMA modeling, extract of time-domain feature, statistical analysis - first - order statistics and high - order statistics, transformation analysis - discrete Fourier transform and wavelet transform and so on [5–9], been used to extracting the quantity of signal characteristic for the structure and regularity of the signal itself. Parametric modeling is much more complex. Existing models, such as AR models, are not suitable for non-stationary signal analysis, but statistics analysis is based on big data, the two methods abovementioned are not ideal for the type of analysis for power quality disturbances [10–13]. Therefore, the relevant scholars will emphasize the method that

© Springer Nature Singapore Pte Ltd. 2018
Y. Bi et al. (Eds.): ESTC 2017, CCIS 857, pp. 157–170, 2018.
https://doi.org/10.1007/978-981-13-1026-3_12

transformation analysis as they research hotspot. And Stockwell proposed the method called S transformation [14, 15], which is not only the fusion between the Windowed Fourier transform and the theory of continuous wavelet transformation, but also an extension on two ideas. Compared with wavelet transform, S transformation not merely can realize the scaling transformation on the specified position and time [16–19], but also can do the translational action with the Gaussian window. The theory and technology of S transformation have aroused great interest of scholars from home and abroad in recent years. However, it is limited to the characteristic vector of the fault to be detected in the S-transform and the characteristics of the larger computational complexity, so that its application in the power electronic system is restricted [20].

Time series similarity plays an important role in the research on the field of power system. It can be used to find similar trends in the time series database to achieve time series prediction, classification and knowledge discovery [21]. The distance function can be used to measure the degree of "similarity" between the distance and the similarity, the smaller the distance between two times series the higher the similarity. Euclidean distance is a widely used time series similarity measure, which is more sensitive to the mutate point of the time series and intuitive easy to calculate, with good mathematical background and significance. Thus, the similarity measure is introduced into the first faulted model in this article, discovers the fault by dividing the confidence interval, and then analyzes the time-frequency characteristic of the segment data by S-transform to extracting the feature quantity related to the faulted type, to improving the efficiency of the algorithm, to making the role of historical databases full used.

To classify and recognize power quality, a new learning algorithm is introduced as ELM (Extreme Learning Machine) for single-hidden layer feedforward neural network [22–28], which has the advantages on easy parameter selection, fast learning and generalization. It avoids the risk of falling into the local optimum, and improves both learning speed and promotion performance of the network.

2   Extraction of Features Based on Time Series Similarity and S Transformation

When the signal feature of power quality is extracted by using S transformation, Euclidean distance is first introduced as the geometric distance of the similarity judgment and measure.

Here is a formula about x_t of time series and Euclidean distance of y_t:

$$D(X, Y) = \sqrt{\sum_{t=1}^{n} |x_t - y_t|^2} \tag{1}$$

The comparison object of Euclidean distance adopts the point-to-point comparison method, which is different from graph or comparison of waveform shapes. It's obvious characteristic that, in view of the normal situation, amplitude and the frequency of energy signal does not change. For two power signals with similarity but with phase difference on both amplitude and frequency, the comparison result should be a huge a difference. In order to eliminate the influence of phase difference between two sequences in the quality of power signal, this paper designs a calculation method that does not affect the calculation result of Euclidean distance and can eliminate the influence of the phase difference, that is: (1) First, the sequence of both studying and reference is taken absolute value operation, to realizing fold of sine wave along the middle line, to eliminating the impact of 180° of the phase difference; (2) The nearest 0 point of the two sequences are aligned, and removing the asymmetric points on the heads and tails of the two series.

By establishing referential signal of the normal state, the metric function of similarity is defined between the time series European distance, and measuring the similarity between study sequence and reference sequence, finding abnormal sequences to monitor the occurrence of fault.

Through similarity found abnormal signal, and then S transformation is used to extracting faulted characteristics of power quality effectively. For a given time series x(t), the S transformation is:

$$S(\tau,f) = \int\limits_{-\infty}^{+\infty} x(t) \frac{|f|}{\sqrt{2\pi}} e^{-\frac{(\tau-t)^2 f^2}{2}} e^{-i2\pi ft} dt \tag{2}$$

In the expression, $S(\tau,f)$ means the sampling sequence, $x(t)$ is complex-time-frequency of two-dimensional matrix after S transformation. The row vector of the two-dimensional matrix represents the frequency value in units of the frequency resolution, and its column vector corresponds to the signal of sampling time at the sampling interval. The matrix, its elements in matrix of S transformation are modeled, is denoted by modulo values of S transformation, and the elements represent the modulo values of a frequency and S transformation of time point. The power signal at a certain point and its distribution of the frequency amplitude, changes with time, is recorded as the row vector of the matrix, meanwhile, signal at a certain point and its distribution of the amplitude, changes in frequency on sampling time, is recorded as the column vector of the matrix.

3 Classification Method Based on Extreme Learning Machine

Compared to other learning machines, ELM classification algorithm has the biggest advantage on learning fast and solving the problem that trapped in the locally best solution. When the number of the hidden layer neuron nodes are determined and its activation function is infinitely differentiable, connection weights and hidden layer neurons threshold of the neuronal input layer and the hidden layer are randomly selected before training, stay the same during the training process [29–31], meanwhile, so the connection weights of the hidden layer and the output layer can be quickly obtained by the regularization principle [32, 33]. ELM algorithms are thousands of times faster than traditional learning machines.

Figure 1 is a mathematical model of ELM for single-hidden layer feedforward neural network.

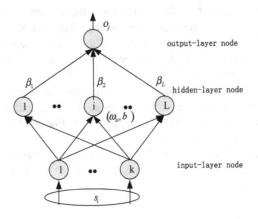

Fig. 1. Single hidden layer feedforward networks

The mathematical model of a single - hidden layer feedforward network with L - hidden layer nodes is:

$$\sum_{i=1}^{L} \beta_i g(\omega_i \bullet s_j + b_i) = o_j \quad j = 1, 2, \cdots, N \tag{3}$$

In this expression, $\beta_i = [\beta_{i1}, \beta_{i2}, \cdots, \beta_{im}]^T$ represents output connection weight vector of the i-th hidden layer and the output layer node; $g(x)$ represents the activation function of hidden layer neurons; $\omega_i = [\omega_{i1}, \omega_{i2}, \cdots, \omega_{ik}]^T$ represents the input connection weight vector between the input layer node and the i-th hidden layer node; s_j represents the j-th input sample; $\omega_i \bullet s_j$ represents inner product between ω_i and s_j; b_i is the threshold of the i-th hidden layer neuron. o_j is the output value of the j-th input sample.

If the hidden layer feedforward neural network approaches the training samples of the same continuous system with zero error, that is $\sum_{i=1}^{N} \|o_i - t_i\| = 0$, there are β_i, ω_i and b_i formula (4) comes into existence:

$$\sum_{i=1}^{L} \beta_i g(\omega_i \bullet s_j + b_i) = t_j, \quad j = 1, 2, \cdots, N \tag{4}$$

The formula (4) also be written as:

$$H\beta = T \tag{5}$$

In the formula,

$$H(\omega_1,\cdots,\omega_L,b_1,\cdots,b_L,s_1,\cdots,s_N) = \begin{bmatrix} g(\omega_1 \bullet s_1 + b_1) & \cdots & \\ \vdots & \vdots & \vdots \\ g(\omega_1 \bullet s_N + b_1) & \cdots & g(\omega_L \bullet s_N + b_L) \end{bmatrix}_{N \times M} \tag{6}$$

H is the matrix of hidden-layer.

$$\omega = \begin{bmatrix} \omega_1^T \\ \vdots \\ \omega_L^T \end{bmatrix}_{L \times m}, \quad T = \begin{bmatrix} t_1^T \\ \vdots \\ t_N^T \end{bmatrix}_{N \times m} \tag{7}$$

The main implementation steps of the ELM learning algorithm are:

(1) Determine the number of hidden layer nodes N, randomly set the connection weight ω_i of input neuron input layer and threshold b_i of the hidden layer neuron, $i = 1,2,\cdots,N$;

(2) According to formula (5) and (6), calculate the connection weights H of hidden layer and output layer;

(3) Figure minimum value $\hat{\beta}$ in the least squares solution of the generalized linear system $H\beta = T$:

$$\hat{\beta} = H^{-1}T \tag{8}$$

H^{-1} is the pseudo inverse of the weight matrix H.

In the case of activation function is differential infinitely, input weight and hidden layer threshold can be randomly selected before training. Keep input weight vector ω_i and hidden layer threshold b_i unchanged during training, and ensure that the hidden layer output matrix H does not change, then only $\hat{\beta}$ in the training network weights is calculated, hence, ELM classification algorithm is equivalent to solving the least squares solution $\hat{\beta}$.

4   Verifying Simulation Experiment

To verify the proposed method by select the voltage swell, voltage dip, voltage interruption, transient oscillation and transient pulse faulted signal.

4.1 Similarity Measurement

Distance between the time series and the template under normal state is conforming to the Gaussian distribution, with more than three times the normal template sequence distance variance of sequence can be regarded as abnormal sequences according to the characteristics of the Gaussian distribution.

Figure 2 shows similarity measure between four kinds of simulation signals and normal state template, and the dotted line in the Figure indicates the moment of failure.

Figure 3 shows the value of similarity measure distribution between the different types of faulted samples and the normal state templates, in which the threshold diagram of the abnormal sequence is represented by the horizontal dotted line.

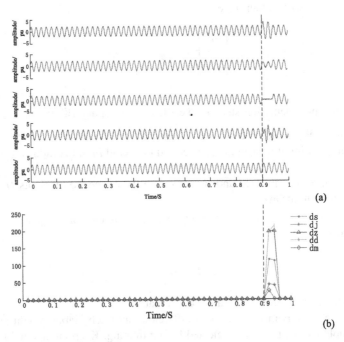

Fig. 2. Similarity measure of five kinds of signals. (a) Temporal characteristics curves of simulation signal. (b) The change of signal similarity measure value.

It can be seen from Figs. 2 and 3 that the similarity measure of the faulted section has changed significantly.

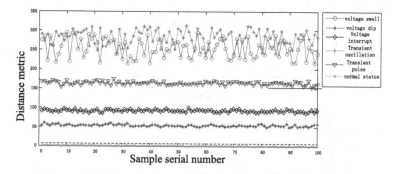

Fig. 3. Similarity measure of five kinds of signals

4.2 Feature Extraction

In order to analyze the time domain and frequency domain characteristics with each disturbed signal, the following two eigenvectors are defined:

(1) time domain feature vector

$$T1(t) = \max(A(t,f)) \tag{9}$$

Where $A(t,f)$ is the modulus matrix of signal S transformation.

(2) frequency domain feature vector

$$T2(f) = \max(A(t,f)) \tag{10}$$

Voltage swell, voltage dip, voltage interruptions, transient oscillation, transient pulse and etcl five types of faulted signal and its S transformation analysis results shown in Figs. 4, 5, 6, 7 and 8.

Figure 4(b), 5(b), 6(b), 7(b) and 8(b) shows the time domain characteristics of the five typical transient disturbance signals after S transformation; Fig. 4(b) shows that the time-domain characteristic curve rises at 0.4 s–0.8 s, reflecting the faulted characteristics of the sudden risen signal; Fig. 5(b) shows that curve to time-domain characteristic decreases at 0.4 s–0.8 s, which reflects the faulted characteristics of the voltage plummeting signal; Fig. 6(b) curve is similar to the voltage collapse curve, which is in line with the signal characteristics of the voltage interrupt, while it is lower at 0.4 s–0.8 s; Fig. 7(b) is an irregular curve reflecting the irregular variation in the time of failure, which is in line with the characteristics of the transient oscillation signal; Fig. 8(b) shows that the energy of the pulse signal in the whole time domain is distributed, which corresponds to the characteristic of transient pulse signal; Fig. 4(c), 5(c), 6(c), 7(c) and 8(c), respectively, shows the five kinds of disturbance signal frequency domain characteristics of S transformation, it is not difficult to find that in addition to the transient oscillation signal (Fig. 7(c)), beyond the base wave frequency 50 Hz where curve of

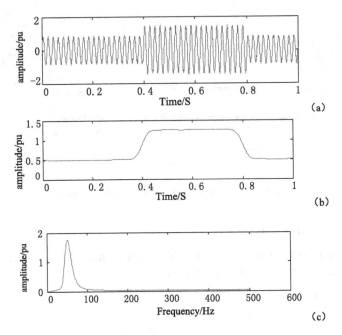

Fig. 4. S transform analysis of voltage swell. (a) The signal of voltage swell. (b) Temporal characteristics curves of S transform. (c) Spectral characteristics curves of S transform.

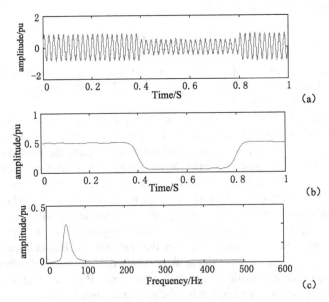

Fig. 5. S transform analysis of voltage dip. (a) The signal of voltage dip. (b) Temporal characteristics curves of S transform. (c) Spectral characteristics curves of S transform

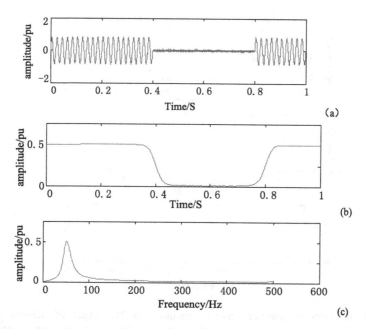

Fig. 6. S transform analysis of voltage interruptions. (a) The signal of voltage interruptions. (b) Temporal characteristics curves of S transform. (c) Spectral characteristics curves of S transform

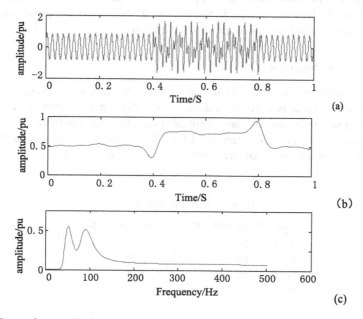

Fig. 7. S transform analysis of transient oscillation. (a) The signal of transient oscillation. (b) Temporal characteristics curves of S transform. (c) Spectral characteristics curves of S transform

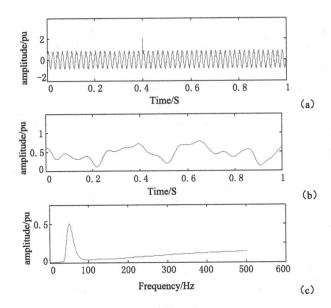

Fig. 8. S transform analysis of transient impulse. (a) The signal of transient impulse. (b) Temporal characteristics curves of S transform. (c) Spectral characteristics curves of S transform.

characteristics in frequency domain is spike, while the other four faulted signals only at the base wave 50 Hz there is a peak. S-transform describes time-frequency character-istics of various faulted signals intuitively and effectively.

4.3   Pattern Recognition

During S transformation, the time domain eigenvector that is the frequency mode matrix and the characteristic vector in the frequency domain are constituted the faulted signal's feature vector, and the faulted signal is detected and classified.

This paper compares the effects of ELM, BP neural network and machine for support vector on the failure of five types of faults, as shown in Table 1.

Table 1. Classification results

Classifier	Recognition rate	Time consuming/s
ELM	93.85%	3.8265
BP	88.41%	4.2245
SVM	93.45%	10.5965

5 Engineering Experiment Analysis

In fact, difference in power signal is huge, while signal with additional noise is non-ideal Gaussian white noise, and noises are diverse and complex. In order to verify the validity of the proposed algorithm in the power signal in actuality processing, an algorithm simulation experiment is carried out for a group of power signals in actuality. This signal is caused by a main circuit voltage interruption and voltage dip fault in Chengde Steel. Figure 9 shows the breakdown signal analysis diagram for this voltage. Figure 10 is the analysis diagram of the voltage drop signal.

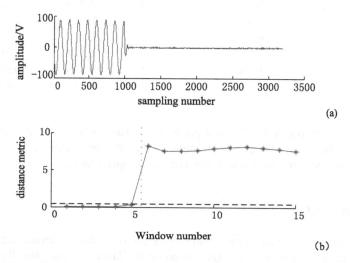

Fig. 9. Analysis of voltage interruptions signal. (a) Temporal Figure of measured signals. (b) Similarity measure of measured signals and template.

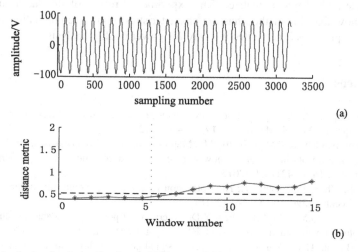

Fig. 10. Analysis of voltage dip signal. (a) Temporal Figure signals. (b) Similarity measure of measured signals and template.

Table 2 compares the effect of the measured signal classification recognition. Among them, the analysis process 1 indicates the method proposed in this paper, and the analysis process 2 indicates that S transformation is directly applied to the signal and the ELM is used for classification.

Table 2. The effects of Classification and recognition by measured signals

Faulted signal length	Analysis process	Similarity prediction accuracy rate	Missed rate	Recognition rate	Time consuming/s
5000	1	100%	0%	95.13%	0.3265
	2	——		94.85%	0.4157
10000	1	99.93%	0%	96.41%	0.4245
	2	——		95.83%	0.9165
20000	1	100%	0%	95.65%	0.5975
	2	——		95.25%	2.0265

It can be seen from Table 2 in this paper, on the basis of the similarity anticipation and analyze the signals can effectively improve the efficiency of operation, especially for data length longer signal, effectively reduce the operation time.

6   Conclusion

In this paper, we use time series similarity, S transformation analysis and ELM to propose a model of failure first judged based on similarity measurement. By dividing the confidence interval, the faulted detection is realized, furthermore through the S-transform time-frequency analysis and the classification learning of ELM the judgment to the faulted type is realized. The experimental results of simulation and engineering show that this method has the characteristics of small computation and high accuracy. It provides a new effective way for power quality analysis.

References

1. Zygarlicki, J., Mroczka, J.: Variable- frequency prony method in the analysis of electrical power quality. Metrol. Meas. Syst. **19**, 39–48 (2012)
2. Belchior, F., Galvão, T.M., Ribeiro, P.F., Márcio Silveira, P.: Comparative analysis of power quality instruments in measuring power under distorted conditions. Int. J. Emerg. Electr. Power Syst. **16**(5), 421–429 (2015)
3. Xia, J.S., Zhao, J.Q., Yang, T.: High precision power quality monitoring system. Electron. Meas. Technol. **39**(01), 134–141 (2016)
4. Luo, A., Xu, Q.M., Ma, F.J., Chen, Y.D.: Overview of power quality analysis and control technology for the smart grid. J. Mod. Power Syst. Clean Energy **4**(1), 1–9 (2016)
5. Sang, B., Liu, H.W., Yin, Z.Y.: Research of signal power quality disturbance identification and classification. Foreign Electron. Meas. Technol. **35**(07), 56–59 (2016)

6. Li, Y.N., Bao, G.Q.: Power quality disturbance signals identification based on wavelet packet and SVM. Electr. Power Sci. Eng. **03**, 21–26 (2012)

7. Liu, G.H., Wu, H.X., Shen, Y.: Novel reconstruction method of power quality data based on regularized adaptive matching pursuit algorithm. Chin. J. Sci. Instrum. **36**(08), 1838–1844 (2015)

8. Hao, Y., Zhen, D., Chen, Y.L., Ge, J.F., Lai, L.L., Vaccaro, A., Meng, A.: An effective secondary decomposition approach for wind power forecasting using extreme learning machine trained by crisscross optimization. Energy Convers. Manag. **150**, 108–121 (2017)

9. Zhao, L.Q., Xie, N.N., Wu, C.M.: Construction of Daubechies complex wavelets and application in power quality detection. Comput. Eng. Appl. **35**, 233–237 (2012)

10. Su, C.L., Yang, M.C., Lin, M.C.: Measurement and analysis of electric power quality for commercial vessels. Adv. Mater. Res. **1566**(433), 6262–6266 (2012)

11. Shin, K.K.: An alternative approach to measure similarity between two deterministic transient signals. J. Sound Vibr. **371**, 434–445 (2016)

12. Kant, S., Mahara, T.: A new similarity measure based on mean measure of divergence for collaborative filtering in sparse environment. Procedia Comput. Sci. **89**, 450–456 (2016)

13. Duraipandy, P., Devaraj, D.: Extreme learning machine approach for on-line voltage stability assessment. In: Panigrahi, B.K., Suganthan, P.N., Das, S., Dash, S.S. (eds.) SEMCCO 2013. LNCS, vol. 8298, pp. 397–405. Springer, Cham (2013). https://doi.org/10.1007/978-3-319-03756-1_36

14. Song, H.J., Huang, C.J., Liu, H.C., Chen, T.J., Li, J.L., Luo, Y.: A new power quality disturbance detection method based on the improved LMD. Proc. CSEE **34**(10), 1700–1708 (2014)

15. Shen, H.B., Zheng, S.S., Qi, X.M.: The embedded system for power quality detection based on FFT and wavelet theory. J. Sun Yat-Sen University (Natural Science Edition) **53**(04), 40–44 (2014)

16. Reddy, J.B., Mohanta, D.K., Karan, B.M.: Power system disturbance recognition using wavelet and S-transform techniques. Int. J. Emerg. Electr. Power Syst. **1**(2) (2011)

17. Zheng, J.D., Pan, H.Y., Cheng, J.S.: Generalized analytical made decomposition for non-stationary analysis. Acta Electronica Sin. **44**(06), 1458–1464 (2016)

18. Mahela, O.P., Shaik, A.G.: Recognition of power quality disturbances using S-transform based ruled decision tree and fuzzy C-means clustering classifiers. Appl. Soft Comput. **59**, 243–257 (2017)

19. Deng, Y., Yu, C.S.: Application of factor analysis and ELM in analog circuit fault diagnosis. J. Electron. Measur. Instrum. **30**(10), 1512–1519 (2016)

20. Zhang, S.Q., Li, P., Shi, R.Y., Hu, Y.T., Jiang, W.L., Liu, Z.Y.: New method for power quality disturbance classification based on modified S transform. Chin. J. Sci. Instrum. **36**(04), 927–934 (2015)

21. Chen, S.M., Cheng, S.H., Lan, T.C.: A novel similarity measure between intuitionistic fuzzy sets based on the centroid points of transformed fuzzy numbers with applications to pattern recognition. Inf. Sci. **343–344**, 15–40 (2016)

22. Wefky, A., Espinosa, F., Santiago, L.D., Revenga, P., Lázaro, J.L., Martínez, M., Wang, W. L.: Electrical drive radiated emissions estimation in terms of input control using extreme learning machines. Math. Prob. Eng. **2012** (2012)

23. Zhang, W.H., Huang, N.T., Yang, J.C., Yang, Y.J., Wang, X.K.: Power quality disturbances classification based on generalized S-transform and differential evolution extreme learning machine. Electr. Meas. Instrum. **53**(20), 50–55 (2016)

24. Yu, R., Xiang, R., Yao, S.W.: Extreme learning machine for fault diagnosis of rotating machinery. Adv. Mater. Res. **3247**(960), 1400–1403 (2014)

25. Ao, H.H., Chen, S.F., Yang, S.S.: Similarity model based on trend of times series. Electron. Meas. Technol. **39**(06), 196–199 (2016)
26. Sun, K., Zhang, J.Z., Zhang, C.X., Hu, J.Y.: Generalized extreme learning machine autoencoder and a new deep neural network. Neurocomputing **230**, 374–381 (2016)
27. Mishra, M., Sahani, M., Rout, P.K.: An islanding detection algorithm for distributed generation based on Hilbert-Huang transform and extreme learning machine. Sustain. Energy Grids Netw. **9**, 13–26 (2016)
28. Zhong, J.Y., Zhang, Y., Wen, F.S., Zhu, H.B., Li, H.C., Fan, H.F.: A fault diagnosing method in power transmission system based on time series similarity matching. Autom. Electr. Power Syst. **39**(06), 60–67 (2015)
29. Nayak, P.K., Mishra, S., Dash, P.K., Bisoi, R.J.: Comparison of modified teaching–learning-based optimization and extreme learning machine for classification of multiple power signal disturbances. Neural Comput. Appl. **27**(7), 2107–2122 (2016)
30. Khokhar, S.H., Mohd Zin, A.A., Memon, A.P., Mokhtar, A.S.: A new optimal feature selection algorithm for classification of power quality disturbances using discrete wavelet transform and probabilistic neural network. Measurement (2016). https://doi.org/10.1016/j.measurement.2016.10.013
31. Ahila, R., Sadasivam, V.: Performance enhancement of extreme learning machine for power system disturbances classification. Soft. Comput. **18**(2), 239–253 (2014)
32. Yang, X.Y., Guan, W.Y., Liu, Y.Q., Xiao, Y.Q.: Prediction intervals forecasts of wind power based on PSO-KELM. Proc. CSEE **35**(S1), 146–153 (2015)
33. Suganyadevi, M.V., Babulal, C.K.: Online voltage stability assessment of power system by comparing voltage stability indices and extreme learning machine. In: Panigrahi, B.K., Suganthan, P.N., Das, S., Dash, S.S. (eds.) SEMCCO 2013. LNCS, vol. 8297, pp. 710–724. Springer, Cham (2013). https://doi.org/10.1007/978-3-319-03753-0_63

Pedestrian Detection with D-CNN

Zhonghua Gao, Weiting Chen$^{(\boxtimes)}$, Guitao Cao, and Peng Chen

MOE Engineering Research Center, for Hardware/Software Co-Design
Technology and Application, East China Normal University Shanghai,
Shanghai 200062, China
wtchen@sei.ecnu.edu.cn

Abstract. Pedestrian detection plays an important role in intelligent analysis of images and videos. In this paper, we propose a deformation model based convolutional neural network(D-CNN) for pedestrian detection. Enlightened by YOLO model, D-CNN network integrates deformation and occlusion handling into the network to improve the accuracy of occluded pedestrian detection. The performance of D-CNN is evaluated on two popular datasets as well as pictures got in daily life. Among the state-of-the-art methods compared in this paper, the comprehensive performance of D-CNN is the best, whose mAP is only 0.4 points lower than the highest one but the detection speed doubles. So our proposed network can get real-time speed while maintaining rather satisfying precision of pedestrian detection.

Keywords: Pedestrian detection · D-CNN · Deformation handling
Occlusion handling

1 Introduction

Pedestrian detection is a technique of locating people and marking them in pictures and videos. Pedestrian detection plays an important role in intelligent analysis of images and videos. In the process of human walking and running, scenes are diverse. The difference in shape, clothing diversification, light changes, object occlusion and complex traffic environments will affect the results of pedestrian detection, producing a multitude of challenges in pedestrian detection.

In order to address these detection issues, a large number of papers have put forward various methods. A great deal of robust features including Haar-like [1], SIFT [2], HOG [3], LBP [4] are extracted from images to catch the most discriminative information of pedestrians. And then classifiers are used to identify whether there are pedestrians in a candidate or sliding window. SVM [5] and boosted models [6] are the most often used classifiers for pedestrian detection. In recent years, deep learning networks such as Fast R-CNN [7, 8], YOLO [9, 10], SSD [11], and GoogLeNet [12] have made even better detection performances. Moreover, occlusion handling [13–16] is applied to determine the existence of a person within a candidate window even when something blocks out certain parts of a pedestrian. Deformation models have also been designed to deal with part detection of a person such as shoulders, legs and hands [14, 17].

© Springer Nature Singapore Pte Ltd. 2018
Y. Bi et al. (Eds.): ESTC 2017, CCIS 857, pp. 171–180, 2018.
https://doi.org/10.1007/978-981-13-1026-3_13

A good feature can improve the accuracy of pedestrian detection. Meanwhile, a good classifier can more effectively utilize features to enhance the sensitivity and robustness of pedestrian detection. Mostly, these two steps of feature extraction and classifiers are designed individually, and then a simple association is made. Although these methods have achieved good performances, researches have shown that just using simple association of several separate approaches in object detection has encountered bottlenecks [14]. Feature extraction and classify methods can be converged into a more effective, glitch-canceling system. Deep neural networks can well take the task of combining and optimizing these two steps by back propagation and get a better pedestrian detector than a simple association of separate components [14].

In this paper, we propose a deformation model based convolutional neural network (D-CNN) to better detect pedestrian. Our proposed D-CNN network is enlightened by the YOLO model [9, 10], and combines deformation model [14] to deal with the occlusion problem and uses Maxout [20] as the activation function to mitigate the disappearance of the gradient.

The rest of this paper is organized as follows. Section 2 introduces the architecture of D-CNN network. Section 3 evaluates the performance of the network on two popular datasets: Caltech dataset [18] and Pascal VOC dataset [19], together with pictures got in daily life. Finally, Sect. 4 concludes the paper.

2 Method

2.1 Network Description

Our proposed D-CNN network is based on YOLOv2 model [10] and UDN [14]. The architecture of D-CNN is shown in Fig. 1. D-CNN network has 20 convolutional layers followed by a softmax layer. In the network, we add a deformation layer, referring to UDN [14], after the second convolutional layer in which we use filters with variable sizes. The part filters in the second convolutional layer of the D-CNN can effectively handle occlusion and improve the performance of pedestrian detection. The deformation handling and occlusion handling refer to UDN [14], but our network architecture is

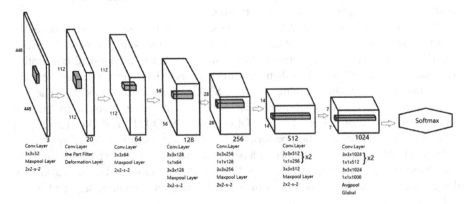

Fig. 1. The architecture of D-CNN.

different from UDN architecture. Moreover, it is helpful to mitigate the disappearance of the gradient when the Maxout [20] is selected as activation function in the D-CNN network.

The D-CNN network solves pedestrian detection as a regression problem, and directly outputs the bounding box of pedestrian in an image. So, the process of using D-CNN to detect pedestrians is simple and straightforward. Firstly, D-CNN framework resizes the original picture to 416 × 416 as the input to the neural network. Secondly, the network gets the bounding boxes containing the coordinates and confidence scores. Finally, Non-maximal suppression filters out redundant boxes. D-CNN network predicts each person using the features extracted from the whole image.

D-CNN model downsamples by a factor of 32. So the network divides the entire picture into 13 × 13 grid cells (as shown in Fig. 2) when a input picture is resized to 416 × 416. Each grid cell generates 5 anchor boxes, which is responsible for predicting the bounding box. A center grid can be got through dividing a picture into 13 × 13 grids. D-CNN first uses the center grid to predict the pedestrian as pedestrians usually occupy the middle part of an image. If no pedestrian is found in the center grid, D-CNN will then search the neighboring grids of the center one. This can increase the efficiency of detection.

Fig. 2. 13 × 13 grid cells of pedestrian detection

2.2 Occlusion Handling and Deformation Model

Generally, the filter size in a network is constant [22, 23]. For pedestrians, there is a certain pattern of human shape, but sometimes people will be blocked by buildings, vehicles, other people and other objects. To better deal with the occlusion problem in pedestrian detection, we use filters with variable sizes in the second convolutional layer of the D-CNN referring to [14]. As shown in Fig. 3, 20 parts with different sizes are used at three levels. There are six small-sized parts in different parts of the body at level 1. There are seven moderate-sized parts in different parts of the people at level 2, each of which is composed of two parts at level 1. And there are seven big-sized parts in different parts of the body at level 3, each of which is composed of two parts at level 2. In the Fig. 3, black color indicates occlusion.

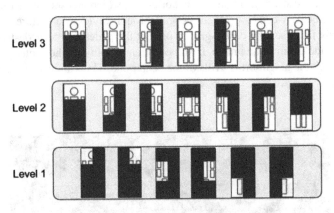

Fig. 3. The model of the part filters [14]

The deformation handling layer [14] in the D-CNN network aims at learning the feature map of different parts. For the neural network, we take the output feature map of the upper layer for the input of the next layer. D-CNN network enters the P parts (P = 20 in this paper) feature map to the deformation layer, and then outputs a summed map. The deformation layer gets the score of deformation map from the p part feature map, denoted by M_p. The deformation layer sums up the part feature map and the deformation map as

$$B_p = M_p + \sum_{n=1}^{N} c_{n,p} D_{n,p}, \tag{1}$$

and then gets a 2D summed map, denoted as B_p. Formula (1) represents $D_{n,p}$ as the nth feature map for the pth part, represents $c_{n,p}$ as the weight for $D_{n,p}$, and represents N as the number of feature maps.

2.3   Activation Function

Sigmoid, Relu, and tanh are popular activation functions used in neuron networks. But Sigmoid saturates and kills gradients, and its outputs are not zero-centered. Tanh is similar to sigmoid but it is zero-centered. Therefore, tanh is better applied than sigmoid in network. ReLu has two significant advantages: the convergence rate of SGD using ReLu will be much faster than that of sigmoid and tanh; Compared to sigmoid and tanh, ReLu only needs a threshold to get the activation value without doing complex calculations. But ReLU units can be fragile during training and can "die". Maxout is excellent in its fitting ability as a learning activation function. It can be interpreted as making a piecewise linear approximation to an arbitrary convex function. Though Maxout has more parameters than Relu, it can relieve the problem of gradient disappearance and the drawback of perceptron's 'die' as that with Relu. So we use Maxout for the activation function of D-CNN network as

$$\max\left(w_1^T + b_1, w_2^T + b_2, \ldots, w_n^T + b_n\right) \tag{2}$$

2.4   Loss Function

At present, the methods for optimizing neural networks are basically based on the idea of back propagation. According to the error calculated by the loss function, the weights of the network are optimized by means of gradient back propagation. D-CNN network uses the following multi-part loss function [9, 21]

$$
\begin{aligned}
&\lambda_{coord} \sum_{i=0}^{S^2} \sum_{j=0}^{B} \mathbb{1}_{ij}^{obj} \left[(x_i - \hat{x}_i)^2 + (y_i - \hat{y}_i)^2\right] \\
&+ \lambda_{coord} \sum_{i=0}^{S^2} \sum_{j=0}^{B} \mathbb{1}_{ij}^{obj} \left[\left(\sqrt{w_i} - \sqrt{\hat{w}_i}\right)^2 + \left(\sqrt{h_i} - \sqrt{\hat{h}_i}\right)^2\right] \\
&+ \sum_{i=0}^{S^2} \sum_{j=0}^{B} \mathbb{1}_{ij}^{obj} \left[(C_i - \hat{C}_i)^2\right] + \lambda_{noobj} \sum_{i=0}^{S^2} \sum_{j=0}^{B} \mathbb{1}_{ij}^{noobj} (C_i - \hat{C}_i)^2 \\
&+ \sum_{i=0}^{S^2} \mathbb{1}_i^{obj} \sum_{c \in classes} (p_i(c) - \hat{p}_i(c))^2
\end{aligned}
\tag{3}
$$

where $\mathbb{1}_i^{obj}$ denotes whether a person exists in cell i and $\mathbb{1}_{ij}^{obj}$ denotes that the jth bounding box predictor of pedestrian in cell i is "responsible". In the loss function, we need to pay more attention to the coordinate prediction and give these losses a greater weight, denoted as λ_{coord}. The confidence loss of the bounding box without pedestrians is given a small loss weight, denoted as λ_{noobj}. In the experiment, $\lambda_{coord} = 5$ and $\lambda_{coord} = 0.5$.

3   Experiments

The performance of our proposed D-CNN network is evaluated on two popular datasets: Caltech dataset [18] and Pascal VOC dataset [19], compared with the state-of-the-art methods.

3.1   Caltech Benchmark

Caltech: The Caltech dataset contains about 350 K pedestrian bounding box annotations across 10 h of urban driving. We evaluate the performance on the reasonable subset of the evaluated datasets in the experiments. This subset consists of pedestrians who are more than 49 pixels in height, and whose occluded portions are less than 35%. In Caltech dataset, the evaluation metrics are MR_{-2} and MR_{-4} [7],corresponding to the log-average Miss Rate on FPPI ranges of $[10^{-2}, 10^{0}]$ and $[10^{-4}, 10^{0}]$. Figure 4 shows the overall experimental results on the Caltech.

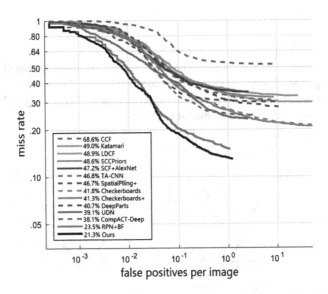

Fig. 4. Comparison of D-CNN with state-of-the-art methods on caltech dataset

As shown in Fig. 4, the miss rate of D-CNN is 21.3% with an IoU threshold of 0.7 on Caltech dataset. Among all the methods compared in the Fig. 4, the comprehensive performance of D-CNN is the best. Compared with other state-of-the-art methods, D-CNN's ROC plot of miss rate against FPPI(false positives per image) is impressive. Particularly, the miss rate of our network is 17.8% lower than that of UDN. Although the deformation and occlusion handling of our network refer to UDN [14], our network architecture and activation function are different from that of UDN. D-CNN network is based on YOLOv2 model and uses Maxout as the activation function to better improve performance. This experiment result indicates that D-CNN has a better performance.

3.2   Pascal VOC Benchmark

Pascal VOC: Pascal VOC provides a complete set of standardized. The Pascal VOC dataset includes 20 classes: person, animal (birds, cats, dogs, horses, cattle, sheep); transport (airplane, ship, bicycle, bus, car, motorcycle, train); indoor (bottles, chairs, tables, potted plants, sofa, TV). Since our focus is on pedestrian detection, we continue to use only the pedestrian class for training and evaluation. Table 1 shows the results on the Pascal VOC dataset.

Table 1. Comparison of performance on pascal VOC.

Methods	Datasets	mAP	FPS
YOLO [9]	VOC2007+2012	63.5	45
Fast R-CNN [7]	VOC2007+2012	72.0	0.5
SSD300 [11]	VOC2007+2012	79.4	46
Faster R-CNN [8]	VOC2007+2012	79.6	7
ResNet [24]	VOC2007+2012	80.7	5
YOLOv2 [10]	VOC2007+2012	81.3	40
SSD512 [11]	VOC2007+2012	83.3	19
D-CNN(Ours)	**VOC2007+2012**	**82.9**	**38**

As can be seen from Table 1, D-CNN achieves 38 FPS, which is double of the 19 FPS of SSD512, with only 0.4 lower in the mAP than SSD512, which has the highest mAP among all the methods evaluated here on Pascal VOC. Although the D-CNN network is based on YOLOv2 architecture, its mAP on pedestrian detection is 19.4 higher than that of YOLO, and is 1.6 higher than that of YOLOv2 on pedestrian detection. Overall, the comprehensive performance of D-CNN is the best among all the methods evaluated on Pascal VOC dataset.

3.3   Performance on Pictures of Daily Life

After training UDN, YOLOv2, and D-CNN on pedestrian datasets of Pascal VOC, we applied the three networks to pedestrian detection in daily life situations. Figure 5 shows the detection results of the three detection networks. Figure 5(a) gives two example pictures got in daily life, both of which contain four occluded people. Figure 5(b), (c), and (d) show the detection results of UDN, YOLOv2, and D-CNN respectively. From the figure we can see that, UDN can only give one bounding box, which means only one pedestrian is detected, and YOLOv2 detects two bounding boxes. Although D-CNN gives three bounding boxes, it detects all the four pedestrians, with two of them detected correctly and the other two treated as one pedestrian. The results indicate that D-CNN perform better than both YOLOv2 and UDN on pedestrian detection in daily life.

(a) Two Pictures in Daily Life

(b) Detection Results of UDN

(c) Detection Results of YOLOv2

(d) Detection Results of D-CNN

Fig. 5. Performance of UDN, YOLOv2, and D-CNN on pedestrian detection in daily life

4 Conclusion

We propose a D-CNN network for pedestrian detection, which integrates deformation model and occlusion handling with YOLOv2 network and applying Maxout as its activation function. Coming after the first convolutional layer and max pooling layer of D-CNN, the part filters of different sizes can effectively handle the problem of occlusion and improve the performance of pedestrian detection. Moreover, the utilizing of Maxout as the activation function helps mitigate the disappearance of gradients. Experiments show that our network achieves better results than other methods compared. Though the D-CNN network focuses on improving the accuracy of pedestrian detection while maintaining high FPS, the framework can also be used for other object detection.

Acknowledgment. This work was supported by National Natural Science Foundation of China (Grant Nos. 81101119 and 61672231).

References

1. Viola, P., Jones, M.J., Snow, D.: Detecting pedestrians using patterns of motion and appearance. In: Proceedings of the IEEE International Conference on Computer Vision (ICCV). IEEE (2003)
2. Lowe, D.G.: Distinctive image features from scale-invariant keypoints. Int. J. Comput. Vis. **60**(2), 91–110 (2004)
3. Dalal, N., Triggs, B.: Histograms of oriented gradients for human detection. In: 2005 IEEE Computer Society Conference on Computer Vision and Pattern Recognition CVPR 2005, vol. 1. IEEE (2005)
4. Ojala, T., Pietikainen, M., Harwood, D.: Performance evaluation of texture measures with classification based on Kullback discrimination of distributions. In: 1994 Pattern Recognition, vol. 1-Conference A: Proceedings of the 12th IAPR International Conference on Computer Vision & Image Processing, vol. 1. IEEE (1994)
5. Cortes, C., Vapnik, V.: Support-vector networks. Mach. Learn. **20**(3), 273–297 (1995)
6. Rojas, R.: AdaBoost and the super bowl of classifiers a tutorial introduction to adaptive boosting. Freie University, Berlin, Technical Report (2009)
7. Girshick, R.: FAST R-CNN. In: Proceedings of the IEEE International Conference on Computer Vision (2015)
8. Ren, S., et al.: Faster R-CNN: Towards real-time object detection with region proposal networks. In: Advances in Neural Information Processing Systems (2015)
9. Redmon, J., et al.: You only look once: Unified, real-time object detection. In: Proceedings of the IEEE Conference on Computer Vision and Pattern Recognition (2016)
10. Redmon, J., Farhadi, A.: YOLO9000: Better, Faster, Stronger (2016). arXiv:1612.08242
11. Liu, W., Anguelov, D., Erhan, D., Szegedy, C., Reed, S., Fu, C.-Y., Berg, Alexander C.: SSD: single shot multibox detector. In: Leibe, B., Matas, J., Sebe, N., Welling, M. (eds.) ECCV 2016. LNCS, vol. 9905, pp. 21–37. Springer, Cham (2016). https://doi.org/10.1007/978-3-319-46448-0_2
12. Szegedy, C., et al.: Going deeper with convolutions. In: Proceedings of the IEEE Conference on Computer Vision and Pattern Recognition (2015)

13. Wang, X.: An HOG-LBP human detector with partial occlusion handling. In: IEEE 12th International Conference on Computer Vision, Kyoto, Japan, 29 September 2009
14. Ouyang, W., Wang, X.: Joint deep learning for pedestrian detection. In: Proceedings of the IEEE International Conference on Computer Vision (2013)
15. Enzweiler, M., et al.: Multi-cue pedestrian classification with partial occlusion handling. In: 2010 IEEE Conference on Computer vision and pattern recognition (CVPR). IEEE (2010)
16. Gao, T., Packer, B., Koller, D.: A segmentation-aware object detection model with occlusion handling. In: 2011 IEEE Conference on Computer Vision and Pattern Recognition (CVPR). IEEE (2011)
17. Felzenszwalb, P.F., et al.: Object detection with discriminatively trained part-based models. IEEE Trans. Pattern Analy. Mach. Intell. 32(9), 1627–1645 (2010)
18. Dollar, P., et al.: Pedestrian detection: An evaluation of the state of the art. IEEE Trans. Pattern Anal. Mach. Intell. 34(4), 743–761 (2012)
19. Everingham, M., et al.: The pascal visual object classes challenge a retrospective. Int. J. Comput. Vis. 111(1), 98–136 (2015)
20. Goodfellow, I.J., et al.: Maxout networks (2013). arXiv preprint arXiv:1302.4389
21. Dai, W., et al.: Co-clustering based classification for out-of-domain documents. In: Proceedings of the 13th ACM SIGKDD International Conference on Knowledge Discovery and Data Mining. ACM (2007)
22. LeCun, Y., et al.: Gradient-based learning applied to document recognition. In: Proceedings of the IEEE 86(11), 2278–2324 (1998)
23. Krizhevsky, A., Sutskever, I., Hinton, G.E.: Imagenet classification with deep convolutional neural networks. In: Advances in Neural Information Processing Systems (2012)
24. He, K., et al.: Deep residual learning for image recognition. In: Proceedings of the IEEE Conference on Computer Vision and Pattern Recognition (2016)

A Novel 3D Human Action Recognition Method Based on Part Affinity Fields

Haipeng Dong, Qingqing Meng, and Tao Hu[(⊠)]

School of Computer Science and Engineering,
Northeastern University, Shenyang, China
{donghaipeng, mengqingqing, hutao}@stu.neu.edu.cn

Abstract. The analysis of human actions based on 3D skeleton data becomes popular recently due to its succinctness, robustness, and view-invariant representation. Recent attempts on this problem suggested to use human body affinity fields to efficiently detect the 2D pose of multiple people in an image. In this paper, we extend this idea to 3D domains and develop a 3D human action recognition system with ability to understand the cooperative action of several people. To achieve this, we firstly extract the human body affinity fields to robustly represent associate 2D human skeleton with individuals in the image. Inspired by the triangulation techniques in stereo vision analysis, 3D human skeleton data can be obtained. To handle the noise in constructed 3D human skeleton data, we introduce an enhanced light-weight matching algorithm based on Dynamic Time Warping (DTW) to compute the matching cost. The real-life experiments demonstrate the efficiency and applicability of our approach.

Keywords: Action recognition · Binocular stereo camera · Part affinity fields
Dynamic time warping

1 Introduction

Human action recognition is the process of detecting human action in the video and labeling it in the image sequences. Robust solutions to this problem has been recognized as an active research topic in the field of computer vision due to the large number of potential applications based on automatic video analysis such as video surveillance, health care, and a variety of systems that involve interactions between persons and machines. Among these applications, one of the promising applications is human-robot interactions. A robot with the ability to understand the action of humans will help the robot to collaborate effectively and efficiently with humans to complete one specific task.

An action is a sequence of human body movements, and may involve several body parts concurrently. Due to the variations in motion performance, recording settings and inter-personal differences, it is in general challenging to solve the problems of human action recognition. With its benefit to many real-life applications, the research topic of human action recognition has received much attention in recent years. In [1, 2], Wang et al. introduce a descriptor based on motion boundary histograms (MBH) which relies on differential optical flow. The experiment shows MBH descriptor consistently

© Springer Nature Singapore Pte Ltd. 2018
Y. Bi et al. (Eds.): ESTC 2017, CCIS 857, pp. 181–192, 2018.
https://doi.org/10.1007/978-981-13-1026-3_14

outperform other state-of-the-art descriptors. But this approach highly relies on the detection effect of human body, and the recognition rate is low in the condition of human motion blur. Recently, deep-learning based approaches, such as ISA(Independent Subspace Analysis) [3, 4] and LSTM (Long-Short Term Memory) [5, 6], have been wildly applied to solve the problem and also have achieved promising performance in 3D action recognition. In [7], the ISA algorithm is applied to learn spatiotemporal features from local regions of joints for the improvement of the training efficiency. Based on these features, an integrated learning approach for the action recognition task is proposed for the action recognition task. In [8], inspired by the observation that the co-occurrences of the joints intrinsically characterize human actions, Zhu et al. proposed fully connected deep LSTM network for skeleton based action recognition. In general, deep learning based algorithms can achieve great improvement in the recognition accuracy compared to the traditional methods. However, deep learning based algorithms require costly computation and therefore suffer from poor real-time performance. This limits the practicability of these approaches in industry. In [9], Tian et al. use DTW algorithms (Dynamic Time Warping) to distinguish the similarity of actions based on the calculation the ratio of the angle differences. However, this method cannot distinguish the body parts with the larger movement and the one that hardly participate in the movement. This results in the accuracy loss of the recognition.

In this paper, we introduce an enhanced light-weight matching algorithm based on DTW for 3D action recognition of multiple peoples. In this approach, we firstly use the human part affinity field to construct 2D pose of multiple people in an image. To achieve robustness and view-invariant representation of human skeleton data, the obtained human skeleton data is transferred from 2D to 3D domain based on the triangulation techniques in stereo vision analysis. Finally, an enhanced DTW based algorithm is proposed to recognize actions. Compared to the original DTW algorithms [10] which cannot deal with the case that the 3D positions of the joints are noisy, our recognition system develops an approach to represent intensity of each joint and integrate this intensity descriptor into DTW to improve the accuracy of the approaches.

The remainder of the paper is organized as follows. Part affinity fields based 2D pose estimation is presented in Sect. 2. Section 3 details the transformation of human skeleton data. Section 4 presents the light-weight matching algorithm based on DTW algorithm for 3D action recognition of multiple peoples. Section 5 presents the experimental results. Section 6 concludes this paper.

2 2D Pose Estimation of Multiple People

2.1 Part Affinity Fields

In this section, we introduce the basic concept of part affinity fields (PAFs), which can be used to extract the 2D key points for each person from an image. The concept of PAF is firstly introduced in [11] Different with traditional methods, Cao et al. [11] use neural network to obtain a set of 2D confidence maps S for body part locations and a set of 2D vector fields L for part affinities. In particular, the set $S = \{S_1, S_2, ..., S_j\}$ has

j body part locations and the set $L = \{L_1, L_2, ..., L_C\}$ has C vector fields. PAFs describes the connections between body parts.

Figure 1 illustrates the overall network structure, which has T stages. Initialized by 10 layers of VGG-19, we can obtain initial set F of feature maps for an image. This initial set F is then injected into the first stage of network for predictions. The network is split into the top branch and the bottom branch, which are shown as green and blue blocks in Fig. 1. Particularly, the top branch is used to predict joints hot maps, while the bottom branch is used to predict the distribution of PAFs.

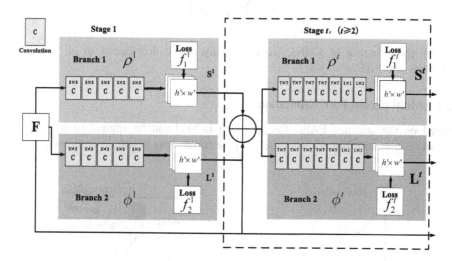

Fig. 1. Network structure [11]

At the first stage, the network produces a set of detection confidence maps $S^1 = \rho^1(F)$ and a set of part affinity fields $L^1 = \varphi^1(F)$, where ρ^1 and φ^1 are the inference of Stage 1. In each subsequent stage, the predictions from both branches in the previous stages, along with the original image features F, are concatenated and used to produce refined predictions,

$$S^t = \rho^t(F, S^{t-1}, L^{t-1}), \forall t \geq 2 \tag{1}$$

$$L^t = \varphi^t(F, S^{t-1}, L^{t-1}), \forall t \geq 2 \tag{2}$$

where ρ^t and φ^t are the inference of stage t.

To guide the iteration of the constructed networks, two loss functions are introduced at the end of each stage. Specifically, the loss functions at stage t are defined as:

$$f_S^t = \sum_{j=1}^{J} \sum_p W(p) * \left\| S_j^t(p) - S_j^*(p) \right\|_2^2 \tag{3}$$

$$f_L^t = \sum_{c=1}^{C} \sum_p W(p) * \left\| L_c^t(p) - L_c^*(p) \right\|_2^2 \tag{4}$$

where S_j^* is the groundtruth part of confidence map, L_c^* is the groundtruth part of affinity vector field, W is a binary mask where $W(p) = 0$ holds when the annotation is missing at an image location p. The overall objective is to minimize the following functions:

$$f = \sum_{t=1}^{T} (f_S^t + f_L^t) \tag{5}$$

By the inference of CNNs, we can finally obtain distribution of all body part locations and PAFs.

2.2 Multi-person Pose Estimation

Based on the obtained PAFs, the approach in [11] can be applied to identify the associate joint and further detect the 2D pose of multiple people in an image.

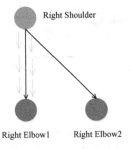

Right Shoulder

Right Elbow1   Right Elbow2

Fig. 2. Joint matching (Color figure online)

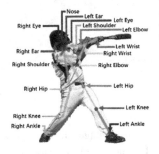

Fig. 3. Human body joints [11]

We now use an example (as presented in Fig. 2) to explain how the scheme of pose estimation works by using PAFs. For simplicity of presentation, we consider 3 joint points structures with right shoulder and two right elbows from two persons which are denoted as right elbow 1 and right elbow 2, respectively. Black lines indicate possible connections between to joint points. Yellow lines indicate PAFs. In practice, we determine part associations by the mapping of PAFs. As shown in Fig. 2, the black line that connects right shoulder joint and right elbow 1 has same direction with yellow line which represents the mapping of PAFs. This confirms the part association among right shoulder joint and right elbow 1. By training neural network in coco dataset, the sequence information of each human body's joints can be successfully obtained, as shown in Fig. 3.

3   3D Human Skeleton Data Transformation

Until now, we have obtained 2D human skeleton data by using the approach in [11]. However, 2D human skeleton data is not robust enough to represent human actions due to view-variant problems. Therefore, we require to transform 2D human skeleton data to 3D domains.

Stereo camera allows the camera to simulate human binocular vision, and therefore gives it the ability to capture three-dimensional images. This process is known as stereo photography. With high efficiency, reasonable precision, and low cost, Stereo camera vision system can be considered as an effective solution to transform 2D human skeleton data to 3D domains.

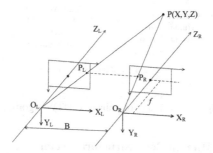

Fig. 4. Binocular ranging method

Figure 4 show the triangulation techniques to capture depth information of an object in an image. In Fig. 4, P is the object point with coordinate (X, Y, Z) in left camera coordinate. $P_L(x_L, y_L)$ and $P_R(x_R, y_R)$ are pixel points on left and right image planes respectively. O_L and O_R are the optical centers of left and right cameras, respectively. We define disparity as:

$$d = x_L - x_R \tag{6}$$

Let us denote B and f as baseline between two cameras and focal distance of the both cameras, respectively. According to pinhole camera model and the principle of similar triangles, we have:

$$Z = \frac{Bf}{d} \tag{7}$$

Now, we can obtain depth information from original images by Eq. (7) and transform 2D human skeleton data to 3D domains, which make the action representation more accurate.

4   Enhanced DTW Algorithms

In this section, we present our enhanced DTW algorithm for 3D human action recognition. The overview of the algorithm is presented in Fig. 5. To handle the noise in constructed 3D human skeleton data, we firstly construct human body structure vector and use variance of vector angles to represent intensity of actions. Based on the analysis of the constructed human body structure vector, the weight of vector angles can be determined and integrated into traditional DTW algorithm for 3D human action recognition.

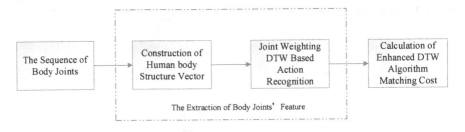

Fig. 5. Overview of enhanced DTW algorithm

4.1   Construction of Human Body Structure Vector

To achieve better representation of pose relationship between movement of extremities and torsos, we construct human body structure vector based on the method in [9]. The joints structure we used in this paper is represented as:

Joints = {nose, neck, left shoulder, left elbow, left wrist, right shoulder, right elbow, right wrist, left hip, left knee, left ankle, right hip, right knee, right ankle, centroid}

The corresponding structure vector between joint points $P_1(x_1, y_1, z_1)$ and $P_2(x_2, y_2, z_2)$ can be obtained as:

$$\overrightarrow{p_1p_2} = (x_2 - x_1, y_2 - y_1, z_2 - z_1) \tag{8}$$

In general, human body movement trend is almost similar. In this paper, we use the angle of body struct vector to eliminate structure vector differences among different individuals. Supposing that there are body structure vectors $v_1(x_1, x_2, x_3)$ and $v_2(y_1, y_2, y_3)$, the angle between the two vectors is defined as:

$$\langle v_1, v_2 \rangle = \arccos \frac{v_1 \cdot v_2}{|v_1||v_2|} \tag{9}$$

where $v_1 \cdot v_2 = x_1 \cdot x_2 + y_1 \cdot y_2 + z_1 \cdot z_2$, $|v_1| = \sqrt{x_1^2 + y_1^2 + z_1^2}$, $|v_1| \neq 0$ and $|v_2| \neq 0$. According to Eq. (9), we can obtain 20 sets of body structure vector angle as listed in Table 1.

Table 1. Body struct vector angle

ID	Body struct vector angle	ID	Body struct vector angle
1	Nose_rshoulder_relbow	11	Rshoulder_centroid_rknee
2	Rshoulder_relbow_rwrist	12	Centroid_rhip_rknee
3	Neck_lshoulder_lelbow	13	Rhip_rknee_rankle
4	Lshoulder_lelbow_lwrist	14	Lshoulder_centroid_lhip
5	Neck_rshoulder_centroid	15	Centroid_lhip_lknee
6	Rshoulder_relbow_centroid	16	Lhip_lknee_lankle
7	Relbow_rhand_centroid	17	Neck_centroid_rhip_rknee
8	Neck_lshoulder_centroid	18	Neck_centroid_rknee_rankle
9	Lshoulder_lelbow_centroid	19	Neck_centroid_lhip_lankle
10	Lelbow_lhand_centroid	20	Neck_centroid_lknee_lankle

4.2 Joint Weighting DTW Based Action Recognition

In traditional action recognition approaches [12], body structure vectors of the intensive and silence actions cannot be well distinguished, which restricts the improvement of accuracy of action recognition. Our approach is inspired by adaptive weighting method presented in [13] and reassigns weight to each body struct vector angle. The intensive body struct vector angles are assigned with smaller weight while almost silence ones are assigned with bigger weight.

We divide the action frame sequence as $P = [p_1, p_2, \ldots, p_i, \ldots p_T]$ into N segments by time, where T denotes the frame number and p_i denotes the angle data of ith frame in the frame sequence, as defined as $p_i = \{a_1, a_2, \ldots, a_j, \ldots a_k\}$. Each frame has k body struct vector angles ($k = 20$ as listed in Table 1) and a_j is the arccosine of the jth body struct vector in each frame. In each segment, we measure active degree by the variance of the vector angle variation, sort the frames in descending order by active degree and derive sequence $T = [T_1, T_2, \ldots, T_n, \ldots, T_N]$, where T_n is the human struct vector angle ID sequence that is corresponding to the nth segment. Taking the first H human struct vector angle IDs from T_n, we have $T^H = [T_1^H, T_2^H, \ldots, T_n^H, \ldots, T_N^H]$. We define function $count(T^H, i)$ to represent the times that the human struct vector angle ID i appears in T^H. Then, we can calculate a ratio for each human struct vector angle i.

$$S_i = \frac{count(T^H, i)}{H \times N}, \quad i = 1, \ldots, k \tag{10}$$

Sorting S_i in descending order, we have $S' = [S'_1, S'_2, \ldots, S'_m, \ldots, S'_M]$. Take the first m elements from S' and select the elements with the sum is greater than α. The corresponding human struct vector angle s are merged into the set C. Therefore, we can derive weight for each body structure vector angle:

$$\omega_i = \begin{cases} S_i \cdot \alpha / \sum_{j=1}^{j=m} S'_j & i \in C \\ (T - m)/(1 - \alpha) & i \notin C \end{cases} \quad i = 1, 2, \ldots, k \tag{11}$$

Here, we refer to the method from paper [13] and conduct several experiments so as to adjust α and H.

4.3 Calculate Matching Cost Using Enhanced DTW Algorithm

DTW algorithm aims to align two length-inconsistent time sequences and calculate the matching cost. We define two sequences A, whose length is n, and B, whose length is m:

$$A = \{a_1, a_2, \ldots, a_i, \ldots, a_n\}$$
$$B = \{b_1, b_2, \ldots, b_i, \ldots, b_m\} \quad (12)$$

To calculate the matching cost, we build a $n \times m$ matrix D, whose element $d_{i,j}$ is the matching distance $d(a_i, b_j)$ between a_i and b_j. Traditional DTW algorithm calculates matching cost by means of Euclidean distance and then use the principle of dynamic programming to find an alignment path in matrix D that minimizes the cost of matching sequence A and sequence B. The dynamic programming can be implemented to find the optimal path in matrix D by the integration of the following matching cost function:

$$cost(a_i, b_j) = d(a_i, b_j) + min\{cost(a_{i-1}, b_j), cost(a_i, b_{j-1}), cost(a_{i-1}, b_{j-1})\} \quad (13)$$

Suppose the length k of the optimal alignment path is derived. Then, the overall matching cost function can be represented as:

$$DTW(A, B) = \frac{\sum_{1}^{k} \cos t_k}{k} \quad (14)$$

In this paper, we integrate the weighted body structure vector angle into traditional DTW algorithm to calculate the matching distance. In particular, the weights are multiplied as coefficients during the calculation of the matching cost. By this way, the dominance of the joint with intensive actions can be improved during the calculation.

Now, we show how the weight can be integrated. We define test sequence a_i and template sequence b_j:

$$a_i = \{acrcos\theta_{i1}, acrcos\theta_{i2}, \ldots, acrcos\theta_{i20}\}$$
$$b_j = \{acrcos\theta_{j1}, acrcos\theta_{j2}, \ldots, acrcos\theta_{j20}\} \quad (15)$$

Then the matching cost can be calculated as:

$$d(a_i, b_j) = \sum_{n=1}^{N} w_n \frac{(acr \cos \theta_{in} - arccos \theta_{jn})^2}{arccos \theta_{in} + arccos \theta_{jn}} \quad (16)$$

where w_n refers to the weight of the nth joint vector angle. With this integration, the overall matching cost is derived by DTW algorithm. If the test sequence has the minimum matching cost with a template sequence from template library, the test sequence and the template sequence refer to the same action.

5 Experiment Results

In this section, we conduct experiments to evaluate the performance of the proposed approaches. We firstly apply the proposed approach to real image sequences and show the applicability of the approach on generating 3D human skeleton data. To evaluate the performance of enhanced DTW algorithms, the standard benchmark is then adopted for demonstration.

5.1 Case Study

In this case study, we show how to use the stereo camera to obtain the 3D human skeleton data by using affinity field. ZED stereo camera [15] is applied in this experiment. We use part affinity field to detect the 2D pose of peoples in the left image of ZED camera [15] and then map the pixel positions of joints to the disparity map generated by ZED camera [15].

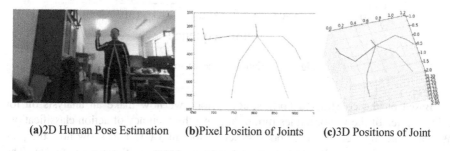

(a)2D Human Pose Estimation   (b)Pixel Position of Joints   (c)3D Positions of Joint

Fig. 6. Result of the experiment

Figure 6(a) shows one student conducts the motion of hand up. The 2D human pose have been successfully detected using part affinity field, as shown Fig. 6(a). Then, the pixel positions of joints as shown in Fig. 6(b) is mapped to the disparity map of ZED [15]. By this operation, the 3D positions of the joints can be successfully obtained as shown in Fig. 6(c).

5.2 Evaluation

In this section, we focus on evaluating the performance of enhanced DTW algorithms. In this experiment, we apply the benchmark of MSR-Action3D [14] for testing, which contains 3D datasets including several real-life human action sequences. We select 5 types of data sets including drinking, calling, eating, throwing, and cheering for the performance evaluation of human action recognition. For the fairness, we use the cross-validation method in which one part of data is selected as template and the others is used as evaluation.

At first, we construct body struct vectors based on joint data and calculate the vector angles. In the experiment, we select 7th body structure vectors in Table 1 for demonstration. We analyze arccosines of this vector angle from various action. The analysis results are presented in Fig. 7. In this figure, x-axis denotes the time instant, whereas y-axis presents the arccosines value of the selected vector. In Fig. 7, we can observe the angle of the same body struct vector in various actions are different.

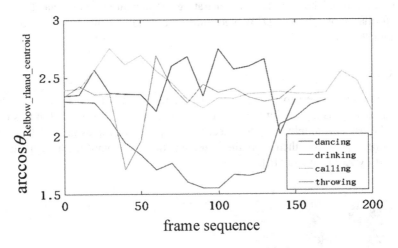

Fig. 7. Variation of the vector angle

Based on the constructed body struct vectors, we now make an analysis on for active degree of the vector angles further improve the accuracy of action classification. We calculate the weight for 20 body struct vectors in Table 1 to show how the proposed approach can efficiently represent active degree of the vector angles. The analysis results are presented in Table 2. The significant movement has smaller weight (as indicated as white cell in Table 2), while the silent movement has bigger weight (as indicated as dark cell in Table 2). Another observation is that the weight of the same vector angle in different action sequences varies significantly.

We now evaluate the performance of enhanced DTW algorithms on MSR-Action3D [14] benchmark including 5 action sequences. In each action sequence, we randomly select 2 samples as template and 1 sample for testing. Each action sequence can conduct 200 experiments. The results are presented in Table 3. As shown in Table 3, our approach outperforms traditional DTW algorithm on the action classification accuracy.

According to Table 3, our method increases the action classification precision and have better performance than traditional DTW algorithm.

Table 2. Weights of the vector angles

ID	cheering	drinking	calling	throwing	Eating
1	0.108	46.667	40.000	0.061	46.667
2	0.148	0.181	0.178	0.198	46.667
3	0.108	46.667	40.000	43.333	46.667
4	0.162	46.667	0.082	0.076	0.086
5	46.667	46.667	40.000	43.333	46.667
6	46.667	0.068	40.000	0.091	46.667
7	0.067	0.135	0.069	0.152	0.111
8	46.667	46.667	40.000	43.333	46.667
9	46.667	46.667	0.055	43.333	46.667
10	46.667	46.667	0.069	43.333	0.098
11	46.667	0.113	40.000	0.061	46.667
12	46.667	46.667	40.000	43.333	46.667
13	46.667	46.667	0.069	43.333	46.667
14	46.667	46.667	40.000	43.333	46.667
15	46.667	46.667	40.000	43.333	46.667
16	0.108	0.068	0.096	0.061	0.160
17	46.667	46.667	40.000	43.333	0.098
18	46.667	46.667	0.082	43.333	46.667
19	46.667	46.667	40.000	43.333	46.667
20	46.667	0.135	40.000	43.333	0.147

Table 3. Analysis result

Behavior Recognition rate Method	cheering	drinking	calling	throwing	eating
Traditional DTW	58%	43.5%	61%	91%	75%
Enhanced DTW	87.5%	57.5%	78.5%	97.5%	98%

6   Conclusion

In this paper, we proposed a novel 3D human action recognition method based on part affinity fields. In this approach, the technique of human body affinity field is applied to construct 2D pose of multiple people in an image. To achieve robustness and view-invariant representation of human skeleton data, the obtained human skeleton data is transferred from 2D to 3D domain based on the triangulation techniques in stereo analysis. Furthermore, an enhanced light-weight matching algorithm based on Dynamic Time Warping (DTW) is proposed for human action recognition. The experiment results show the applicability and efficiency of the proposed approaches.

References

1. Wang, H., Schmid, C.: Action recognition with improved trajectories. In: Proceedings of IEEE International Conference Computer Vision, pp. 3551–3558 (2013)
2. Wang, H., Kläser, A., Schmid, C., Liu, C.L.: Dense trajectories and motion boundary descriptors for action recognition. Int. J. Comput. Vis. **103**(1), 60–79 (2013)
3. Geng-Dai, L., Ming-Liang, X., Ming-min, Z.: Human motion synthesis based on independent spatio-temporal feature space. Chinese J. Comput. **34**(3), 464–472 (2011)
4. Tao, Q., Dexiang, D., Hui, L., Lian, Z., Yifeng, L.: Extracting spatio-temporal features via multi-layer independent subspace analysis for action recognition. Geomatics Inf. Sci. WuHan Univ. **41**(4) (2016)
5. Zhang, S., Liu, X., Xiao, J.: On geometric features for skeleton-based action recognition using multilayer LSTM networks. In: Proceedings of 2017 IEEE Winter Conference on Applications of Computer Vision, WACV 2017, pp. 148–157 (2017)
6. Liu, J., Shahroudy, A., Xu, D., Wang, G.: Spatio-temporal LSTM with trust gates for 3D human action recognition. In: Leibe, B., Matas, J., Sebe, N., Welling, M. (eds.) ECCV 2016. LNCS, vol. 9907, pp. 816–833. Springer, Cham (2016). https://doi.org/10.1007/978-3-319-46487-9_50
7. Chen, G., Giuliani, M., Clarke, D., Gaschler, A., Knoll, A.: Action recognition using ensemble weighted multi-instance learning. In: Proceedings of IEEE International Conference on Robotics and Automation, pp. 4520–4525 (2014)
8. Zhu, W., et al.: Co-occurrence feature learning for skeleton based action recognition using regularized deep LSTM networks, no. 2, pp. 3697–3703 (2016)
9. Guohui, T., Jianqin, Y., Xu, H., Jing, Y.: A novel human activity recognition method using joint points information. Robot **36**(3), 285–292 (2014)
10. Sempena, S., Maulidevi, N.U., Aryan, P.R.: Human action recognition using dynamic time warping. In: Proceedings of 2011 International Conference on Electrical Engineering Informatics, no. July, pp. 1–5 (2011)
11. Cao, Z., Simon, T., Wei, S.-E., Sheikh, Y.: Realtime Multi-Person 2D Pose Estimation using Part Affinity Fields (2016)
12. Galna, B., Barry, G., Jackson, D., Mhiripiri, D., Olivier, P., Rochester, L.: Accuracy of the Microsoft Kinect sensor for measuring movement in people with Parkinson's disease. Gait Posture **39**(4), 1062–1068 (2014)
13. Chengfeng, W., Hong, C., Ruixuan, Z., Dehai, Z., Qing, W., Shuli, M.: Research on DTW action recognition algorithm with joint weighting. J. Graph. **37**(4) (2016)
14. Liu, Z.: Zicheng Liu at Microsoft Research (2017). https://www.microsoft.com/en-us/research/people/zliu/#!projects
15. ZED Stereo Camera: https://www.stereolabs.com

Channel Feature Extraction and Modeling Based on Principal Component Analysis

Biyuan Yao[1], Jianhua Yin[1], Hui Li[1(✉)], Hui Zhou[1], and Wei Wu[2]

[1] College of Information Science and Technology,
Hainan University, Haikou 570228, China
yaobiyuanyy@163.com, {yinjh,lihui,zhouhui}@hainu.edu.cn
[2] Institute of Deep-sea Science and Engineering,
Chinese Academy of Sciences,
Sanya 572000, China
wuwei@sidsse.ac.cn

Abstract. The research aims to solve the problem of wireless channel feature extraction and modeling in mobile communications. According to the real channel measurement pulse results of three scenes, this study employs a digital signal processor to analyze the characterization of multi-path channel parameters and subsequently extract effective features. Through extracting feature parameters of channels in these scenes, we identify three different scenes, and analyze the trend and performance of different parameters on the channel features. The study then draws on principal component analysis to build a fingerprint of the wireless channel characteristic model. Finally, the research shows that the model features are in good agreement with the measured data.

Keywords: Channel characteristics · Channel feature extraction
Channel modeling · Principal component analysis

1 Introduction

Mobile communications industry has been rapidly developing at an alarming rate and has become one of the major high-tech industries that have spurred the development of the global economy. It has also had a huge impact on human life and social development. In mobile communications, the transmitter and the receiver transmit signals by electromagnetic waves. We can imagine some invisible electromagnetic paths between the two, and these electromagnetic paths called wireless channel [1]. Digital transmission system is the transmission capacity of the transmitter by the signal input from the receiver through the transmission path. The two main aspects affecting digital signal transmission are the transmission loss and the characteristics of wireless channel. The digital transmission system is widely used in dispatching communication in our life. Therefore, it is necessary to continuously develop communication technology to improve the function of the dispatching communication system to meet the

© Springer Nature Singapore Pte Ltd. 2018
Y. Bi et al. (Eds.): ESTC 2017, CCIS 857, pp. 193–209, 2018.
https://doi.org/10.1007/978-981-13-1026-3_15

needs of various users. Studying the features and the utilization of the channel is the need to meet the increasing of communication volume. In mobile communication, the signal will encounter many buildings, trees and undulating terrain. These obstacles cause energy absorption, penetration and reflection of wireless waves, scattering and diffraction. The distance in various paths of the wireless wave propagation is different, which results in different arrival time for each of reflection path. The superposition of multiple signals appears at the receiver with the direction of different phases. It will enhance if the signals are with phase in the same direction and decrease with the opposite one. And a change of the amplitude of the received signal occurs a fading phenomenon at the same time. This decline is caused by the multi-path, and is accordingly called the multi-path decay [2]. The propagation process of wireless channel is shown in Fig. 1.

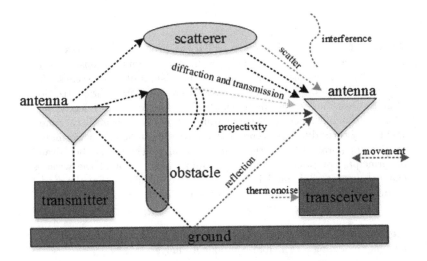

Fig. 1. Schematic diagram of wireless channel propagation

The channel propagation model takes into account the phenomenon of the propagation environment [3]. Fingerprint of a wireless channel is the difference between the characteristics of various wireless channels [4]. Using these features one can effectively identify different channels, which can then be applied to optimize wireless communication modeling. Channel modeling is a combination of mathematics, communication theory, electromagnetic field technology, microwave technology, and cross-disciplinary random process theory. The fingerprint of a wireless channel model is used to analyze the mathematical model of fingerprint characteristics [5] and based on the priori model as well as on the measured data of the differences between different channels. Channel modeling is used to identify, analyze and model the main features of the system, which then lays the foundation for the deployment and optimization of digital transmission systems [6].

2   Preliminary Results

Taking the multi-path coefficients and multi-path delay into account, discrete linear systems are usually used in wireless channel modeling. The signal and multi-path coefficients in this model are complex. The ideal channel measurement pulse through a wireless channel can be represented as an unit "$\delta[k]$" after the transmission. The ideal measurement of channel can be using the following formula.

$$h[k] = \sum_{l=0}^{L-1} h_l \cdot \delta[k - \tau_l],$$
$$\delta[k] = \begin{cases} 0, k \neq 0 \\ 1, k = 0 \end{cases} \tag{1}$$
$$k = 0, 1, ..., K - 1; k \geq \max\{\tau_l\}$$

Where k is the sample of discrete signal identification, it is assumed that there is a total of K sample points. L is the total number of paths at the current moment. h_l is the channel coefficient for the current l path, which is usually complex. τ_l is the time delay for the current l path and is converted into sample points that is delayed τ_l sample points. Obviously, the complex signal $h[k]$ gives the current time of the complete channel. Nevertheless, the calculation of the measurement of ideal channel does not result in a direct calculation for $h[k]$. Because in the real wireless communication systems, it usually requires transmission and reception of a filter within the system in order to improve the transmission quality of the signal. The effect of all filters in real measurements of channel can be represented by a function $g[k]$. At this time, the results of channel measurement are the following formula.

$$r[k] = \sum_{m=0}^{M-1} h[k - m] \cdot g[m], k = 0, 1, ..., K - 1 \tag{2}$$

Where M is the length of the filter, and $g[k]$ is the number of samples. Taking into account the time-varying channel and the noise in the measurement, the real measurement of channel at different time and their corresponding wireless channel is the following formula.

$$\begin{cases} r[k, n] = \sum_{m=0}^{M-1} h[k - m] \cdot g[m] + u[k, n] \\ h[k, n] = \sum_{l=0}^{L-1} h_l[n] \cdot \delta[k - \tau_l[n]] \\ k = 0, 1, ..., K - 1; n = 0, 1, ..., N - 1; \end{cases} \tag{3}$$

where n represents the testing sample of identification, it is assumed that there is a total of N samples. $h_l[n]$ denotes the channel coefficients for the current n time and the l-path, which is usually complex. $\tau_l[n]$ indicates the path delay for the current n time and the l-path of the sampling number. $u[k, n]$ indicates complex Gauss white noise, which is introduced into the n time and the test sample of kth. $r[k, n]$ indicates n time unit pulse sequentially through the transmission filter, the channel and the receiving filter after the actual signal. Obviously, we can obtain a complete time-varying channel $h[k, n]$ from $r[k, n]$.

2.1 Basic Assumptions

In order to make the channel fingerprint model as similar to the actual wireless channel model as possible, we present the following basic assumptions used in modeling: (1) We assumed each scene contains a single transmitter with a single receiver and that there is no interference from multiple transmitters or receivers. Each path is linear. (2) Supposing the electromagnetic wave is transmitted to the whole space with a spherical wave, we assumed the emission signal is stable. (3) We assumed all channels are scalar channels.

2.2 Multipath Channel Parameters

The channel can be subdivided into several sub-channels based on two characteristics: the multi-path time delay spread (signal envelope) and timing variations (random fading of the signal phase). The main parameters of the multi-path channel are characterized as follows:

(1) Power delay spectrum. The power delay spectrum $P(\tau)$ intuitively reflects the delay spread of the signal, and it is a function of the delay of τ. It can be obtained by observing the instantaneous power delay distribution.

(2) Time dispersion parameter. The parameter of channel time dispersion is usually used to describe the average delay $\bar{\tau}$ and the root means square (RMS) delay spread σ_τ. $\bar{\tau}$ describes the discrete degree of multi-path signals, which is defined as the first-order moment of the power delay spectrum $P(\tau)$ in the following formula.

$$\bar{\tau} = E(\tau) = \frac{\sum_k a_k^2 \cdot \tau_k}{\sum_k a_k^2} = \frac{\sum_k P(\tau_k)\tau_k}{\sum_k P(\tau_k)} \tag{4}$$

Where a_k is the attenuation factor of the kth path, $k = 1, 2, \ldots, n$, where n is the number of paths. And $P(\tau_k)$ is the relative power of the multi-path fading at delay time τ_k. σ_τ is the square root of the second-order or central moment by power delay spectrum $P(\tau)$, which describes the standard deviation of the average delay. This is calculated by the following formula.

$$\sigma_\tau = \sqrt{\overline{\tau^2} - (\bar{\tau})^2}$$
$$\overline{\tau^2} = \frac{\sum_k a_k^2 \cdot \tau_k^2}{\sum_k a_k^2} = \frac{\sum_k P(\tau_k)\tau_k^2}{\sum_k P(\tau_k)} \tag{5}$$

(3) Coherent bandwidth. The delay spread is caused by the reflection and scattering propagation path, and the coherent bandwidth B_c is determined from

the root mean square delay. If the correlation function is greater than 0.5 [8], the correlation is defined as follows.

$$B_c = \frac{1}{5\sigma_\tau} \tag{6}$$

(4) Doppler expansion and coherence time. Doppler-extended B_d is a measure of the degree of spectral spreading caused by the mobile radio channel. The spectral range of the signal after Doppler expansion is calculated as follows.

$$B_d = [f_c - f_{dmax}, f_c + f_{dmax}] \tag{7}$$

Where $f_{dmax} = v/\lambda$ is the maximum Doppler frequency shift, f_c is carrier frequency, and v and λ are relative motion velocity and wave length, respectively. The coherence time of the channel impulse response is a statistical average of all time intervals and remains unchanged. The correlation is defined as follows.

$$T_c \approx \frac{1}{f_{dmax}} \tag{8}$$

(5) Multi-path number. The multi-path quantity is a relative value, and an intensity parameter can be set to evaluate the intensity of the monitored information and carry out the count.

(6) Sampling refers to a process in which a continuous analog signal becomes a discrete sample of time on time. Sampling theorem: if a time-limited continuous analog signal is sampled for a band, the signal can be reconstructed based on its sample value when the sampling rate reaches a certain value.

2.3   Principal Component Analysis

In the experiment carried out here, a moving target will cause the different response due to obstacles. The response data can be divided into two groups, groups A is affected by buildings apparently, while groups B is not. As a result, the PCA is introduced to filter those properties from those fuzzy factors.

Principal component analysis (PCA) is used to extract the principal components by the coordinate transformation, deletes redundant variables and establishes as few new variables as possible, so that these new variables are paired uncorrelated [7]. Since each parameter of the channel changes little between adjacent samples n, the channel can be considered quasi-static, which allows us to use the PCA method to extract channel features. This means that the Doppler channel expansion is much smaller than the signal bandwidth in the frequency domain.

The specific process of PCA as follows:

1. The original data is standardized. Variables are selected for factor analysis.

Suppose that there are m variables of principal component analysis, they are $x_1, x_2, \ldots, x_m$, and there is n assessed objectives. The value of the jth index of the ith evaluation object is a_{ij}. The index value a_{ij} is converted into the standardized index value $\widetilde{a}_{ij}$.

$$\widetilde{a}_{ij} = \frac{(a_{ij} - u_j)}{s_j}, i = 1, 2, ..., n; j = 1, 2, ..., m \tag{9}$$

Among them, u_j is the sample mean of the jth index, s_j is the the standard deviation of the jth index. $\widetilde{x}_j$ is the standardized index variable.

$$u_j = \frac{1}{n} \sum_{i=1}^{n} a_{ij}, j = 1, 2, ..., m \tag{10}$$

$$s_j = \sqrt{\frac{1}{n-1} \sum_{i=1}^{n} (a_{ij} - u_j)^2}, j = 1, 2, ..., m \tag{11}$$

$$\widetilde{x}_j = \frac{(x_j - u_j)}{s_j}, j = 1, 2, ..., m \tag{12}$$

2. Eigenvalues and eigenvectors of the correlation coefficient of matrix R are analyzed.

$$R = \begin{bmatrix} r_{11} & r_{12} & \cdots & r_{1p} \\ r_{21} & r_{22} & \cdots & r_{2p} \\ \cdots & \cdots & \ddots & \cdots \\ r_{p1} & r_{p2} & \cdots & r_{pp} \end{bmatrix}; i, j = 1, 2, ..., p \tag{13}$$

$r_{ij}(i, j = 1, 2, ..., p)$ is the correlation coefficient between the original variable x_i and x_j after standardization, and $r_{ij} = r_{ji}$. p is number of factors of PCA. This is calculated using the following formula.

$$r_{ij} = \frac{\sum_{k=1}^{n} (x_{ki} - \overline{x}_i)(x_{kj} - \overline{x}_j)}{\sqrt{\sum_{k=1}^{n} (x_{ki} - \overline{x}_i)^2 \sum_{k=1}^{n} (x_{kj} - \overline{x}_j)^2}} \tag{14}$$

3. The correlation of matrix eigenvalue and eigenvector is solved, determining the principal components.

(1) Solve the characteristic equation $| \lambda \cdot I - R |= 0$. Calculate the eigenvalues and make them according to the size of the order $\lambda_1 \geq \lambda_2 \geq \cdots \lambda_p \geq 0$. (2) Solve the eigenvalues λ_i of the eigenvectors respectively, which requires $\sum_{j=1}^{p} e_{ij}^2 = 1$, where the unit vector e_{ij} represents the vector e_i of the jth component.

4. The main components are evaluated comprehensively, and the contribution rate of the principal component and the cumulative contribution rate are obtained.The contribution rate b_j and the cumulative contribution rate a_p of the eigenvalues λ_i $(j = 1, 2, \ldots, m)$ are calculated.

$$b_j = \frac{\lambda_j}{\sum\limits_{k=1}^{m} \lambda_k}, \ j = 1, 2, ..., m, \ a_p = \frac{\sum\limits_{k=1}^{p} \lambda_k}{\sum\limits_{k=1}^{m} \lambda_k} \qquad (15)$$

2.4   Performance Analysis

In order to measure the performance of the fingerprint, we define a performance function Y, which is expressed as follows.

$$Y = \sum_{i=1}^{n} a_i \cdot \left\| \bar{b}_i^j \right\|_F^2 \qquad (16)$$

where a_i and $\bar{b}_i^j$ are expressed as follows.

$$\begin{cases} a_i = \dfrac{1}{\sum\limits_{j=1}^{k} \mathrm{var}(b_j^{(j,m)}) + C} \\ \bar{b}_i^j = mean(b_j^{(j,m)}) \end{cases} \qquad (17)$$

Where $i = 1, 2, ..., n$ denotes the channel fingerprint in the ith feature characteristic parameters. $j = 1, 2, ..., k$ represent the jth scene, where $k = 3. m = 1, 2, ..., l$ represent the mth channel, where $l = 5$. a_i is the weight of the ith characteristic parameter. $b_i^{(j,m)}$ is the ith parameter value of the jth scene in the mth channel. $\bar{b}_i^j$ is the mean of $b_i^{(j,m)}$.

The physical meaning of the performance function Y is the follows: Euclidean distances of the same parameters of feature in different scenes are measurement criteria. The larger the Euclidean distance is, the better the performance of the characteristic parameter is. At the same time, we used the reciprocal of the characteristic parameters variance as the weights. The performance of the characteristic parameters is better, if they have relatively stable values for different channels in the same scene. Accordingly, we can compare the features of fingerprint distilled from each of the three channels. As a result, the values of different fingerprint characteristic parameters can be obtained, which can ultimately provide some references for the weight selection of environmental identifications with multiple fingerprint parameters.

3   Model Establishment

Scene 1, scene 2, scene 3 correspond to the signal acquisition of three scenes respectively, each 5 channels of every scenes. The results contain 1,500 channel samples in 1 s, and the interval time of adjacent channels are 2/3 ns, and each sample of channel are corresponding with $K = 100$ points, with the interval time of adjacent points is 65 ns.

In order to extract the "fingerprint" characteristic of the channel, we select the delay power spectrum, root-mean-square (RMS) of delay, the signal envelope, random fading of signal phase and the associated domain as the extracted features of channels.

The received signal $r[k, n]$ (where $k = 0, 1, \ldots, K - 1$ denote the discrete signal of sample identification. $n = 0, 1, \ldots, N - 1$ represent the test time of the testing sample of identification. $r[k, n]$ represents the unit pulse of time n sequentially through the transmission filter, the actual received signal after channel and received filter. It is the binary function of k and n.) shows that each scene is measured five times, and each measurement of the sampling points is 1500×100. We extract the parameters of each measurement in each scene, and construct the fingerprint model of wireless channel.

3.1   Digital Signal Processing

The characteristics of wireless channel are studied from three perspectives: time domain, frequency domain and correlation domain. From time point of view, temporal dispersion is the frequency selective fading of wireless channel, and the related parameters of channel include power delay spectrum and delay spread. From the analysis of frequency domain, frequency dispersion leads to time selective fading in wireless channels, and the related parameters of channel include root mean square delay expansion and random fading of signal phase.

(1) Power Delay Spectrum

The parameters of the power delay spectrum are extracted from each measurement, and based on this information, a fingerprint parameter is used as a representation of the scene. Three scenes of the power delay spectrum are shown in Fig. 2.

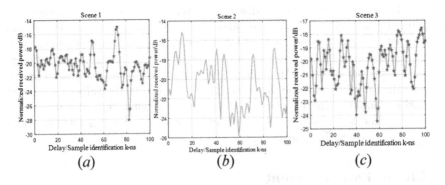

Fig. 2. Delay power spectrum

From the delay power spectrum given in Fig. 2, it can be seen that each scene has multiple transmission paths, but the multi-path structures are completely different from each other. Figures 2(a), (b) and (c) show that of the three scenes, the second scene has the largest delay in Fig. 2(b), followed by the first scene in Fig. 2(a), and then the third scene in Fig. 2(c), which has the smallest delay. In Fig. 2, each peak corresponds to a real signal, and it can be seen that there is a big difference between the scenes 1, 2 and 3. When the source of the pulse width is very narrow, the antenna transmission system can keep the invariant transmission waveform in the wireless channel. Since the pulse width is very narrow, its spectrum density of the peak frequency is higher, hence it avoids the poor frequency of bands in the transmission function.

(2) RMS Delay Expansion

Considering the measurement data of 1500 sampling duration is 1s, sampling sample can't be independent, and they should have a certain correlation. Therefore, the measurements for each scene are carried out by extracting the RMS delay expansion parameter. The results are shown in Table 1. The RMS of mean and variance of delay spread in the three scenes is shown in Table 2.

Table 1. RMS delay expansion

Scene	Test1	Test2	Test3	Test4	Test5
1	3117.41	2465.87	3967.47	2926.09	3308.75
2	2943.46	3380.85	2681.88	2688.89	2295.11
3	4806.56	2916.44	4047.15	3483.16	3708.79

Table 1 shows that the RMS delay of the measurement component in each scene is different. When the time dispersion and frequency-selective decay are caused by multi-path transfer, the Doppler spread will cause the frequency dispersion and time-selective decay.

Table 2. RMS delay expanding of the mean and variance in three scenes

Scene	1	2	3
Mean	3157.12	2798.04	3792.42
Variance	2943.46	3380.85	2681.88

Table 2 shows that during the wireless channel transmission process, the value of RMS delay is about 3100 ns. The RMS delay of scene 2 is less than that of the other two.

(3) Delay Spread

Due to the influence of reflection, refraction and diffraction on the signal at the receiving end, the received signal will be drastic changes, resulting in multi-path expansion. Therefore, the multi-path extension of the channel is described by delay spread, as shown in Fig. 3.

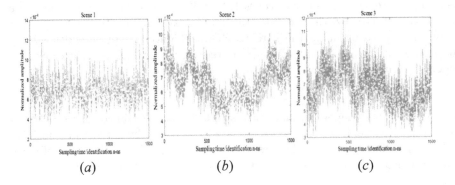

Fig. 3. Multi-path time delay spread characteristics

Figure 3 shows that the envelopes of the three scenes are different. Channel decay is also a result of the Doppler Effect originated from movement of the transmitter and receiver. The envelope of the first scene is the smallest one, therefore the quality of the received signal is best. The envelope in the second scene, on the other hand, is the largest one, so the quality of the received signal is worst. As we know, Doppler extension causes frequency dispersion, which leads to signal distortion. So in the frequency domain, signal distortion deteriorates with the increasing of Doppler spread of the transmitted signal.

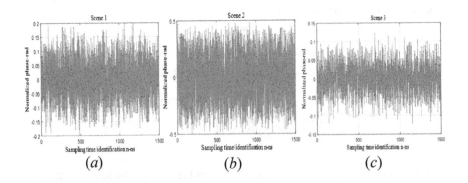

Fig. 4. Timing variations characteristics

(4) Random Fading of Signal Phase

As can be seen in Fig. 4, the phase of scene 1 ranges primarily from -0.15 rad to 0.15 rad. Short-term rapid changes and peak position changes in the channel phase and amplitude are nearly uniformly distributed, indicating that there are continuous changes regarding the phase and Doppler Effect. In the time domain, the Doppler Effect means that the channel impulse response varies with time, and the mobile wireless channel is usually considered to be a linear time-varying system. The phase of scene 2 ranges primarily from -0.4 rad to 0.4 rad, meaning the phase distribution of the signal is extended. This extension and slow changes of amplitude indicate that there is a serious multi-path effect at the same time. The phase of scene 3 is concentrated mainly in the range of -0.07 rad to 0.08 rad. The phase distribution of the signal is more concentrated and its amplitude change is relatively slow with the sampling time, indicating that a severe Doppler Effect does not exist.

(5) Correlation Domain

By using the observational data in the scene, the channel impulse response $h_k(1500 \times 100)$ can be obtained. Using these channel coefficients one can calculate the correlation coefficient between the groups, which then forms the symmetric matrix. The third matrix of all twelve impulse response matric is taken from three scenes respectively. The correlation coefficient matrix for every data is obtained by using the corresponding sample of value (1×100), h_k to calculate every sampling time n. Two-dimensional diagrams of the correlation coefficient matrix diagram are shown in Fig. 5.

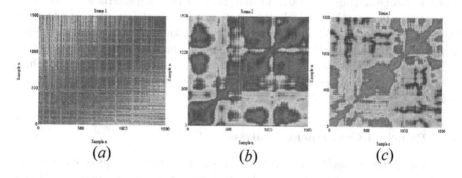

(a)   (b)   (c)

Fig. 5. Correlation coefficient matrix of scenes 1, 2 and 3

Figure 5 shows that the correlation coefficient matrix of the channel in scene 1 has very fine texture characteristics, which means the correlation intensity changes rapidly. This rapid change represents the channel characteristics changing in a short time. The texture characteristics of the channel correlation coefficient matrix in scene 2 are fuzzier than that in scene 1, which shows the sample values in a scene have no impact on the channel correlation, so the numerical fluctuation in the correlation coefficient matrix is small and has strong continuity. The correlation between the channels of scene 3 changes over time and is not related to the sample values. The correlation coefficient matrix chart reflects the irregular shape of the texture.

From what has been discussed above, we conclude the channel fingerprint features and scene criterion shown in Table 3.

Table 3. Channel fingerprint characteristics and criterion of three scenes

Fingerprint feature	Feature matching	Matching results
Time-varying features of amplitude	Short-term rapid change (fast time-varying channel)	Scene 1
	Change relatively slow (slow time-varying channel)	Scene 2, scene 3
Distribution features of position	Concentration (No multipath)	Scene 1, scene 3
	Dispersion (Multipath effect)	Scene 2
Sloping law of the line	Slash (Doppler effect)	Scene 1
	Nearly linear (weak Doppler effect)	Scene 2, scene 3
Frequency features	No obvious frequency selective fading	Scene 1, scene 2
	Obviously the frequency selective fading	Scene 3

Table 3 shows that the extracted parameters of signal feature have good discrimination to the three scenes. In Table 3, the magnitude of scene 1 witnessed a rapid change during a short-time margin, and the characteristic of the moving position is smoothed, which indicates that its phase is continuous and the Doppler is significant. While in scene 2, the magnitude is evenly distributed relatively, and it is not a fast time-varying signal under slow time-varying channel. In scene 3, the magnitude is spread different from scene 1 and scene 2, which shows the multi-path scenario characteristic. These different cases are helpful for analyzing a given case.

3.2   Principal Component Analysis

The measurement results are given in the process of data acquisition, and the interference will be subject to the stability of the external environment and internal noise of the measurement system. Additionally, contribution of a multi-path signal with smaller amplitude is less significant in establishing a wireless channel model. In order to ensure the credibility of the modeling of various statistical parameters including delay, we used three scenes of fifteen real channels processed by the SPSS (Statistical product and service solutions) software kit for principal components analysis. According to output of the Kaiser-Meyer-Olkin (KMO) values and Sig. values, we use the forth measurement results of the channel, which is biggest than others, as representatives of scenes 1, 2 and 3.

1) Correlation Analysis

In the correlation matrix, the bigger the correlation coefficient is, the more significant the characteristic factor correlation is. The time series data of communication channel is highly correlated. We use PCA method to analysis those representative samples. The coefficient in correlation matrix of most variables of the measured data is greater than 0.5, which means the characteristic factor has a strong correlation. In order to further study the correlation between variables, we use a detailed KMO/Bartlett analysis of the relevant test methods, which is shown in Table 4.

Table 4. Distance between the final cluster centers

		Scene		
		1	2	3
KMO measurements		0.701	0.563	0.786
Bartletts spherical test	df	1275	4950	1975
	Sig.	0	0	0

Table 4 shows that the KMO values of scene 1, scene 2 and scene 3 are 0.701, 0.563, and 0.786, respectively. They are all greater than 0.5, indicating that the data is suitable for factor analysis. Sphericity test results of Bartlett show scene 1, scene 2 and scene 3 of Sig. values are all 0.00 as indicated in the last row of Table 4, the Sig. values are less than 0.05. There is a significant difference in the correlation coefficient between the correlation matrix and the variable, and it is a big correlation between the measured data. We need analysis the channel model based on principal component analysis.

(2) Eigenvalue

Getting the features of the wireless channel in different environments, namely through the unit to the response sequence of the channel are processed to get the characteristic parameters under the conditions of different scenes. Analysis of the difficulty in this problem has validation on the rationality of channel features. Due to the difference between the participation of statistical data, they lack sufficient data to verify the features of the whole channel. In addition, it is difficult to select the index to evaluate the channel features. Therefore, we use part of the data to extract parameters and combine with the remainder to obtain the parameters of validation and evaluation, which improve the effectiveness of the parameter selection. According to the correlation coefficient matrix of the original variables, PCA is used to select the main factor. We select the main factor of the eigenvalue which is more than 1. The main factor of scene 1, scene 2 and scene 3 are extracted and shown in Table 5.

In Table 5, we extracted the significant eigenvector with characteristic root above 1, thus to balance efficiency by reducing computational complexity. The results of the characteristic root below 1 implies that it is not sufficient to explain the observation data persuasively, in this case, it will be removed from further

Table 5. Distance between the final cluster centers

Scene element	Scene 1		Scene 2		Scene 3	
	var%	accu%	var%	accu%	var%	accu%
1	11.87	11.86	19.73	19.73	14.11	14.11
2	9.33	21.2	7.25	26.97	10.37	24.49
3	6.16	27.35	6.24	33.21	7.78	32.27
4	6.04	33.39	5.64	38.85	5.78	38.04
5	5.24	38.64	5.2	44.05	5.44	43.48
6	4.53	43.16	4.73	48.78	4.51	47.99
7	4.45	47.61	4.67	53.45	4.2	52.19
8	4.4	52.01	4.21	57.65	4.18	56.37
9	3.92	55.93	4.17	61.83	3.58	59.95
10	3.67	59.6	3.91	65.74	3.51	63.47
11	3.62	63.22	3.41	69.15	3.37	66.83
12	3.51	66.73	3.08	72.23	3.16	69.99
13	3.26	70	2.97	75.21	2.99	72.97
14	3.09	73.08	2.88	78.09	2.72	75.7
15	2.93	76.01	2.68	80.76	2.68	78.38
16	2.83	78.84	2.35	83.11	2.64	81.02
17	2.78	81.62	2.29	85.4	2.26	83.29
18	2.5	84.12	2.07	87.47	1.99	85.27
19	2.27	86.39	1.95	89.42	1.92	87.19
20	2.2	88.59	1.82	91.24	1.77	88.96
21	1.93	90.52	1.64	92.88	1.55	90.51
22	1.82	92.39	1.33	94.21	1.45	91.96
23	1.57	93.9	1.22	95.43	1.33	93.29
24	1.28	95.18	1.01	96.43	1.29	94.58
25	1.11	96.3	0.78	97.21	1.1	95.67
26	0.95	97.25	0.63	97.84	0.94	96.61

analyzing. The contribution rates of elements of each channel are varying in accumulation gradually, the final data of level 96.30%, 96.43% and 95.67% is only one reference set, and it cannot reflect the overall status. Therefore, the main factors distilled in scenes 1, 2 and 3 are 25, 24, and 25, respectively, which provides most of the information on the original data and reflects the real situation more comprehensively. We used the scree plot to verify and describe the selected feature eigenvalues more vividly and accurately.

Figure 6 shows that the smaller the number of channel components, the greater the eigenvalues of its corresponding scene is. Figure 6 indicates that if a

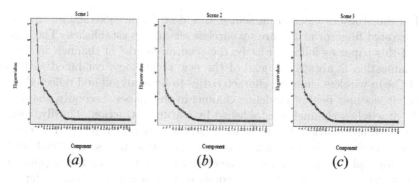

Fig. 6. Scree plot of three scenes

channel contains less factor (or sub channels), and the characteristic root will bigger. The characteristic values of the three scenes extracted by PCA are different, and so it is used as a fingerprint to identify the channel. In order to further illustrate the differences between the eigenvalues of these three scenes, we used the first-order statistics of their eigenvalues. The results are shown in Table 6.

Table 6. Statistical features of characteristic value in three scenes

Scene	Total factor		Principal component factors	
	Mean	Variance	Mean	Variance
1	1	4.189	3.85	5.83
2	1	6.102	3.89	13.24
3	1	4.902	3.83	8.86

Table 6 shows that the eigenvalues of the three scenes extracted by PCA can be used to characterize the fingerprint of the channels, especially by using the extraction of the main factor. The characteristic root in these senses are different from each other, in Table 6, the mutation index is varying at 2.05, 2.47 and 2.21. If the mutation index is near 1, the communication will be more stable. This result can be used to identify if a given communication is effective.

4   Conclusion and Future Work

Multipath parameters of a wireless channel, including multipath time delay, RMS delay expansion, Doppler spread, random fading of signal envelope, random fading of signal phase, and correlation domain can be used as fingerprint features of a channel to recognize the scene. We can identify if a certain channel of communication is qualified through the parameters examined here, thus to provide improving suggestions to it. In this paper, the wireless channel is analyzed and reflected in the model by combining DSP with PCA, which is a new field in the study of channel modeling. Based on feature extraction, the model of integrated fingerprint feature by wireless channel is established. The innovation of this paper as follows. Firstly, the accurate model of channels in wireless communication is always the goal of the new technology, combined with DSP and PCA in wireless channels characteristics to be analyzed and reflected in the model, it is a new field of modeling channel in this paper. Secondly, the feature model of wireless channel is established by feature extraction. Thirdly, without losing much information, the main information is extracted from numerous real channels results of measurement, and the data structure is simplified. In this article, we typically use wireless channel fingerprint to expand the application, and research on its application in mobile communication system in-depth. In general, the fingerprint of a wireless channel is a valuable research. Our research serves as a starting point, hoping to help guide further wireless channel research and make greater progress on wireless channel technology.

Acknowledgements. This work is supported by National Natural Science Foundation of China (No. 61661018 and 61662019); Natural Science Foundation of Hainan Province (No. 2016CXTD004); High Tech. of Key Research and Development Project of Hainan Province (No. ZDYF2016010); Scientific Research Foundation of Hainan University (No. kyqd1536); Key Project on Science Research of Higher School from Hainan Department of Education (No. Hnky2016ZD-5).

References

1. Yao, M.: Digital Image Processing, pp. 293–344. Machinery Industry Press, Beijing (2006)
2. Liu, Y.: Pedestrian Detection Based on Shallow Learning to Guide Deep Learning. Wuhan University (2016)
3. Hao, M.: Breakthrough in computer intelligent image recognition technology is analyzed. China New Telecommun. **19**, 3–3 (2014)
4. Lécun, Y., Bottou, L., Bengio, Y., Haffner, P.: Gradient-based learning applied to document recognition. Proc. IEEE **86**(11), 2278–2324 (1998)
5. Hinton, G.E., Salakhutdinov, R.R.: Reducing the dimensionality of data with neural networks. Science **313**(5786), 504 (2006)
6. Lee, H., Grosse, R., Ranganath, R., Ng, A.Y.: Unsupervised learning of hierarchical representations with convolutional deep belief networks. Commun. ACM **54**(10), 95–103 (2011)
7. Breakthrough Technologies 2013. MIT Technology Review, 23 April 2013 (2013)
8. Moody, J., Darken, C.J.: Fast learning in networks of locally-tuned processing units. Neural Comput. **1**(2), 281–294 (1989)
9. Liu, Y., Zhan, F.: MATLAB Image and Video Processing Practical Examples. Publishing House of Electronics Industry, China (2015)
10. Du, Y.: Research on Edge Detection Algorithm of Deep Image Based on Genetic Neural Network. Harbin University of Science and Technology (2009)
11. Yang, D., Zhao, H., Long, Z.: Detailed Explanation of MATLAB Image Processing. Tsinghua University Press, Beijing (2013)
12. Gonzalez, R.C., Woods, R.E., Eddins, S.L.: MATLAB Implementation of Digital Image Processing. Tsinghua University Press, China, Beijing (2013)

13. Xu S.: Video Analysis Based on Sequence Depth Learning: Modeling Expression and Application. University of Science and Technology of China (2017)
14. Zhang, S., Gong, Y., Wang, J.: Development of deep convolution neural network and its application in the field of computer vision. Chin. J. Comput., 1–29 (2017). http://kns.cnki.net/kcms/detail/11.1826.TP.20170918.2025.006.html
15. Xu, W.: Research on ECG Identification Technology Based on Convolution Neural Network. Northeast Forestry University (2016)
16. Feng, X.: Research of Image Recognition Algorithm Based on Depth Learning. Taiyuan University of Technology (2015)
17. Macdonald, R.D.R.: Design and implementation of a dual-energy x-ray imaging system for organic material detection in an airport security application, vol. 4301, pp. 31–41 (2001)
18. Kawano, Y., Yanai, K.: ILSVRC on a Smartphone. IPSJ Trans. Comput. Vis. Appl. 6, 83–87 (2014)
19. Shengwei, Y.: Case Analysis and Application of MATLAB Optimization Algorithm. Tsinghua University Press, Beijing (2014)
20. Yan, Y., Mo, Y.: Deep Learning Principle and TensorFlow Practice. Publishing House of Electronics Industry, Beijing (2017)
21. Abrahams, S., Hafner, D., Erwitt, E., Scarpinelli, A.: TensorFlow Practice for Machine Intelligence. China Machine press, Beijing (2017)
22. Huang, W., Tang, Y.: TensorFlow of Actual Combat. Publishing House of Electronics Industry, Beijing (2017)
23. Luo, J., Jiang, M., Liu, X., Zhou, L.: Multi-scale convolutional-recursive neural networks for RGB-D object recognition. Appl. Res. Comput. 34(9), 2834–2837 (2017)

A Real-Time Embedded Localization in Indoor Environment Using LiDAR Odometry

Genghang Zhuang[1,2], Shengjie Chen[1,2], Jianfeng Gu[1,2], and Kai Huang[1,2(✉)]

[1] Key Laboratory of Machine Intelligence and Advanced Computing,
Sun Yat-sen University, Ministry of Education, Guangzhou, China
[2] School of Data and Computer Science, Sun Yat-sen University, Guangzhou, China
{zhuanggh2,chenshj35,gujf5}@mail2.sysu.edu.cn, huangk36@mail.sysu.edu.cn

Abstract. Localization for mobile robots in a pre-structured environment with a given prior map is considered as the essential problem to perform the further autonomous navigation. For indoor environments without the access to external localization system like GPS, we present a localization method based on the Monte Carlo Localization (MCL), only utilizing a modern 2D LiDAR of high update rate and low measurement noise, to locate the mobile robot in the prior map without giving a starting point. A LiDAR pseudo-odometry is proposed to compute pose changes in movements of the robot, in which the scan point clouds are matched against a locale map to reduce the cumulative errors. In localization iterations, the LiDAR odometry provides motion data to predict the position hypotheses distribution, which is corrected by incorporating the current LiDAR observation to update and yield the localization estimates. The experiments performed on a car-like mobile robot in the real indoor environment demonstrate the accuracy and the real-time performance of the proposed localization system.

Keywords: Mobile robots · Indoor localization · LiDAR · Real-time

1 Introduction

There has been increasing interest in developing autonomous operating ground vehicles in mobile robotics, which can be deployed in extensive scenarios to accomplish civilian and military tasks, including unknown area exploring, natural disaster rescue, and uninhabited district patrol. In addition, it is also getting great attention in public because of its service applications in indoor environments.

The localization with a prior map is essential for a robot to perform autonomous navigation to a given destination. Many simultaneous localization and mapping (SLAM) methods and algorithms are successfully applied on ground vehicle robots to build a map for the environment and estimate the pose changes and the position relative to the origin of the built map. Different from

Y. Bi et al. (Eds.): ESTC 2017, CCIS 857, pp. 210–222, 2018.
https://doi.org/10.1007/978-981-13-1026-3_16

SLAM, localization with a prior map is to determine where the robot is on the pre-charted map at the beginning of navigation and during the movements heading to the destination. In the urban environment, the problem is often solved with the Global Positioning System (GPS) and the Inertial Navigation System (INS) [8]. However, mobile robots in indoor environments without access to the external localization system such as GPS must rely on other approaches to locate itself.

In this paper, we propose a novel localization method based on Monte Color Localization (MCL) using a high update rate and low measurement noise 2D LiDAR, without other sensors like wheel encoders or IMU involved. Different from normal MCL methods deployed on ground robots, we utilize LiDAR as the only sensor to generate pseudo-odometry data of robot pose changes as the robot motion model in the prediction phase, in which locale map is built during movements to reduce the accumulating error. In the next correction phase, we use the laser scan data as the measurement model to correct the prediction. After a number of iterations with particle re-sampling, a sufficiently accurate pose estimation will be yielded from the system.

Experimental results on our car-like mobile robot platform, running on an embedded ECU, demonstrate the accuracy of the localization, also the robustness and real-time capability of the system. The results running on the car-like robot further show that this method with only one main sensor can greatly endow the autonomous robot platform a high integration and portability.

2   Related Works

Many kinds of research attempted to solve the problem of mobile robot localization in indoor environments with various sensors. One of the common methods is path dead reckoning using internal odometry such as wheel encoders and gyroscopes in [6,11] with the given outset position from the beginning of robot movements. But it is hard to determine some physical parameters of the robot including the scale factors of the wheels and gears, and the robot kinematics model with high accuracy. These problems can cause large accumulating errors in the dead reckoning localization process. The approach cannot be applied in cases starting from an unknown position in the map, without access to environment references.

Some methods focus on providing an external reference system in indoor environments, based on the electromagnetic signal strength like the WiFi in [7]. Though the methods based on the wireless signal are successfully deployed on mobile robots [2], the requirements and effort of the pre-deployment and the accuracy subject to the variant medium and non-deterministic interference are the key challenges for these solutions.

Monte Carlo Localization [3] is a probabilistic approach with particle-based density representation for robot position estimates, which is able to localize a mobile robot without knowledge of its starting location. Methods proposed in [1,12] apply the Monte Carlo Localization to fuse both the odometry and laser scan data, which can greatly eliminate the cumulative errors of odometry by utilizing probabilistic correction approach with LiDAR measurement model. However, these methods still require the odometry of sufficient accuracy, which is subject to the external affection from the environment like driving wheels slipping and driven wheels getting stuck. In addition, the solution implementations of these systems are hardware platform specific because of their invasiveness in odometry pre-deployment.

3　System Overview

3.1　Software System Overview

The proposed localization system mainly consists of two components. The LiDAR odometry part takes in laser scan point clouds and estimates the pose changes from the robot motion, while the MCL part takes in the motion data from the LiDAR virtual odometry to update position estimation in the given prior map of the environment.

The Fig. 1 illustrates the framework of the localization system. LiDAR odometry processes the incoming laser scan data from a high update rate and low measurement noise 2D LiDAR. To reduce the accumulating errors in registering two consecutive scan point clouds in a long time period, registering scan data to a locale map is applied. At the beginning of robot movements, a locale map is initialized with the first scan. Every frame of scans in later will be registered to the

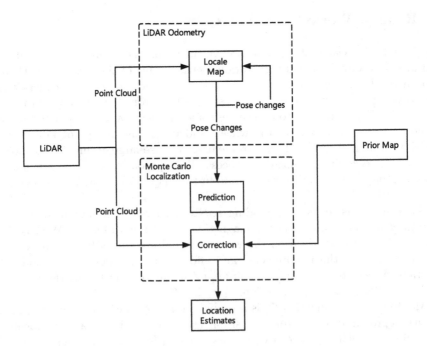

Fig. 1. Overview of system

locale map, to compute the pose change and update the locale map recursively for the next incoming scan.

Monte Carlo Localization is based on the Bayes' Theorem using a set of particles to represent the robot position hypotheses distribution. In recursive estimation process, MCL do the following works to update and approximate the position in reality:

- Prediction: Predict the new set of particles according to the robot motion model. In our method, the motion model is obtained from the LiDAR odometry above.
- Correction: Update the weight of each particle according to the real-time observation from the LiDAR.
- Re-sampling: Re-sample the particles in set depending the weight of each particle in a period of time.

The LiDAR odometry is involved in the prediction step to do coarse position update for every particle, by which a localization system taking advantage of modern LiDAR as the only sensor gets completed.

3.2 Mobile Robot Platform

The proposed method is tested and validated on a car-like mobile robot at a size of 0.70 m × 0.52 m × 0.35 m, which is motivated by a driving motor for the four wheels and a steering motor for two front wheels, controlled by an Arduino single-board microcontroller, as shown in the Fig. 2a.

A *Hokuyo UTM-30LX-EW* LiDAR of high update rate and accuracy is installed at the front of the upper platform, as the only main sensor of the localization system, which can provide measurement data in a range of 270° with a resolution of 0.25°, per 25 ms. The LiDAR is fixed on a metal platform with spring suspension to obtain 2D point clouds from the environment at a relatively stable height.

(a) Car-like Mobile Robot   (b) Hokuyo 2D LiDAR

Fig. 2. Hardware platform

The software system is running on an Electronic Control Unit (ECU) with an Intel ultra-low power processor embedded in. The software platform is based on the Robot Operating System [9], which can provide highly efficient communication for local processes and also the remote computational nodes. For real-time robustness, the localization iteration is resolved on the ECU platform, and the status and position estimates are transmitted to a PC or laptop for display and interacting purposes.

4   LiDAR Odometry

The pose of a robot in a 2D map can be defined as a three degrees of freedom variable $\mathbf{x} = (x, y, \theta)^T$ indicating the position coordinate and the heading angle relative to the origin of the given prior map, which is finally estimated in the MCL iteration introduced in the next section.

The LiDAR odometry in this part serves as a pseudo-odometry to give transitions of robot state in motion model, fed with consecutive point clouds from LiDAR scans.

To compute pose change over two successive scans or a period of time, defined as $\Delta\xi = (\Delta x, \Delta y, \Delta\theta)^T$, in our approach the scan from the LiDAR observation is matched against the locale map using the nonlinear optimization method, similar to the sub-problem of SLAM. In further the state of the LiDAR odometry is defined as a tuple $O = \langle M, \xi, \{\langle \Delta\xi_t, t \rangle_{t=0,1,\dots} \} \rangle$, composed of maintained locale map which keeps tracking robot movements in period of time, accumulated pose change from local movement origin to the current robot position, and the pose changes sequence over time.

4.1   Pre-processing

The raw data from LiDAR of a full range scan consists of a sequence of values indicating distances to endpoints in range finder scope stepping by scanning angular resolution. Therefore, each endpoint can be intuitively presented as $e = (d, \theta)$ in the polar coordinate form. For further processing, the endpoints are transformed into the $\mathbb{R}^2$ Cartesian coordinate form.

$$\mathbf{e} = \begin{pmatrix} x \\ y \end{pmatrix} = \begin{pmatrix} d \cdot cos(\theta_o - \theta) \\ d \cdot sin(\theta_o - \theta) \end{pmatrix} \tag{1}$$

Note that the scan starting angular offset θ_o and increasing direction of θ is LiDAR and software platform specific, and should be taken into account in implementation. The transformed endpoints here are in the LiDAR reference frame, whose origin indicates the LiDAR center.

4.2   Locale Map

Point clouds of scans are registered to construct and update the locale map and yield the pose change estimates at the same time. The major motivation for adopting locale map is to track and keep surroundings details and features in a range of vicinity for further refinement in point cloud matching with less accumulated errors, rather than considering only two point clouds from the adjoin scans.

The locale map uses occupancy grids to represent the environment surroundings information, which is a prevalent approach in 2D SLAM for mobile robots [10]. The occupancy grid map down-sample endpoints into discrete grids to greatly reduce computational consumption, and tolerate observation noise with probabilistic strategy [4].

For a grid g, the occupancy to describe the probability of being occupied is usually given as a log-odds:

$$M(g) = log\frac{p(g)}{1 - p(g)} \tag{2}$$

where the $p(g)$ is the probability of being occupied for the grid g. At the beginning, the grids are initialized with $M(g) = 0$ inferring $p(g) = 0.5$ for the unknown area. When updating the grid map with a given scan point cloud, the occupancy values of grids which beams go through are updated with:

$$M(g) = M_{curr}(g) + log\frac{p_{free}}{1 - p_{free}} \tag{3}$$

while values of the grids where endpoints drop in are set to:

$$M(g) = M_{curr}(g) + log\frac{p_{occ}}{1 - p_{occ}} \tag{4}$$

where the $log\frac{p_{free}}{1-p_{free}}$ and $log\frac{p_{occ}}{1-p_{occ}}$ are constants referred as the measurement model beliefs.

In practice, a locale map only tracks a period of robot movements to reach agreement on both accuracy and memory consumption, especially in a large scale environment. The maintained part of the locale map is constrained in a size of window in our method, which shifts to keep around to the robot position in a long time movement, trimming the unconcerned far away part.

4.3   Pose Change Estimating

To compute pose change in LiDAR Odometry processing iteration, the scan point cloud is matched against the locale map, by solving the nonlinear optimization problem as follow:

$$\Delta\xi = \underset{\Delta\xi'}{argmax} \sum_{i=0}^{N} M^{\star}(\mathbf{T}_{\Delta\xi'} \cdot \mathbf{T}_{\xi} \cdot \mathbf{e}_i) \tag{5}$$

This optimization is to find the best pose change $\Delta\xi$, which the point cloud $\{\mathbf{e}_i; i = 1\dots N\}$ applies, getting most overlaid and coincided with the locale map around the pose in the last iteration.

Firstly, the scan point cloud gets projected to the last robot pose with $\mathbf{T}_\xi$, intuitively referred as a coarse match. Then the $\Delta\xi$ is optimized as the objective refinement for best matching. The $\mathbf{T}_{\Delta\xi}$ is defined as the transformation for the corresponding pose change $\Delta\xi$:

$$\mathbf{T}_{\Delta\xi} = \begin{pmatrix} cos(\Delta\theta) & -sin(\Delta\theta) & \Delta x \\ sin(\Delta\theta) & cos(\Delta\theta) & \Delta y \\ 0 & 0 & 1 \end{pmatrix} \tag{6}$$

Note there are implicit conversions between homogeneous coordinates and Cartesian coordinates.

The $\mathbf{0}$ will be a good initial estimate for $\Delta\xi$ with the belief that the pose change between two scans is minor, owing to the high update rate of the LiDAR, and also the gentle movements of the ground robot in indoor scenarios.

Note that since the accuracy of scan is highly superior to the locale grid map, an up-sampled map M^* for M is necessary for the optimization process. A bilinear interpolation introduced in [5] is adopted in this work.

Registering scans to locale map rather than taking account of only two consecutive scans like the typical ICP method, can greatly minimize the cumulative errors, and avoid unexpected immense deviation in results caused by symmetry in the environment, by giving a good initial estimate closed to the global minima yielded from the locale map approach.

The $\Delta\xi$ serves as the output of the LiDAR odometry in the iteration. Subsequently, the state of the LiDAR odometry, defined above as $O = \langle M, \xi, \{\langle\Delta\xi_t, t\rangle_{t=0,1,\dots}\}\rangle$, gets updated. The scan point cloud projected on the estimate is registered into the locale map M applying the method mentioned above, while the $\Delta\xi$ is inserted into the sequence of the pose changes $\{\langle\Delta\xi_t, t\rangle_{t=0,1,\dots}\}$, updating the pose change ξ relative to the movement origin:

$$\xi = \sum_{i=0}^{N} \Delta\xi_i = \xi_{last} + \Delta\xi \tag{7}$$

5   Monte Carlo Localization

With the input pose change estimates from the LiDAR odometry, the Monte Carlo Localization resolves the global localization problem based on the probabilistic method.

The Monte Carlo Localization approach can be considered as an implementation of the Bayesian filter, in which the pose of the robot at a moment t, defined as $\mathbf{x}_t = (x, y, \theta)^T$, is estimated based on the perception data in the past time, modeled as a posterior density:

$$p(\mathbf{x}_t | Z^t) \tag{8}$$

where the Z^t is the measurement knowledge up to the current moment.

The conditional density is solved in recursive iterations. In the prediction phase, the motion model $p(\mathbf{x}_t|\mathbf{x}_{t-1}, \mathbf{u}_{t-1})$ is involved to give the prediction density:

$$p(\mathbf{x}_t|Z^{t-1}) = \int p(\mathbf{x}_t|\mathbf{x}_{t-1}, \mathbf{u}_{t-1})p(\mathbf{x}_{t-1}|Z^{t-1})d\mathbf{x}_{t-1} \qquad (9)$$

By applying the Bayes theorem, the posterior density in (8) is obtained recursively with the measurement model $p(\mathbf{z}_t|\mathbf{x}_t)$ incorporated in the correction phase:

$$p(\mathbf{x}_t|Z^t) = \frac{p(\mathbf{z}_t|\mathbf{x}_t)p(\mathbf{x}_t|Z^{t-1})}{p(\mathbf{z}_t|Z^{t-1})} \qquad (10)$$

In the MCL method, the posterior density $p(\mathbf{x}_t|Z^t)$ is sampled as a set of particles:

$$S_t = \left\{ <\mathbf{x}_t^i, w_t^i>; i = 1\ldots N \right\} \qquad (11)$$

Each particle in the set represents a candidate hypothesis for robot pose $\mathbf{x}$, with a weight w which indicates the corresponding probability.

In the prediction phase, the pose change $\Delta\xi = (\Delta x, \Delta y, \Delta\theta)^T$ obtained from the LiDAR odometry serves as the motion model, to approximately motivate the particles in respect of the robot motion in reality. The set of particles S_t' describing the predictive density $p(\mathbf{x}_t|Z^{t-1})$ derives from the S_{t-1} in the last iteration, with the pose change $\Delta\xi$ applied.

In the correction phase, the weight of each particle in S_t' is updated according to the match level with the current measurement model. The LiDAR scan data is taken into account as the measurement model in this phase to compute the probability of particle belief with the given prior map. The weighted set then is re-sampled to yield the resulting sample set S_t as the distribution of the robot position hypotheses.

6   Experiments

6.1   Experimental Setup

The proposed localization system in this paper has been tested on a car-like robot with a high frequency and low noise LiDAR in a real indoor environment. The method is implemented on the ROS framework and deployed on an ultra-low power processor.

The indoor environment in the experiments is a laboratory office composed of four rooms and a side corridor. For localization and reference purposes, an environment map was obtained preceding the further experiments by driving the mobile manually in the office. The pre-built map is an occupancy grid map generated by applying the 2D SLAM algorithms with LiDAR. The Fig. 3 shows the pre-built grid map and the environment picture in the camera scene. The size of the area is about $7\,\mathrm{m} \times 9\,\mathrm{m}$, represented in the prior map with the grids of $5\,\mathrm{cm}$ resolution.

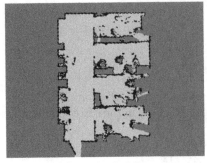

(a) Pre-built Map   (b) Environmet Picture

Fig. 3. Experiment environment

The experiments consist of three parts, focusing on the two subsystems in this work. The first part is intended for validating and testing the LiDAR odometry capacity of computing pose changes in robot movements. The second part verifies and demonstrates the proposed localization approach only utilizing the LiDAR sensor, and the third part presents the performance analysis of the localization system.

6.2 LiDAR Odometry

To evaluate the accuracy of the proposed LiDAR pseudo-odometry, we performed the path dead reckoning with the pose changes from the LiDAR odometry in the movements of patrolling in the experiment area. For comparison, a physical odometry embedded in the car-like robot including rotary encoders in the rear wheels and steering motor was used to draw an independent path in the same period of movements.

Figure 4 shows the comparison of drawn paths obtained from reckoning of LiDAR and encoder odometry, with a given starting point in the reference map. In the patrolling movements of the car-like mobile robot in the four rooms, the trajectory path of LiDAR odometry reveals the relatively high accuracy even over a long time move, while the path of physical encoder odometry drafts and deviates quickly over time, showing high cumulative errors of the physical odometry, especially in the angular pose estimates.

The deviation in the physical odometry could be caused by various factors, including wheel slipping, inaccuracy in measurements of parameters like turning radius in this case and the internal errors in encoders, which further suggests the high invariance and portability in different hardware platforms the presented method has endowed.

6.3 Localization

This part carries out the localization experiments based on the LiDAR odometry, aiming to validate the ability of the localization system to locate the mobile

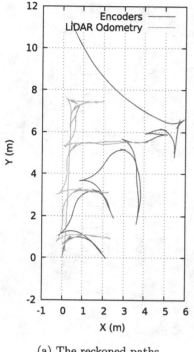

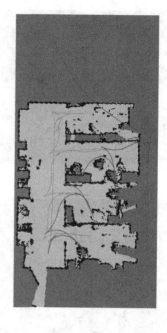

(a) The reckoned paths

(b) The paths in reference map

Fig. 4. Comparison of paths reckoned with proposed LiDAR odometry and physical encoders. The path in green color is obtained by accumulating pose changes from the LiDAR odometry, while the red path indicates the trajectory drawn by collecting the encoder data from wheels and steering motor rotating. (Color figure online)

robot in the prior map without a given starting position and to keep tracking the position of the robot in succeeding movements.

The experimental result was attained in the same laboratory office area. The Fig. 5 shows the iterations of the localization process, where the arrows indicate the particle hypotheses for the position and heading of the robot in the MCL.

Initially, the distribution of arrows is uniform over the space without giving a known position. After a while, in the period of movements, the particle arrows begin to converge on several position beliefs because of the symmetry in the environment. In further movements, the distribution of the arrows concentrates in the true position of the robot and trace the robot in the following moves.

Figure 6 shows the tracking path of another localization process after a converged distribution was obtained. To evaluate the accuracy of the localization in tracking, we drove the car-like robot passing by a series of preset label points, measuring the distance errors between the trajectory and reference points, as shown in the Table 1. Since the footprint size of the car-like mobile robot is 0.70 m × 0.52 m, the result of localization could be considered to be sufficiently accurate.

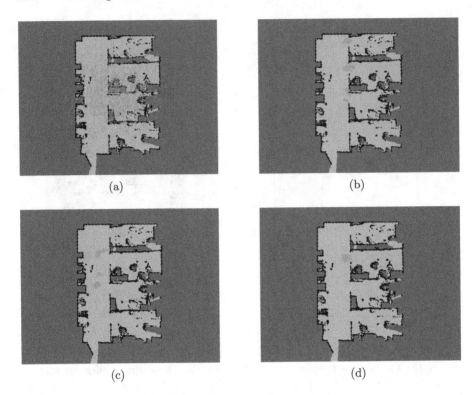

Fig. 5. The iterations of the localization process. The arrows in green color indicate the particles in MCL. (a) Initial distribution of particles. (b) Converged particles on several high probabilities of location. (c), (d) Particles distributed on the correct position after further movements. (Color figure online)

Table 1. Average errors in meters on preset reference points

Point	A	B	C	D	E	F	G
Error (cm)	9.07	2.15	9.54	9.95	1.95	3.02	6.51

6.4   Performance Analysis

The experiments were running on an ECU with an ultra-low power processor *Intel i7 7500U*. To exclude the effects from irrelevant variations in the environment and other parameters, we perform the analysis based on simulations on the same recorded LiDAR scan data.

The statistics in Table 2 show the time cost of the pose change computation in the LiDAR odometry, which reveals the real-time capacity of the LiDAR odometry to provide motion data of the mobile robot at a sufficient update rate. Because of the up-sampling function in the nonlinear optimization process, the time costs remain steady in the limited range of available resolutions, which

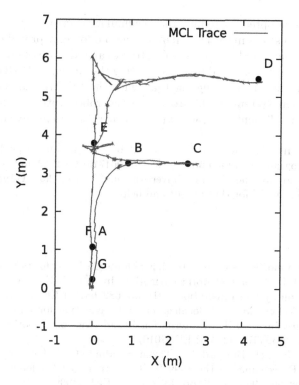

Fig. 6. The localization trajectory in MCL with preset reference points.

Table 2. Average time costs in iteration of LiDAR odometry

Resolution of locale map (cm)	3–15
Average iteration time cost (ms)	2.33539

depends on the measurement noise of the LiDAR and the moving velocity of the mobile robots. In practice, since the MCL only corrects the localization errors after a certain distance movement, the correction rate is about 1 Hz–5 Hz, depending on the moving velocity. Therefore, with the LiDAR odometry, the localization system can provide location estimates at an adequate accuracy and update rate at least 100 Hz.

7   Conclusion

In this paper, we propose a novel localization method in indoor environments based on the Monte Carlo Localization (MCL), only utilizing a high update rate and low measurement noise LiDAR. A LiDAR odometry is introduced to estimate the pose changes during the movements of the mobile robot, in which a locale map is adopted to reduce the accumulating errors by matching scan point clouds against the map. The LiDAR pseudo-odometry provides the motion model in the prediction phase of the MCL, to give a prediction of pose hypotheses distribution, which is corrected by incorporating the current LiDAR observation.

The experimental results suggest that, with the LiDAR odometry, the proposed localization system is able to locate the robot within a given map in real-time with a sufficient accuracy, without other sensors involved.

Acknowledgment. This work was supported by the National Key Research and Development Program of China under grant No. 2017YFB1001703 and the Fundamental Research Funds for the Central Universities under grant No. 171gjc40. We are appreciated and grateful for the support and help.

References

1. Akai, N., Hoshino, S., Inoue, K., Ozaki, K.: Monte Carlo localization using magnetic sensor and LiDAR for real world navigation. In: 2013 IEEE/SICE International Symposium on System Integration (SII), pp. 682–687. IEEE (2013)
2. Biswas, J., Veloso, M.: Wifi localization and navigation for autonomous indoor mobile robots. In: 2010 IEEE International Conference on Robotics and Automation (ICRA), pp. 4379–4384. IEEE (2010)
3. Dellaert, F., Fox, D., Burgard, W., Thrun, S.: Monte Carlo localization for mobile robots. In: Proceedings of the 1999 IEEE International Conference on Robotics and Automation, 1999, vol. 2, pp. 1322–1328. IEEE (1999)
4. Elfes, A.: Using occupancy grids for mobile robot perception and navigation. Computer **22**(6), 46–57 (1989)
5. Kohlbrecher, S., Von Stryk, O., Meyer, J., Klingauf, U.: A flexible and scalable slam system with full 3D motion estimation. In: 2011 IEEE International Symposium on Safety, Security, and Rescue Robotics (SSRR), pp. 155–160. IEEE (2011)
6. Komoriya, K., Oyama, E.: Position estimation of a mobile robot using optical fiber gyroscope (OFG). In: Proceedings of the IEEE/RSJ/GI International Conference on Intelligent Robots and Systems 1994. Advanced Robotic Systems and the Real World, IROS 1994, vol. 1, pp. 143–149. IEEE (1994)
7. Olivera, V.M., Plaza, J.M.C., Serrano, O.S.: Wifi localization methods for autonomous robots. Robotica **24**(4), 455–461 (2006)
8. Qi, H., Moore, J.B.: Direct Kalman filtering approach for GPS/INS integration. IEEE Trans. Aerosp. Electron. Syst. **38**(2), 687–693 (2002)
9. Quigley, M., Conley, K., Gerkey, B., Faust, J., Foote, T., Leibs, J., Wheeler, R., Ng, A.Y.: ROS: an open-source robot operating system. In: ICRA Workshop on Open Source Software, vol. 3, p. 5. Kobe (2009)
10. Thrun, S., Burgard, W., Fox, D.: Probabilistic Robotics. MIT Press, Cambridge (2005)
11. Watanabe, Y.: Estimation of position and its uncertainty in the dead reckoning system of the wheeled mobile robot. In: Proceedings of the 20th ISIR, Tokyo, pp. 205–212 (1990)
12. Zhang, L., Zapata, R., Lépinay, P.: Self-adaptive Monte Carlo localization for mobile robots using range sensors. In: IEEE/RSJ International Conference on Intelligent Robots and Systems, 2009, IROS 2009, pp. 1541–1546. IEEE (2009)

A Sufficient Criterion for Termination of Multi-path Linear Assignment Loops

Yi Li[⊠], Tianxun Cai, and Yong Feng

Key Laboratory of Automated Reasoning and Cognition, CIGIT, CAS,
Chongqing 400714, China
{liyi,caitianxun,yongfeng}@cigit.ac.cn

Abstract. Termination of loop programs is a hot research in these years. In this paper, we focus on the termination of multi-path linear assignment (MPLA) loop programs. A sufficient criterion is presented to check that such a MAPL loop will terminate. Experimental results show that the proposed method can prove certain MPLA loop will terminate, which cannot be proven by existing approach that tries to find global linear ranking functions or lexicographic linear ranking functions.

Keywords: Termination analysis · redlog · Local ranking function
Multi-paths linear assignment loop programs

1 Introduction

Termination analysis of loop programs has received a considerable attention. Guaranteed termination of program loops is necessary in many settings, such as safety critical software and embedded systems. For a generic loop

$$while \quad (conditions) \quad \{updates\}$$

it is well known that the termination problem is undecidable in general. A standard technique for termination analysis is to find a ranking function. Ranking functions maps vector to an element of some well-founded set such that the execution of the updates causes the value of the function to decrease in order. The existence of the ranking functions for a loop program implies that the corresponding loop program is terminating. How to automatically generate ranking functions has been widely studied in [1, 2, 5–7, 9, 10, 12, 13].

For example, in 2001, Colón and Sipma introduced the linear ranking functions to the proof of program termination in [7]. Podelski and Rybalcheko [13] proposed a complete method for synthesizing linear ranking functions of linear loop program. In [6], Chen et al. gave a method to synthesize non-linear ranking functions for polynomial programs by solving semi-algebraic systems. Chen et al. extends

This research is supported by the National Natural Science Foundation of China NNSFC (61572024, 61103110, 11471307).

the work of Podelski and Pybalchenko in [5]. [1] presented the notion of eventual ranking functions and gave an algorithm to compute such ranking functions. In [2], Ben-Amram and Genaim analyzed the complexity of the Linear Ranking problem when the variables range over the integers and presented a complete algorithm for synthesizing linear ranking functions over the integers. In 2005, Bradley et al. presented a method for synthesizing lexicographic linear ranking functions($LLRFs$ for short) with supporting linear invariants in [3,4].

In this paper, we investigate the termination of multi-path linear assignment loops (MPLA for short) and give a sufficient criterion for MPLA loop programs to be terminating. The multi-path loop programs means the loop update of loop program have more than one paths to execute, such as if $\cdots$ else $\cdots$ structure in C language.

The Experimental results show that for some MPLA loop programs which have no global linear ranking functions, lexicographic linear ranking functions, they indeed can be proven to be terminating by our method.

The rest of paper is organized as follows. In Sect. 2, we give the definitions of traditional global ranking functions and lexicographic linear ranking functions. In Sect. 3, we establish a sufficient criterion for MPLA loops with m paths to be terminating, and prove that if such criterion is satisfied, then MPLA loops with m paths must be terminating. In Sect. 4, we show that the termination of an MPLA loop with nonhomogeneous linear assignments can always be equivalently reduced to that of its homogeneous version obtained by introducing a new variable. In addition, an algorithm is given to check if a given MALP loop terminates. In Sect. 5, we conclude this paper.

2   Preliminaries

In this paper, we focus on the termination of multi-path linear assignment (MPLA for short)loops, whose loop guard is a conjunction of linear inequalities, and loop body is the update of the variables in an linear way. Consider the following program GCD,

$$\mathbf{int}\ gcd(\mathbf{int}\ y_1 > 0,\ \mathbf{int}\ y_2 > 0):$$
$$\mathbf{while}\ y_1 \neq y_2\ \mathbf{do}$$
$$\mathbf{if}\ y_1 > y_2\ \mathbf{then}$$
$$y_1 := y_1 - y_2$$
$$\mathbf{else}$$
$$y_2 := y_2 - y_1$$
$$\mathbf{return} y_1$$

The program GCD computes the greatest divisor of two positive integers. Because the strict inequalities can be translated into weak inequalities based on the integer type of the variables, the corresponding transition system can be abstracted from this program, as follows:

loop:

$$\tau_1 : 1 \le y_1 \wedge 1 \le y_2 \wedge y_1 \ge y_2 + 1 \Rightarrow \begin{cases} y_1 := y_1 - y_2 \\ y_2 := \quad y_2 \end{cases}$$

$$\tau_2 : 1 \le y_1 \wedge 1 \le y_2 \wedge y_2 \ge y_1 + 1 \Rightarrow \begin{cases} y_1 := \quad y_1 \\ y_2 := y_2 - y_1 \end{cases}$$

where τ_1, τ_2 corresponds to the first path and the second path of program GCD, respectively. In the following, we identify an MPLA program with its transition system. Thus, in this paper, we consider the termination of the following multiple-path linear assignment loop P_m,

loop:

$$P_m : \begin{array}{l} \tau_1 : \bigvee_{\mu_1} (\bigwedge_{\nu_1} P^{(1)}_{\mu_1\nu_1}(\mathbf{x}) \triangleright 0) \quad \Rightarrow \mathbf{x} := \mathbf{A_1}\mathbf{x} \\ \tau_2 : \bigvee_{\mu_2} (\bigwedge_{\nu_2} P^{(2)}_{\mu_2\nu_2}(\mathbf{x}) \triangleright 0) \quad \Rightarrow \mathbf{x} := \mathbf{A_2}\mathbf{x} \\ \quad\vdots \qquad\qquad\qquad\qquad\quad \vdots \quad \vdots \\ \tau_m : \bigvee_{\mu_m} (\bigwedge_{\nu_m} P^{(m)}_{\mu_m\nu_m}(\mathbf{x}) \triangleright 0) \Rightarrow \mathbf{x} := \mathbf{A_m}\mathbf{x}, \end{array}$$

where P_m have m paths and $\mathbf{x} = (x_1, ..., x_n)^T$, $\mathbf{x} \in \mathbb{R}^n$, $\mathbf{A}_j \in \mathbb{R}^{n \times n}$, τ_j denotes the jth path. $P^{(j)}_{\mu_j\nu_j}(\mathbf{x})$ is the vector of polynomials in $\mathbf{x}$, for $1 \le j \le m$ and $\triangleright \in \{\ge, >\}$. $\bigvee_{\mu_j} (\bigwedge_{\nu_j} P^{(j)}_{\mu_j\nu_j}(\mathbf{x})\triangleright 0)$ is the loop condition of τ_j, $\mathbf{A_j}$ is the assignment matrix of τ_j. Let $\Omega_j = \{\mathbf{x} \in \mathbb{R}^n | \bigvee_{\mu_j} (\bigwedge_{\nu_j} P^{(j)}_{\mu_j\nu_j}(\mathbf{x}) \triangleright 0)\}$, for $j = 1, 2, \cdots, m$. Let $\Omega = \bigcup_{j=1}^m \Omega_j$, Where $\Omega_i \cap \Omega_j = \varnothing(i \ne j)$. Denote $P_m(\tau) = \{\tau_1, \tau_2, \cdots, \tau_m\}$. We say P_m is terminating over the reals, if for any $\mathbf{x} \in \Omega$, there exists a positive integer $k_{\mathbf{x}}$, such that $\mathbf{x}$ falls outside Ω after $k_{\mathbf{x}}$ times iterations of the loop. Such $\mathbf{x}$ is called the terminating point of P_m.

Next, we introduce the definition of traditional ranking function which can also be found in [6,8,11].

Definition 1 (Global ranking functions for Multi-path Linear Assignment Loops). *A function $\rho(\mathbf{x})$ is a global ranking function for program P_m, if the following formula is true over the reals.*

$$\bigwedge_{j=1}^m (\forall \mathbf{x}, \mathbf{x}' (\mathbf{x} \in \Omega_j \wedge \mathbf{x}' = \mathbf{A}_j\mathbf{x} \Rightarrow \rho(\mathbf{x}) \ge 0 \wedge \rho(\mathbf{x}) - \rho(\mathbf{x}') \ge 1)) \quad (1)$$

When $m = 1$, Definition 1 can also be applicable to single-path loops. The existence of the global ranking functions for P_m implies that Program P_m is terminating. That is, if global ranking functions exist for P_m, then any point in $\Omega = \cup_{j=1}^m \Omega_j$, must fall into $\overline{\cup_{j=1}^m \Omega_j}$ after finite iterations. For convenience, we also call such $\rho(\mathbf{x})$ the ranking function over $\cup_{j=1}^m \Omega_j$.

It is easy to see that Formula (1) holds if and only if the following Formulas hold.

$$(\textbf{Bounded})\forall \mathbf{x}.(\mathbf{x} \in \Omega_1 \cup \Omega_2 \cup \cdots \cup \Omega_m \Rightarrow \rho(\mathbf{x}) \geq 0),$$
$$(\textbf{Ranking})\forall \mathbf{x}.\mathbf{x}'.(\mathbf{x} \in \Omega_j \wedge \mathbf{x}' = \mathbf{A}_j\mathbf{x} \Rightarrow \rho(\mathbf{x}) - \rho(\mathbf{x}') \geq 1),$$

$$(2)$$

for all $1 \leq j \leq m$.

Next, we take an example to illustrate how to compute global ranking functions for a given multipath loop by the tool *redlog*.

Example 1. Consider the following linear assignment loop P_1 with two paths:

loop:

$$\text{P1:} \quad \tau_1 : 0 \leq x \leq 5 \wedge 6 \leq y \leq 12 \Rightarrow \begin{cases} x := x + y \\ y := \quad 2y \end{cases}$$

$$\tau_2 : 6 \leq x \leq 10 \wedge 1 \leq y \leq 9 \Rightarrow \begin{cases} x := \quad 3x \\ y := x - y \end{cases}$$

Let us consider Example 1 and formally ask whether there exists a global linear ranking function of the form $\rho(\mathbf{x}) = ax + by + c$.

$\forall x, y : (0 \leq x \leq 5 \wedge 6 \leq y \leq 12) \vee (6 \leq x \leq 10 \wedge 1 \leq y \leq 9) \Rightarrow ax + by + c >= 0$

$\forall x, y : (0 \leq x \leq 5 \wedge 6 \leq y \leq 12) \Rightarrow ax + by + c - (a(x + y) + b(2y) + c) >= 1$

$\forall x, y : (6 \leq x \leq 10 \wedge 1 \leq y \leq 9) \Rightarrow ax + by + c - (a(3x) + b(x - y) + c) >= 1$

And then, we compute the value of a, b, c. This formulation of the problem is executable by quantifier elimination on a symbolic computation system like Reduce:

$1 : load\_package$ *"redlog"*;

$2 : rlset\ r;$

$3 : F := all(\{x, y\}, (((0 <= x <= 5)and(6 <= y <= 12))or((6 <= x <= 10)$
$and(1 <= y <= 9)))impl(a * x + b * y + c >= 0));$

$4 : t1 := rlqe\ F;$

$5 : F := all(\{x, y\}, (0 <= x <= 5)and(6 <= y <= 12)impl((a * x + b * y + c)$
$-(a * (x + y) + b * (2 * y) + c) >= 1));$

$6 : t2 := rlqe\ F;$

$7 : F := all(\{x, y\}, (6 <= x <= 10)and(1 <= y <= 9)impl((a * x + b * y + c)$
$-(a * (3 * x) + b * (x - y) + c) >= 1));$

$8 : t3 := rlqe\ F;$

$9 : F := ex(\{a, b, c\}, (t1)\ and\ (t2)and\ (t3));$

$10 : rlqe\ F;$

Statement 1 loads the *redlog*. Statement 2 defines **R** as the domain of discourse. Statement 3 and Statement 4 correspond to the (**bound**) conditions in (2). Statement 3 initializes formula F. Statement 4 runs elimination over F and returns an equivalent formula, and the result is stored in t1. Statement 5 and Statement 6 correspond to the (**ranking**) conditions in (2) of τ_1. The result is stored in t2. Statement 7 and Statement 8 correspond to the (**ranking**) conditions in (2) of τ_2. The result is stored in t3. Statement 9 checks if there exist a, b, c satisfying $t1 \wedge t2 \wedge t3$. Statement 10 runs elimination and returns true. This means that there exists at least one global linear ranking function for $P1$.

By further computing, we get $\rho(\mathbf{x}) = -3x - y + 39$. The existence of the global ranking functions for $P1$ implies that Program $P1$ is terminating.

Another way to prove the termination of the multi-paths program is to synthesize the Lexicographic Linear Ranking Functions in [3,4]. A lexicographic linear ranking function is an n-tuple of linear expressions $(\mathbf{r}_1^T \mathbf{x}, \cdots, \mathbf{r}_m^T \mathbf{x})$ satisfying the following conditions.

$$(\textbf{Bounded})\tau \rightarrow \mathbf{r}_i^T \mathbf{x} \geq 0$$
$$(\textbf{Ranking})\tau \rightarrow \mathbf{r}_i^T \mathbf{x} - \mathbf{r}_i^T \mathbf{x}' \geq \epsilon \tag{3}$$
$$(\textbf{Unaffecting}) for j < i, \tau \rightarrow \mathbf{r}_j^T \mathbf{x} - \mathbf{r}_j^T \mathbf{x}' \geq 0$$

It is well known that the existence of lexicographic linear ranking functions for P_m implies that program P_m is terminating.

The methods for synthesize global linear ranking functions and lexicographic linear ranking functions have been implemented in the tool $iRankFinder$[1] due to Ben-Amram et al. [2].

3   Local Ranking Functions for MPLA Loops with m Paths

In the previous section, we recall the definitions of global ranking functions and lexicographic ranking functions. For a given loop program, if it has a global ranking function or a lexicographic ranking function, then the program must terminate. However, if the program has no such ranking functions defined in (1) and (3), then we can not say that the program does not terminate. This can be seen by Example 2.

Example 2. Consider the following MPLA loop P_2:

> **loop:**
> P2: $\tau_1 : 9 \geq x \geq 1 \wedge y \geq x \quad \Rightarrow x := 3x, y := 2y;$
> $\tau_2 : y \leq x - 1 \wedge 9 \geq y \geq 1 \Rightarrow x := 2x, y := 3y;$

For the program, we find that $P2$ has no global linear ranking functions (GLRFs for short) and lexicographic linear ranking functions by quantifier elimination tool *redlog*. Can we conclude that the loop does not terminate? No. because it may admit a non-linear ranking function, but how to give a template of non-linear ranking function is an intractable problem. Next, we will give a new approach to show that $P2$ is terminating.

We first introduce the definition of local ranking functions and then give a sufficient criterion for an MPLA loop to be terminating.

Before the formal discussion, let us slightly analyze why the global linear ranking function fail. By the definition of global ranking function, we can see that a global ranking function maps Ω to a well-founded set such that the every execution of the updates will cause the value of the function to decrease in order.

---

[1] http://www.loopkiller.com/irankfinder/linrf.php.

This is a strict condition such that sometimes the synthesis of global ranking function may fail. According to the idea of divide-and-conquer method, we find that not all points in Ω will iterate between different path, so we can divide Ω into some subsets, and synthesize corresponding ranking function in the subsets to ensure the termination of the loop program.

First, we give some necessary notations. For P_m, define

$$S_j = \{\mathbf{x} \in \Omega_j | \mathbf{A_j x} \in \bigcup_{\substack{i=1 \\ i \neq j}}^{m} \Omega_i\}.$$

$$\Omega_j'' = \{\mathbf{x} \in \Omega_j | \exists n \in Z^+ . (\mathbf{A_j^n x} \in S_j \wedge \bigwedge_{i=0}^{n-1} (\mathbf{A_j^i x} \in \Omega_j))\}$$

$$\Omega_j' = \Omega_j - S_j - \Omega_j''$$

for $j = 1, 2, \cdots, m$, where Z^+ denotes the set of positive integers. Clearly, $S_j, \Omega_j', \Omega_j''$ are the subsets of Ω_j, for $j = 1, 2, \cdots, m$, and each point in S_j must fall into $\Omega_i (i \neq j)$ after only one iteration. The points in Ω_j'' must fall into S_j after a finite number of iterations. That is to say, the points in Ω_j'' fall into $\Omega_i (i \neq j)$ after at least two iterations. Therefore, $S_j \cap \Omega_j'' = \emptyset$. When $m = 2$, the schematic diagram of $S_j, \Omega_j', \Omega_j''$ is shown in Fig. 1,

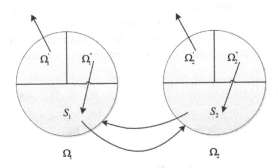

Fig. 1. Schematic diagram of partition

In this figure, we consider the case when m = 2. By the definitions of $S_i, \Omega_i''(i = 1, 2)$, each point in $S_1(resp.S_2)$ must fall into $\Omega_2(resp.\Omega_1)$ after one iteration, and the points in $\Omega_1''(resp.\Omega_2'')$ must fall into $S_1(resp.S_2)$ after a finite number of iterations. That is to say, the points in $\Omega_1''(resp.\Omega_2'')$ fall into $\Omega_2(resp.\Omega_1)$ after at least two iterations. Moreover, the points of Ω_1' must fall into $\overline{\Omega_1 \cup \Omega_2}$ after finite times iterations. This will be shown in proposition 2.

It is easy to see that Ω_j'' can be further expressed as the following form:

$$\Omega_j'' = \bigcup_{k_j=1}^{\infty} \Omega_j''(k_j)$$

$$\Omega_j''(k_j) = \{\mathbf{x} \in \Omega_j | \mathbf{A}_j^{k_j}\mathbf{x} \in S_j \wedge \bigwedge_{i=0}^{k_j-1} (\mathbf{A}_j^i\mathbf{x} \in \Omega_j)\}$$

where $k_j \in Z^+$, for $j = 1, 2, \cdots, m$. Clearly, $\Omega_j''(k_j)$ is a subset of Ω_j'' and any point of $\Omega_j''(k_j)$ fall into S_j after k_j times iterations. It is easy to see that $\Omega_j''(\alpha) \cap \Omega_j''(\beta) = \varnothing$ (for $\alpha \neq \beta, \alpha, \beta \in Z^+$).

Proposition 1. *If there exists a positive integer k_j, such that $\Omega_j''(k_j) = \varnothing$, then $\Omega_j''(k_j + 1) = \varnothing$, for $j = 1, 2, \cdots, m$.*

Proof. Suppose $\Omega_j''(k_j + 1) \neq \varnothing$. Then, there must exist a point $\mathbf{x} \in \Omega_j''(k_j + 1)$. By the definition of $\Omega_j''(k_j + 1)$, we have $\mathbf{A}_j^{k_j+1}\mathbf{x} \in S_j \wedge \bigwedge_{i=0}^{k_j}(\mathbf{A}_j^i\mathbf{x} \in \Omega_j)$. That is, $\mathbf{A}_j^{k_j}(\mathbf{A}_j\mathbf{x}) \in S_j \wedge \bigwedge_{i=0}^{k_j-1}(\mathbf{A}_j^i(\mathbf{A}_j\mathbf{x}) \in \Omega_j)$. Let $\mathbf{x}^* = \mathbf{A}_j\mathbf{x}$, by the definition of $\Omega_j''(k_j)$, we know $\mathbf{x}^* \in \Omega_j''(k_j)$. Hence, $\Omega_j''(k_j) \neq \varnothing$. This contradicts with the hypothesis that $\Omega_j''(k_j) = \varnothing$. $\square$.

Remark 1. By Proposition 1, we know if there exists a positive integer N_j, such that $\Omega_j''(N_j) = \varnothing$, then, $\Omega_j''(n_j) = \varnothing$, for any $n_j \geq N_j + 1$. Therefore, if such N_j exists, then we have

$$\Omega_j'' = \bigcup_{k_j=1}^{\infty} \Omega_j''(k_j) = \bigcup_{k_j=1}^{N_j} \Omega_j''(k_j)$$

According to Proposition 1, we can give a heuristic method to compute Ω_j'', for $j = 1, 2, \cdots, m$. We next will take an example to illustrate how to compute Ω_j''.

Example 3. Following Example 2, consider the MPLA loop $P2$. According to the above definition, we have
$$\Omega_1 = \{(x, y) | 9 \geq x \geq 1 \wedge y \geq x\}.$$
$$\Omega_2 = \{(x, y) | 9 \geq y \geq 1 \wedge y \leq x - 1\}.$$
According to the definitions of $S_j, \Omega_j', \Omega_j''$ for $j = 1, 2, \cdots, m$. We have

$$S_1 = \{\mathbf{x} \in \Omega_1 | \mathbf{A_1}\mathbf{x} \in \Omega_2\}.$$

$$\Omega_1'' = \{\mathbf{x} \in \Omega_1 | \exists n \in Z^+.(\mathbf{A_1^n}\mathbf{x} \in S_1 \wedge \bigwedge_{i=0}^{n-1} (\mathbf{A_1^i}\mathbf{x} \in \Omega_1))\}$$

$$\Omega_1' = \Omega_1 - S_1 - \Omega_1''$$
$$S_2 = \{\mathbf{x} \in \Omega_2 | \mathbf{A_2}\mathbf{x} \in \Omega_1\}.$$

$$\Omega_2'' = \{\mathbf{x} \in \Omega_2 | \exists m \in Z^+.(\mathbf{A_2^m}\mathbf{x} \in S_2 \wedge \bigwedge_{j=0}^{m-1} (\mathbf{A_2^j}\mathbf{x} \in \Omega_2))\}$$

$$\Omega_2' = \Omega_2 - S_2 - \Omega_2''$$

To compute Ω_j'', we first construct S_1, as follows,

$$S_1 = \{\mathbf{x} \in \Omega_1 | \mathbf{A_1x} \in \Omega_2\}.$$
$$= \{\mathbf{x} | 9 \geq x \geq 1 \wedge y \geq x \wedge 9 \geq 2y \geq 1 \wedge 2y \leq 3x - 1\}$$

By S_1 and the tool redlog, we get

$$\Omega_1''(1) = \{\mathbf{x} \in \Omega_1 | \mathbf{A_1x} \in S_1\}.$$
$$= \{\mathbf{x} | 9 \geq x \geq 1 \wedge y \geq x \wedge 9 \geq 3x \geq 1 \wedge 2y \geq 3x \wedge 9 \geq 4y \geq 1 \wedge 4y \leq 9x - 1\}$$
$$\Omega_1''(2) = \{\mathbf{x} \in \Omega_1 | \mathbf{A_1x} \in \Omega_1 \wedge \mathbf{A_1^2x} \in S_1\}.$$
$$= \{\mathbf{x} | 9 \geq x \geq 1 \wedge y \geq x \wedge 9 \geq 3x \geq 1 \wedge 2y \geq 3x \wedge 9 \geq 9x \geq 1 \wedge 4y \geq 9x \wedge$$
$$9 \geq 8y \geq 1 \wedge 8y \leq 27x - 1\} = \varnothing$$

Because $\Omega_1''(2) = \varnothing$, by Proposition 1 and its remark, we get $\Omega_1'' = \Omega_1''(1) \cup \Omega_1''(2) = \Omega_1''(1)$.

Similarly, we can compute S_2, Ω_2'' of Ω_2, as follows.

$$S_2 = \{\mathbf{x} | 9 \geq y \geq 1 \wedge y \leq x - 1 \wedge 9 \geq 2x \geq 1 \wedge 3y \geq 2x\}$$
$$\Omega_2''(1) = \{\mathbf{x} | 9 \geq y \geq 1 \wedge y \leq x - 1 \wedge 9 \geq 3y \geq 1 \wedge 3y \leq 2x - 1 \wedge 9 \geq 4x \geq 1 \wedge$$
$$9y \geq 4x\}.$$
$$\Omega_2''(2) = \{\mathbf{x} | 9 \geq y \geq 1 \wedge y \leq x - 1 \wedge 9 \geq 3y \geq 1 \wedge 3y \leq 2x - 1 \wedge 9 \geq 9y \geq 1 \wedge$$
$$9y \leq 4x - 1 \wedge 9 \geq 8x \geq 1 \wedge 27y \geq 8x\} = \varnothing$$

Because $\Omega_2''(2) = \varnothing$, by Proposition 1 and its remark, we have $\Omega_2'' = \Omega_2''(1)$.

Since $\Omega_j' = \Omega_j - S_j - \Omega_j''$ for $j = 1, 2, \cdots, m$, it is not difficult to see that $\Omega_j' = C_{j0} \cup C_{j\infty}$, where $C_{j0} = \{\mathbf{x} \in \Omega_j | \exists n \in Z^+, (\mathbf{A_j^n x} \in \overline{\Omega}_j \wedge \bigwedge_{i=0}^{n-1} \mathbf{A_j^i x} \in \Omega_j \wedge \mathbf{A_j^{n-1}x} \notin S_j)\}$ and $C_{j\infty} = \{\mathbf{x} \in \Omega_j | \forall n \in Z^+, \mathbf{A_j^n x} \in \Omega_j\}$. That is, C_{j0} consists of points which fall into $\overline{\Omega}_j$ after finite iterations and cannot fall into S_j before falling into $\overline{\Omega}_j$. $C_{j\infty}$ consists of points which always fall into Ω_j for any times iterations. Clearly, any point in $C_{j\infty}$ does not fall into S_j for any times iterations, since any point in S_j must fall into $\overline{\Omega}_j$ after one iterations. In addition, any point in $C_{i\infty}$ do not fall into Ω_j'' too, because any point in Ω_j'' will fall into S_j after finite iterations. By the above arguments, we get that the points in $\bigcup_{j=1}^m \Omega_j'$ can not fall into $\bigcup_{j=1}^m S_j$ and $\bigcup_{j=1}^m \Omega_j''$.

Proposition 2. *For each $\Omega_j, j = 1, 2, \cdots, m$, if there exists a ranking function $\rho_j(\mathbf{x})$ over Ω_j for $j \in \{1, 2, \cdots, m\}$, then the point of Ω_j' will fall into the $\overline{\bigcup_{i=1}^m \Omega_i}$ after finite times iterations.*

Proof. Without loss of generality, we just consider the case when $j = 1$, and similar analysis can be applied to the case when $j = 2, 3, \cdots, m$. Because there exists a ranking function $\rho_1(\mathbf{x})$ over Ω_1, we have that for any $\mathbf{x_0} \in \Omega_1$, there must exist a positive integer n, such that $\mathbf{A_1^n x_0} \notin \Omega_1$. Since $\Omega_1' \subseteq \Omega_1$, we also have that for any $\mathbf{x_0} \in \Omega_1'$, there must exist a positive integer n, such that $\mathbf{A_1^n x_0} \notin \Omega_1$. This immediately implies that $C_{1\infty} = \varnothing$. Hence $\Omega_1' = C_{10}$. By the definition of

C_{10}, for any $\mathbf{x_0} \in C_{10}$, $\mathbf{x_0}$ will fall into $\overline{\Omega}_1$ after finite iterations and cannot fall into S_1 before falling into $\overline{\Omega}_1$. Next, we will show that for any $\mathbf{x_0} \in C_{10}$, $\mathbf{x_0}$ will fall into $\overline{\cup_{i=1}^m \Omega_i}$. Because $\overline{\cup_{i=1}^m \Omega_i} = \overline{\Omega}_1 \cap \overline{\cup_{i=2}^m \Omega_i}$, by the above arguments, we know that to prove for any $\mathbf{x_0} \in C_{10}$, $\mathbf{x_0}$ will fall into $\overline{\cup_{i=1}^m \Omega_i}$ is equivalent to prove that for any $\mathbf{x_0} \in C_{10}$, $\mathbf{x_0}$ will fall into $\overline{\cup_{i=2}^m \Omega_i}$, by the definition of C_{10}. Therefore, the remaining thing is to prove that for any $\mathbf{x_0} \in C_{10}$, $\mathbf{x_0}$ always falls into $\overline{\cup_{i=2}^m \Omega_i}$.

For any $\mathbf{x_0} \in C_{10}$, by the definition of C_{10}, there must exist a positive integer $k_{\mathbf{x_0}}$ associated with $\mathbf{x_0}$, such that $\mathbf{A}_1^{k_{\mathbf{x_0}}} \mathbf{x_0} \in \overline{\Omega}_1 \wedge \bigwedge_{j=0}^{k_{\mathbf{x_0}}-1} \mathbf{A}_1^j \mathbf{x_0} \in \Omega_1 \wedge \mathbf{A}_1^{k_{\mathbf{x_0}}-1} \mathbf{x} \notin S_1$. Clearly, since $\mathbf{x_0} \in C_{10} \subseteq \Omega_1$, $\mathbf{A}_1^{k_{\mathbf{x_0}}} \mathbf{x_0} \notin \cup_{i=2}^m \Omega_i$. This is because, if $\mathbf{A}_1^{k_{\mathbf{x_0}}} \mathbf{x_0} \in \cup_{i=2}^m \Omega_i$, then we have $\mathbf{A}_1^{k_{\mathbf{x_0}}-1} \mathbf{x} \in S_1$, this contradicts with the definition of points in C_{10}. Therefore, for any $\mathbf{x_0} \in C_{10}$, $\mathbf{x_0}$ will fall into $\cup_{i=2}^m \Omega_i$ after finite times iterations.

In summary, when there is a ranking function $\rho_j(\mathbf{x})$ over Ω_1, the point of Ω_1' will fall into the $\overline{\cup_{i=1}^m \Omega_i}$ after finite times iterations, i.e., the points in Ω_1' are all terminating points for program P_m. □

Remark 2. If the hypothesis of Proposition 2 is fulfilled, the points of $\bigcup_{j=1}^m \Omega_j'$ are all terminating points of Program P_m.

Example 4. Following Example 3, by the tool *redlog*, we compute Ω_1', Ω_2' over Ω_1, Ω_2, respectively, as follows,

$$\Omega_1' = \Omega_1 - S_1 - \Omega_1'' = \Omega_1 \cap \overline{S_1} \cap \overline{\Omega_1''}$$
$$= \{\mathbf{x} | 1 \le x \le 9 \wedge x \le y \wedge (2y > 9 \vee 2y < 1 \vee 3x - 2y < 1) \wedge (4y > 9 \vee 4y < 1 \vee$$
$$x > 3 \vee 3x - 2y > 0 \vee 9x - 4y < 1)\}$$
$$\Omega_2' = \Omega_2 - S_2 - \Omega_2'' = \Omega_2 \cap \overline{S_2} \cap \overline{\Omega_2''}$$
$$= \{\mathbf{x} | 1 \le y \le 9 \wedge x - y \ge 1 \wedge (y > 3 \vee 2x - 3y < 1 \vee 4y > 9 \vee 4y < 1 \vee 4x$$
$$- 9y > 0) \wedge (2x > 9 \vee 2x < 1 \vee 2x - 3y > 0)\}$$

We next compute the ranking functions $\rho_1(\mathbf{x})$, $\rho_2(\mathbf{x})$ on Ω_1, Ω_2, respectively. To do this, predefine a ranking functions template that $\rho_1(\mathbf{x}) = ax + by + c$. Then, by the definition of ranking functions, we have following formulas:

$$\forall x, y \; (9 \ge x \ge 1 \wedge y \ge x) \Rightarrow \begin{cases} ax + by + c \ge 0 \\ ax + by + c \ge a(3x) + b(2y) + c + 1. \end{cases}$$

Eliminating x,y from the above formulas, we get a set of constraints on a,b,c. Solving the constraints, we can get a sample point $(-\frac{1}{2}, 0, \frac{9}{2})$. We therefore obtain $\rho_1(\mathbf{x}) = -\frac{1}{2}x + \frac{9}{2}$. Similarly, we can obtain $\rho_2(\mathbf{x}) = -\frac{1}{2}y + \frac{9}{2}$.

Since there exist ranking functions $\rho_1(\mathbf{x})$, $\rho_2(\mathbf{x})$ over Ω_1, Ω_2, respectively, according to the Proposition 2, we know that $\forall \mathbf{x_0} \in \Omega_1' \cup \Omega_2'$, $\mathbf{x_0}$ will fall into $\overline{\Omega_1 \cup \Omega_2}$ after finite times iterations. That is to say, all the points in $\Omega_1' \cup \Omega_2'$ are terminating points of $P2$.

Let $\Phi_m = (S_1 \cup \Omega_1'') \cup (S_2 \cup \Omega_2'') \cup \cdots \cup (S_m \cup \Omega_m'')$. Next, we give the definition of local ranking function for MPLA loops with m paths.

Definition 2 *(Local ranking functions for MPLA loops with m paths).*
Given an MPLA loop P_m. We call $\rho(\mathbf{x})$ the local ranking function for Program P_m over Φ_m, if the following conditions are satisfied.

$$\exists N_j \in Z^+, \Omega_j'' = \bigcup_{k_j=1}^{N_j} \Omega_j''(k_j), \text{ for } j = 1, 2, \cdots, m \tag{4a}$$

$$\forall \mathbf{x} \in \Phi_m \Rightarrow \rho(\mathbf{x}) \geq 0 \tag{4b}$$

$$\bigwedge_{j=1}^{m} (\forall \mathbf{x} \in S_j \Rightarrow \rho(\mathbf{x}) - \rho(\mathbf{A_j x}) \geq 1) \tag{4c}$$

$$\bigwedge_{j=1}^{m} (\bigwedge_{k_j=1}^{N_j} (\forall \mathbf{x} \in \Omega_j''(k_j) \Rightarrow \rho(\mathbf{x}) - \rho(\mathbf{A_j^{k_j} x}) \geq 0)) \tag{4d}$$

Theorem 1 *(Termination for MPLA loops with m paths).* Let Φ_m be defined as above. For Program P_m, if the following conditions are all satisfied,
   (i) there exists a ranking function $\rho_j(\mathbf{x})$ over Ω_j, for $j = 1, 2, \cdots, m$,
   (ii) there exists a local ranking function $\rho(\mathbf{x})$ over Φ_m,
then Program P_m terminates.

Proof. To prove Program P_m is terminating is equivalent to prove that the points in $\bigcup_{j=1}^{m} \Omega_j$ are all terminating points of P_m. Note that $\bigcup_{j=1}^{m} \Omega_j = (\Omega_1' \cup S_1 \cup \Omega_1'') \cup \cdots \cup (\Omega_m' \cup S_m \cup \Omega_m'') = (\bigcup_{j=1}^{m} \Omega_j') \cup \Phi_m$. By Proposition 2 and Remark 2, we know when hypothesis (i) is satisfied, the points of $\bigcup_{j=1}^{m} \Omega_j'$ are all terminating points of Program P_m. Next, we will show that all the points in Φ_m are terminating points of P_m. Suppose that there exist a point $\mathbf{x_0} \in \Phi_m$ which is a non-terminating point of P_m. Then, there must exist an infinite iteration sequence $L = \{\mathbf{x_0}, \mathbf{x_1}, \mathbf{x_2}, \cdots\} = \{\mathbf{x_i}\}_{i=0}^{+\infty} \subseteq \bigcup_{j=1}^{m} \Omega_j$. Obviously, $L \cap (\bigcup_{j=1}^{m} \Omega_j') = \varnothing$, since any point in $\bigcup_{j=1}^{m} \Omega_j'$ is non-terminating points of P_m, which will fall outside $\bigcup_{j=1}^{m} \Omega_j$ after finite times iterations. Thus, such L just can lie in Φ_m, i.e., $L \subseteq \Phi_m$. Let $\triangle$ be an empty set, i.e., $\triangle = \{\}$. For the infinite sequence L, without loss of generality, assume $\mathbf{x_0} \in (S_{j_0} \cup \Omega_{j_0}'')$ for a certain $j_0 \in \{1, \cdots, m\}$. Since any point in Ω_{j_0}'' will fall into S_{j_0} after finite times iterations, without loss of generality, we can further assume $\mathbf{x_0} \in S_{j_0}$. Let $\mathbf{y_0} = \mathbf{x_0}$ and $\triangle = \{\mathbf{y_0}\}$. By the definition of S_{j_0}, we get $\mathbf{x_1} = \mathbf{A_{j_0} x_0}$ and $\mathbf{x_1}$ must be in $S_{j_1} \cup \Omega_{j_1}''$ for a certain $j_1 \in \{1, \cdots, m\} \setminus \{j_0\}$. Let $\mathbf{y_1} = \mathbf{x_1}$ and add $\mathbf{y_1}$ to $\triangle$ and get $\triangle = \{\mathbf{y_0}, \mathbf{y_1}\}$. By (ii), since $\rho(\mathbf{x})$ is the local ranking function over Φ_m and $\mathbf{x_0} \in S_{j_0}$, by (4c), we have $\rho(\mathbf{x_0}) - \rho(\mathbf{x_1}) \geq 1$. It immediately follows that $\rho(\mathbf{y_0}) - \rho(\mathbf{y_1}) \geq 1$. For $\mathbf{x_1}$, there will be two cases to consider. (a). If $\mathbf{x_1} \in S_{j_1}$, then by the definition of S_{j_1}, we have $\mathbf{x_2} = \mathbf{A_{j_1} x_1} = \mathbf{A_{j_1} A_{j_0} x_0} \in S_{j_2} \cup \Omega_{j_2}''$ for $j_2 \in \{1, \cdots, m\} \setminus \{j_1\}$. Since $\rho(\mathbf{x})$ is the local ranking function over Φ_m and $\mathbf{x_1} \in S_{j_1}$, by (4c), we have $\rho(\mathbf{x_1}) - \rho(\mathbf{A_{j_1} x_1}) \geq 1$. (b). If $\mathbf{x_1} \in \Omega_{j_1}''$, then by the definition of Ω_{j_1}'', there must exist $k_{\mathbf{x_1}} \in Z^+$, such that $\mathbf{x_{k_{\mathbf{x_1}}+1}} = \mathbf{A_{j_1}^{k_{\mathbf{x_1}}} x_1} = \mathbf{A_{j_1}^{k_{\mathbf{x_1}}} A_{j_0} x_0} \in S_{j_1}$. Since $\rho(\mathbf{x})$ is the local ranking function over Φ_m and $\mathbf{x_1} \in \Omega_{j_1}''$, by (4d), we have

$$\rho(\mathbf{x_1}) - \rho(\mathbf{x_{k_{\mathbf{x_1}}+1}}) \geq 0 \tag{5}$$

Hence, if case (b) occurs, then $\mathbf{x}_{k_{\mathbf{x}_1}+2} = A_{j_1}(\mathbf{x}_{k_{\mathbf{x}_1}+1}) = A_{j_1}^{k_{\mathbf{x}_1}+1}\mathbf{x}_1 = A_{j_1}^{k_{\mathbf{x}_1}+1}A_{j_0} \cdot \mathbf{x}_0 \in S_{j_2} \cup \Omega_{j_2}''$ for $j_2 \in \{1, \cdots, m\} \setminus \{j_1\}$. Since $\mathbf{x}_{k_{\mathbf{x}_1}+1} \in S_{j_1}$ and $\rho(\mathbf{x})$ is the local ranking function over Φ_m, by (4c), we have

$$\rho(\mathbf{x}_{k_{\mathbf{x}_1}+1}) - \rho(\mathbf{x}_{k_{\mathbf{x}_1}+2}) \geq 1 \tag{6}$$

Therefore, when $\mathbf{x}_1 \in \Omega_{j_1}''$, by (5) and (6), we get $\rho(\mathbf{x}_1) - \rho(\mathbf{x}_{k_{\mathbf{x}_1}+2}) = \rho(\mathbf{x}_1) - \rho(A_{j_1}^{k_{\mathbf{x}_1}+1}\mathbf{x}_1) \geq 1$. To sum up, if $\mathbf{x}_1 \in (S_{j_1} \cup \Omega_{j_1}'')$, then there must exist k_1, $k_1 \in \{1, k_{\mathbf{x}_1}+1\}$, such that $\mathbf{x}_{k_1+1} = A_{j_1}^{k_1}\mathbf{x}_1 = A_{j_1}^{k_1}A_{j_0}\mathbf{x}_0 \in S_{j_2} \cup \Omega_{j_2}''$ and $\rho(\mathbf{x}_1) - \rho(\mathbf{x}_{k_1+1}) \geq 1$. Let $\mathbf{y}_2 = \mathbf{x}_{k_1+1}$ and add $\mathbf{y}_2$ to $\triangle$, and get $\triangle = \{\mathbf{y}_0, \mathbf{y}_1, \mathbf{y}_2\}$. Clearly, $\rho(\mathbf{y}_1) - \rho(\mathbf{y}_2) \geq 1$. In the same way, since L is an infinite sequence, we can pick up an infinite number of points from L to construct an infinite sequence $\triangle = \{\mathbf{y}_0, \mathbf{y}_1, \mathbf{y}_2, \cdots\} \subseteq L \subseteq \Phi_m$, which has the property that

$$\rho(\mathbf{y}_i) - \rho(\mathbf{y}_{i+1}) \geq 1 \tag{7}$$

Moreover, since $\rho(\mathbf{x})$ is the local ranking function over Φ_m, by (4b), we have $\forall \mathbf{x} \in \Phi_m \Rightarrow \rho(\mathbf{x}) \geq 0$. Thus, since $\triangle$ is an infinite sequence, by (7), there must exist $k \in Z^+$ such that $\rho(\mathbf{y}_k) < 0$ which clearly contradicts with that $\rho(\mathbf{x}) \geq 0$ for all $\mathbf{x} \in \Phi_m$. □

Example 5. Following Example 3, we know $\Omega_1'' = \Omega_1''(1)$ and $\Omega_2'' = \Omega_2''(1)$. Thus, condition (4a) of Definition 2 is met. Following Example 4, next, we will compute the linear local function $\rho(\mathbf{x})$ on $S_1, S_2, \Omega_1'', \Omega_2''$. To do this, we predefine a linear function template $\rho(\mathbf{x}) = ax + by + c$. According to the Definition 2, we construct the following formulas:

$$\forall \mathbf{x} \in S_1 \cup \Omega_1'' \cup S_2 \cup \Omega_2'' \Rightarrow ax + by + c \geq 0$$
$$\forall \mathbf{x} \in S_1 \Rightarrow -2ax - by \geq 1$$
$$\forall \mathbf{x} \in \Omega_1''(1) \Rightarrow -2ax - by \geq 0$$
$$\forall \mathbf{x} \in S_2 \Rightarrow -ax - 2by \geq 1$$
$$\forall \mathbf{x} \in \Omega_2''(1) \Rightarrow -ax - 2by \geq 0$$

All the computation are implemented by using *redlog*. Eliminating x,y from the above formulas, we get the constraints on a,b,c. Solving such constraints, we get a sample point $(1, -3, 26)$. We therefore obtain the desired local ranking function $\rho(\mathbf{x}) = x - 3y + 26$. According to the example 4, since there exist ranking functions $\rho_1(\mathbf{x})$ and $\rho_2(\mathbf{x})$ over Ω_1 and Ω_2, respectively, by Theorem 1, the program $P2$ is terminating.

4   MPLA Loops with Nonhomogeneous Linear Assignments

In this section, we consider the MPLA loops with nonhomogeneous assignment statements, as follows,

loop:

$$\tau_1 : \bigvee_{\mu_1}(\bigwedge_{\nu_1} P^{(1)}_{\mu_1\nu_1}(\mathbf{x}) \rhd 0) \Rightarrow \mathbf{x} := \mathbf{A_1}\mathbf{x} + \mathbf{c_1}$$

$$\tau_2 : \bigvee_{\mu_2}(\bigwedge_{\nu_2} P^{(2)}_{\mu_2\nu_2}(\mathbf{x}) \rhd 0) \Rightarrow \mathbf{x} := \mathbf{A_2}\mathbf{x} + \mathbf{c_2}$$

$P'_m :$ $\qquad\vdots\qquad\qquad\vdots\qquad\qquad\vdots$

$$\tau_m : \bigvee_{\mu_m}(\bigwedge_{\nu_m} P^{(m)}_{\mu_m\nu_m}(\mathbf{x}) \rhd 0) \Rightarrow \mathbf{x} := \mathbf{A_m}\mathbf{x} + \mathbf{c_m}$$

By introducing an additional variable z, the termination of P'_m can be equivalently reduced to that of Q_m.

loop:

$$\tau_1 : (\bigvee_{\mu_1}(\bigwedge_{\nu_1} P^{(1)}_{\mu_1\nu_1}(\mathbf{x}) \rhd 0)) \wedge (z = 1) \Rightarrow \mathbf{x}' := \mathbf{A}'_1\mathbf{x}'$$

$$\tau_2 : (\bigvee_{\mu_2}(\bigwedge_{\nu_2} P^{(2)}_{\mu_2\nu_2}(\mathbf{x}) \rhd 0)) \wedge (z = 1) \Rightarrow \mathbf{x}' := \mathbf{A}'_2\mathbf{x}'$$

$Q_m :$ $\qquad\vdots\qquad\qquad\vdots\qquad\qquad\vdots$

$$\tau_m : (\bigvee_{\mu_m}(\bigwedge_{\nu_m} P^{(m)}_{\mu_m\nu_m}(\mathbf{x}) \rhd 0)) \wedge (z = 1) \Rightarrow \mathbf{x}' := \mathbf{A}'_m\mathbf{x}'$$

where

$$\mathbf{A}'_\mathbf{j} = \begin{pmatrix} \mathbf{A_j} & \mathbf{c_j} \\ 0 & 1 \end{pmatrix}, \mathbf{x}' = \begin{pmatrix} \mathbf{x} \\ z \end{pmatrix} \tag{8}$$

Let $\Psi_j = \{\mathbf{x} | (\bigvee_{\mu_j}(\bigwedge_{\nu_j} P^{(j)}_{\mu_j\nu_j}(\mathbf{x}) \rhd 0)) \wedge (z = 1)\}$, for $j = 1, 2, \cdots, m$ and $\Psi = \bigcup_{j=1}^{m} \Psi_j$. Let $\Omega_j = \{\mathbf{x} \in \mathbb{R}^n | \bigvee_{\mu_j}(\bigwedge_{\nu_j} P^{(j)}_{\mu_j\nu_j}(\mathbf{x}) \rhd 0)\}$, for $j = 1, 2, \cdots, m$ and let $\Omega = \bigcup_{j=1}^{m} \Omega_j$.

Theorem 2. P'_m *does not terminate over the reals if and only if* Q_m *does not terminate over the reals.*

Proof. ($\Leftarrow$) Let $\overline{\mathbf{A}_\mathbf{i}}(\mathbf{x}) = \mathbf{A_i}\mathbf{x} + \mathbf{c_i}$, for $i = 1, 2, \cdots, m$. If P'_m does not terminate over the reals, then there must exist a point $\mathbf{x_0} \in \Omega$ and an index set $S = \{j_i\}_{i=1}^{+\infty}$, where $j_i \in \{1, 2, \cdots, m\}$ for any $i \in Z^+$, such that

$$\mathbf{x_0} \in \Omega,$$
$$\mathbf{x_1} = \overline{\mathbf{A}}_{\mathbf{j_1}}(\mathbf{x_0}) \in \Omega,$$
$$\mathbf{x_2} = \overline{\mathbf{A}}_{\mathbf{j_2}}(\mathbf{x_1}) = \overline{\mathbf{A}}_{\mathbf{j_2}} \circ \overline{\mathbf{A}}_{\mathbf{j_1}}(\mathbf{x_0}) \in \Omega,$$
$$\vdots \tag{9}$$
$$\mathbf{x_k} = \overline{\mathbf{A}}_{\mathbf{j_k}}(\mathbf{x_{k-1}}) = \overline{\mathbf{A}}_{\mathbf{j_k}} \circ \overline{\mathbf{A}}_{\mathbf{j_{k-1}}} \circ \cdots \circ \overline{\mathbf{A}}_{\mathbf{j_2}} \circ \overline{\mathbf{A}}_{\mathbf{j_1}}(\mathbf{x_0}) \in \Omega,$$
$$\vdots$$

Let $\mathbf{x_0}' = (\mathbf{x_0}, 1)^T$. Then, by (9), it follows that $\mathbf{x_0}' \in \Psi$, $\mathbf{x_1}' = \mathbf{A}'_{\mathbf{j_1}} \mathbf{x_0}' = \begin{pmatrix} \mathbf{A}_{\mathbf{j_1}} & c_{\mathbf{j_1}} \\ 0 & 1 \end{pmatrix} \mathbf{x_0}' = \begin{pmatrix} \mathbf{A}_{\mathbf{j_1}} & c_{\mathbf{j_1}} \\ 0 & 1 \end{pmatrix} \begin{pmatrix} \mathbf{x_0} \\ 1 \end{pmatrix} = \begin{pmatrix} \overline{\mathbf{A}}_{\mathbf{j_1}}(\mathbf{x_0}) \\ 1 \end{pmatrix} = \begin{pmatrix} \mathbf{x_1} \\ 1 \end{pmatrix} \in \Psi$, $\mathbf{x_2}' = \mathbf{A}'_{\mathbf{j_2}} \mathbf{x_1}' = \begin{pmatrix} \mathbf{A}_{\mathbf{j_2}} & c_{\mathbf{j_2}} \\ 0 & 1 \end{pmatrix} \mathbf{x_1}' = \begin{pmatrix} \mathbf{A}_{\mathbf{j_2}} & c_{\mathbf{j_2}} \\ 0 & 1 \end{pmatrix} \begin{pmatrix} \mathbf{A}_{\mathbf{j_1}} & c_{\mathbf{j_1}} \\ 0 & 1 \end{pmatrix} \begin{pmatrix} \mathbf{x_0} \\ 1 \end{pmatrix} = \begin{pmatrix} \mathbf{A}_{\mathbf{j_2}} & c_{\mathbf{j_2}} \\ 0 & 1 \end{pmatrix} \begin{pmatrix} \mathbf{x_1} \\ 1 \end{pmatrix} = \begin{pmatrix} \overline{\mathbf{A}}_{\mathbf{j_2}}(\mathbf{x_1}) \\ 1 \end{pmatrix} = \begin{pmatrix} \mathbf{x_2} \\ 1 \end{pmatrix} \in \Psi$. In the same way, we get $\mathbf{x_k}' = \mathbf{A}'_{\mathbf{j_k}} \mathbf{x}'_{k-1} = \begin{pmatrix} \mathbf{A}_{\mathbf{j_k}} & c_{\mathbf{j_k}} \\ 0 & 1 \end{pmatrix} \begin{pmatrix} \mathbf{x_{k-1}} \\ 1 \end{pmatrix} = \begin{pmatrix} \overline{\mathbf{A}}_{\mathbf{j_k}}(\mathbf{x_{k-1}}) \\ 1 \end{pmatrix} = \begin{pmatrix} \mathbf{x_k} \\ 1 \end{pmatrix} \in \Psi$, for all $k = 1, 2, 3, \cdots$. Therefore, there exist $\mathbf{x_0}' \in \Psi$ and an index set $S' = \{j_i\}_{i=1}^{+\infty}$, $j_i \in \{1, 2, \cdots, m\}$. Such that $\mathbf{x_k}' = \mathbf{A}'_{\mathbf{j_k}} \mathbf{A}'_{\mathbf{j_{k-1}}} \cdots \mathbf{A}'_{\mathbf{j_2}} \mathbf{A}'_{\mathbf{j_1}} \mathbf{x_0}' \in \Psi$, for all $k = 1, 2, 3, \cdots$. This indicates that Q_m is non-terminating on $\mathbf{x_0}'$.

($\Rightarrow$) If Q_m does not terminate, then there must exist $\mathbf{x_0}' = \begin{pmatrix} \mathbf{x_0} \\ z_0 \end{pmatrix} \in \Psi$ and an index set $S' = \{j_i\}_{i=1}^{+\infty}$, $j_i \in \{1, 2, \cdots, m\}$, such that

$$\mathbf{x_0}' \in \Psi, \mathbf{x_k}' = \mathbf{A}'_{\mathbf{j_k}} \mathbf{A}'_{\mathbf{j_{k-1}}} \cdots \mathbf{A}'_{\mathbf{j_2}} \mathbf{A}'_{\mathbf{j_1}} \mathbf{x_0}' \in \Psi \tag{10}$$

for $k = 1, 2, 3, \cdots$. Therefore, $z_0 \equiv 1$. By (10), we get $\mathbf{x_0}' = (\mathbf{x_0}, 1)^T \in \Psi$, $\mathbf{x_1}' = \mathbf{A}'_{\mathbf{j_1}} \mathbf{x_0}' = \begin{pmatrix} \mathbf{A}_{\mathbf{j_1}} & c_{\mathbf{j_1}} \\ 0 & 1 \end{pmatrix} \begin{pmatrix} \mathbf{x_0} \\ 1 \end{pmatrix} = \begin{pmatrix} \overline{\mathbf{A}}_{\mathbf{j_1}}(\mathbf{x_0}) \\ 1 \end{pmatrix} \in \Psi$, Let $\mathbf{x_1} = \overline{\mathbf{A}}_{\mathbf{j_1}}(\mathbf{x_0})$. By the definition of Ψ, we know that $\mathbf{x_0} \in \Omega$ and $\mathbf{x_1} = \overline{\mathbf{A}}_{\mathbf{j_1}}(\mathbf{x_0}) \in \Omega$. By (10), $\mathbf{x_2}' = \mathbf{A}'_{\mathbf{j_2}} \mathbf{x_1}' = \begin{pmatrix} \mathbf{A}_{\mathbf{j_2}} & c_{\mathbf{j_2}} \\ 0 & 1 \end{pmatrix} \begin{pmatrix} \mathbf{x_1} \\ 1 \end{pmatrix} = \begin{pmatrix} \overline{\mathbf{A}}_{\mathbf{j_2}}(\mathbf{x_1}) \\ 1 \end{pmatrix} \in \Psi$. By the similar arguments as above, we have $\mathbf{x_2} = \overline{\mathbf{A}}_{\mathbf{j_2}}(\mathbf{x_1}) \in \Omega$. In the same way, we obtain that $\mathbf{x_k}' = \mathbf{A}'_{\mathbf{j_k}} \mathbf{x}'_{k-1} = \begin{pmatrix} \mathbf{A}_{\mathbf{j_k}} & c_{\mathbf{j_k}} \\ 0 & 1 \end{pmatrix} \begin{pmatrix} \mathbf{x_{k-1}} \\ 1 \end{pmatrix} = \begin{pmatrix} \overline{\mathbf{A}}_{\mathbf{j_k}}(\mathbf{x_{k-1}}) \\ 1 \end{pmatrix} \in \Psi$. Let $\mathbf{x_k} = \overline{\mathbf{A}}_{\mathbf{j_k}}(\mathbf{x_{k-1}})$. Then, by the similar arguments as above, we have $\mathbf{x_k} \in \Omega$. This immediately implies that there exist a point $\mathbf{x_0}$ and an index set $S = \{j_i\}_{i=1}^{+\infty}$, $j_i \in \{1, 2, \cdots, m\}$, such that $\mathbf{x_k}' = \overline{\mathbf{A}}_{\mathbf{j_k}}(\mathbf{x_{k-1}}) = \overline{\mathbf{A}}_{\mathbf{j_k}} \circ \overline{\mathbf{A}}_{\mathbf{j_{k-1}}} \circ \cdots \circ \overline{\mathbf{A}}_{\mathbf{j_1}}(\mathbf{x_0}) \in \Omega$ for any $k = 1, 2, 3, \cdots$. Hence, P'_m is nonterminating on $\mathbf{x_0}$. $\qquad\square$

Next, we present an algorithm to check if an MPLA loop programs is terminating.

Algorithm. **Determination of termination of MPLA loops.**

Input: an MPLA loop program P'_m

Output: If the hypothesis of Theorem 1 can be satisfied, then return Terminating; otherwise, return unknown.

1. Introduce a new variable z to translate P'_m to Q_m.
2. Synthesize the ranking functions $\rho_j(\mathbf{x})$, for $j = 1, 2, \cdots, m$.
3. Compute the $S_j, \Omega'_j, \Omega''_j$, for $j = 1, 2, \cdots, m$.
4. Synthesize the local ranking function $\rho(\mathbf{x})$ over Φ_m.
5. **if** $\rho_j(\mathbf{x})$, for $j = 1, 2, \cdots, m$ and $\rho(\mathbf{x})$ exist, **then**
6.   **return terminating;**
7. **else**
8.   **return unknown;**
9. **end if**

In the following table, we compare our method with methods based on the synthesis of GLRFs and LLRFs. Notes that GLRF (resp.LLRF) is the abbreviation of global linear ranking functions(resp.lexicographic linear ranking functions). Here, "unknown" represents that the termination of a given loop cannot be determined by the methods based on synthesizing GLRFs and LLRFs. This is because, for the following three examples, by computation, we find that all of them have no GLRFs and LLRFs. Thus, the methods based on GLRFs and LLRFs cannot check if any of the three loops is terminating. However, by our method, all of the three loops are verified to be terminating.

MPLA loops			GLRF-based method	LLRF-based method	Our method
P3: $\tau_1 : x \geq 1 \wedge y \leq -1 \Rightarrow$	$\begin{cases} x := x + y \\ y := y - 1 \end{cases}$		unknown	unknown	terminating
$\tau_2 : \begin{array}{c} -5 \leq x \leq -1 \\ \wedge -4 \leq y \leq -1 \end{array} \Rightarrow$	$\begin{cases} x := x - y \\ y := \quad y \end{cases}$				
P4: $\tau_1 : 2x + y \geq 2 \wedge x \leq 0 \Rightarrow$	$\begin{cases} x := x + 1 \\ y := y - x \end{cases}$		unknown	unknown	terminating
$\tau_2 : -x \geq y \wedge y \leq 0 \wedge x > 0 \Rightarrow$	$\begin{cases} x := x - y \\ y := y + 2 \end{cases}$				
P5: $\tau_1 : \begin{array}{c} y \geq 5 \wedge x \geq 2 \\ \wedge 7 \leq x + y \leq 10 \end{array} \Rightarrow$	$\begin{cases} x := x - y \\ y := y - x \end{cases}$		unknown	unknown	terminating
$\tau_2 : \begin{array}{c} x \leq -1 \wedge y \geq 2 \\ \wedge -5 \leq x - y \leq -3 \end{array} \Rightarrow$	$\begin{cases} x := x + y \\ y := \quad 2y \end{cases}$				

5 Conclusion

In this paper, we have given a sufficient criterion for P_m to be terminating. Our method depends on the partition of Ω_j, i.e., $\Omega_j = S_j \cup \Omega'_j \cup \Omega''_j$ for $j = 1, 2, \cdots, m$. We first compute three subsets $S_j, \Omega'_j, \Omega''_j$ of Ω_j. Then, we compute the global ranking function $\rho_j(\mathbf{x})$ over Ω_j, which guarantee the points in Ω'_j are terminating points of P_m. Finally, we synthesize a so-called local ranking functions to guarantee the points in S_j, Ω''_j are terminating points of P_m. Experimental results show that for some MPLA loop programs which have no global linear ranking functions or lexicographic ranking functions over $\cup_{j=1}^{m} \Omega_j$, they indeed can be proven to be terminating by our method.

Acknowledgment. This research is supported by the National Natural Science Foundation of China NNSFC (61572024, 61103110, 11471307).

References

1. Bagnara, R., Mesnard, F.: Eventual linear ranking functions. In: Proceedings of the 15th Symposium on Principles and Practice of Declarative Programming, pp. 229–238. ACM, Madrid (2013)
2. Ben-Amram, A.M., Genaim, S.: On the linear ranking problem for integer linear-constraint loops. In: POPL 2013 Proceedings of the 40th Annual ACM SIGPLAN-SIGACT Symposium on Principles of Programming Languages, pp. 51–62. ACM. Rome (2013)
3. Bradley, A.R., Manna, Z., Sipma, H.B.: Linear ranking with reachability. In: Etessami, K., Rajamani, S.K. (eds.) CAV 2005. LNCS, vol. 3576, pp. 491–504. Springer, Heidelberg (2005). https://doi.org/10.1007/11513988_48
4. Bradley, A.R., Manna, Z., Sipma, H.B.: The polyranking principle. In: Caires, L., Italiano, G.F., Monteiro, L., Palamidessi, C., Yung, M. (eds.) ICALP 2005. LNCS, vol. 3580, pp. 1349–1361. Springer, Heidelberg (2005). https://doi.org/10.1007/11523468_109
5. Chen, H.Y., Flur, S., Mukhopadhyay, S.: Termination proofs for linear simple loops. In: Miné, A., Schmidt, D. (eds.) SAS 2012. LNCS, vol. 7460, pp. 422–438. Springer, Heidelberg (2012). https://doi.org/10.1007/978-3-642-33125-1_28
6. Chen, Y., Xia, B., Yang, L., Zhan, N., Zhou, C.: Discovering non-linear ranking functions by solving semi-algebraic systems. In: Jones, C.B., Liu, Z., Woodcock, J. (eds.) ICTAC 2007. LNCS, vol. 4711, pp. 34–49. Springer, Heidelberg (2007)
7. Colóon, M.A., Sipma, H.B.: Synthesis of linear ranking functions. In: Margaria, T., Yi, W. (eds.) TACAS 2001. LNCS, vol. 2031, pp. 67–81. Springer, Heidelberg (2001). https://doi.org/10.1007/3-540-45319-9_6
8. Cousot, P.: Proving program invariance and termination by parametric abstraction, Lagrangian relaxation and semidefinite programming. In: Cousot, R. (ed.) VMCAI 2005. LNCS, vol. 3385, pp. 1–24. Springer, Heidelberg (2005). https://doi.org/10.1007/978-3-540-30579-8_1
9. Heizmann, M., Hoenicke, J., Leike, J., Podelski, A.: Linear ranking for linear lasso programs. In: Van Hung, D., Ogawa, M. (eds.) ATVA 2013. LNCS, vol. 8172, pp. 365–380. Springer, Cham (2013). https://doi.org/10.1007/978-3-319-02444-8_26
10. Leike, J., Heizmann, M.: Ranking templates for linear loops. Logical Methods Comput. Sci. **11**, 1–27 (2015)
11. Li, Y., Zhu, G., Feng, Y.: The L-depth eventual linear ranking functions for single-path linear constraint loops. In: 2016 10th International Symposium on Theoretical Aspects of Software Engineering, Shanghai, pp. 30–37 (2016)
12. Kersten, R., Van Eekelen, M.: Ranking functions for loops with disjunctive exit-conditions. In: Proceedings of the 2nd International Workshop on Foundational and Practical Aspects of Resource Analysis, pp. 111–126 (2011)
13. Podelski, A., Rybalchenko, A.: A complete method for the synthesis of linear ranking functions. In: Steffen, B., Levi, G. (eds.) VMCAI 2004. LNCS, vol. 2937, pp. 239–251. Springer, Heidelberg (2004). https://doi.org/10.1007/978-3-540-24622-0_20

Education and Surveys

LearnDroid: An Exclusive Tool for Online Learning on Customized Android Platform

Qingcheng Li, Heng Cao, Guangming Zheng, Ye Lu$^{(\boxtimes)}$, and Qi Du

Nankai University, Tianjin, China
luye@nankai.edu.cn

Abstract. Learning should be a process of concentration. Now, the tablet operating system, which is full of irrelevant software, greatly interferes with the concentration of students' learning. To address this problem, we designed a dedicated Android desktop launcher to mask interference from irrelevant software. At the same time, considering that students are learning video or reading e-books, they may need to wake up the note taking application at any time to take notes. This paper focuses on how to improve the ease of use of the homework management system. By studying the process of Android's Home key, we design home key event monitoring module and system status management module to achieve the goal of waking up the note-taking app by pressing one keystroke.

Keywords: Online learning · Customized Android launcher
Home key

1 Introduction

The growth of online autonomous learning has been developing rapidly, especially in recent years, because of the outbreak of online education software, which has led to people constantly upgrading their knowledge through online platforms. More and more Internet service providers are beginning to provide online information. Study from [2] shows that The online learning population is exploding within this year around the whole world. For example, Udacity, with industry giants Google, AT&T, Facebook, Salesforce, Cloudera, etc., is building an online university, by Silicon Valley that teaches the skills that industry employers need today, delivers credentials endorsed by employers and educates at a fraction of the coast of traditional schools. DEDAO a famous online learning software in China gained 5.58 million users in a year, with more than 450,000 daily active users.

However, the current online learning platform is not enough to guarantee the effectiveness of online learning. Since in order to really master the knowledge, people need to maintain a high degree of attention in the course of learning,

© Springer Nature Singapore Pte Ltd. 2018
Y. Bi et al. (Eds.): ESTC 2017, CCIS 857, pp. 241–257, 2018.
https://doi.org/10.1007/978-981-13-1026-3_18

and keep a record of what they have learned, and review it in time. The current online education platform is made up of software that runs on mobile phones, and is often interrupted by social software, push, and even phone calls in the course of learning. Even such devices offer more entertainment, and a large number of entertainment software will continue to attract learners, so that online learning cannot maintain a high degree of attention. At the same time, the current online learning software only provides a large number of online learning resources, but did not provide good notes function, lead learners not to contact the new knowledge review, easy to forget, greatly affected the efficiency and effectiveness of online learning.

Online education has become the people to acquire new knowledge and skills to master the most commonly used way, so, in order to ensure the efficiency and effectiveness of online learning, we need to solve the following two problems: (1) in the process of online learning, how to ensure a high degree of attention of students. (2) how to provide a convenient and quick way to take notes, so as to help students review the main points of knowledge learned.

To this end, this paper innovatively designed a set of customized firmware based on Android – LearnDroid. The system provides an immersive, portable learning device solution. Specifically, the original custom Android system, Learn-Droid has a complete set of online learning system softwares, and when the system is running, first load the customized learning launcher application, which is the entrance of LearnDroid. And, the software in the LearnDroid system is all related to the provision of online education services. This mechanism greatly reduces the likelihood that students will be disturbed during the learning process and ensures a high degree of attention during the learning process. In addition, LearnDroid provides a portable and efficient mechanism for note taking. We had a customization on Home control keys on intelligent hardware platforms, through a simple operation on the home key, we can achieve fast wake-up notes function, and through the design of touch operation, we provide a convenient and intelligent way to take notes on smart platforms.

Specifically, the core of our LearnDroid system design is to improve the effectiveness of online education. By redesigning the application level, system level and hardware level of Android system, this paper implements an immersive online education customization system LearnDroid. Through the LearnDroid system, we can realize the independent management of educational application, construct the application ecology with education as the core, and build a closed-loop learning environment. Customization and management can improve the efficiency of online learning and promote the development of online education technology.

One point should be stressed is that since the LearnDroid system is implemented by modifying the Android system, it should coexist with the Android device on the mobile device and schedule the dual system over the Android system kernel. And the existing educational software can also be run on LearnDroid without any modification. Users can choose to run different systems according to their own needs.

At the end of this paper, we implemented the LearnDroid system on the current mobile development platform, and tested the performance of the system comprehensively. The experimental results show that LearnDroid can efficiently run on mobile devices currently on the online education environment and provide can make learners maintain a high degree of attention, and provides a convenient way of taking notes, thereby greatly improving the user's learning efficiency.

2   Related Work

With the development of information technology, online education is more and more widely used because of its convenience and diversity. According to an 8 years' study on responses from more than 2,500 colleges and universities, [1] says sixty-three percent of all reporting institutions said that online learning was a critical part of their institution's long term strategy. [8] defines distance education as institution-based formal education where the learning group is separated, and where interactive telecommunications systems are used to connect learners, resources, and instructors.

At the same time, a lot of research has focused on the development and construction of online education platform. [2] has designed a platform names WebAssign, it provides a flexible platform for different kinds of assignments and correctionmodes ranging from automatically assessed multiple-choice tasks to manually correctedwritten assignments. [3] extended the Technology Acceptance Model to include technical support as a precursor and then investigated the role of the extended model in user acceptance of WebCT (Web Course Tools). [5] reported the results of a comparison of student understanding of physics concepts with and without online homework, as measured by the force concept inventory. They compared students in large introductory courses taught by interactive engagement and noninteractive engagement methods and with ungraded homework and with online homework. KK, Cheng et al. studied the online home work system and showed that the online homework system enhances the students' understanding of key concepts in the course [14].

At present, the research focus of ubiquitous mobile learning, since the smart platform is widely used in daily life which can make online learning happen in anywhere at any time. According a report from Kantar Worldpanel [13], by March 2017, 86.4% of mobile devices were based on Android system. Because Android system is an open project [9], we can customize the function according to our requirements. According to [10,11], we can customize the function of the home key to launch the online learning environment quickly and realize a scheme of quick wake-up note-taking function.

3   Online Application Environment

We provide teachers and students a digital learning terminal running on Android devices. The learning devices deliver video-watching behavior to a dedicate module. A teaching video functions to separate video learning applications; a

Internet forum is designed to share learning experiences and act as a part of homework subsystem. The client's operating system is based on a deeply customized android learning private system, which allows students to perform learning related applications and lock learning unrelated applications when they are learning in the classroom. Digital operating system terminal with wireless access function, so students are not subject to site constraints, at home, in the library or in the school room, can access the digital school operating system network and access to learning resources.

The characteristics of students' digital homework system client for elementary education stage of the corresponding interface customization provides massive video teaching and experimental demonstration video for mathematics, physics and chemistry and other subjects. Students in the classroom can better understand the corresponding theoretical knowledge by watching these experimental video demonstrations. Digital operating system client applications are very rich, in addition to the core application, there are a lot of studying applications, all of these applications are downloaded from education application store, which provides a useful platform for the management of application developers and student users.

4   Dedicated Launcher

Students in the classroom use Android tablet computers to learn and do homework, and the applications used in the teaching and learning environment need to be run in a closed operating environment, so as not to be disturbed by non-learning applications. In order to build a closed learning environment, we make a priority distinction between educational applications and entertainment applications. Students are guaranteed to use educational applications as long as when they are studying in class.

We put forward a method of customized dedicated learning launcher. The learning launcher is customized with learning features, and replaces Android native launcher to present an exclusive learning environment for students who are lack of self control. Because the launcher starter is the first application of Android system when starting up and boot directly into the application, the dedicated learning launcher performs a high level priority to the system. This solution needs to modify the Android system source code and recompile the mirror image.

Learning launcher is the first application when the Android system is started. It is the entrance of the digital learning terminal and the interface between the teacher and the student. They directly interact with the digital learning terminals. First of all, the launcher plays an vital important role of the whole scheme, we can put learning applications in the top level of the system; more importantly, before the devices is activated, installation and configuration of various learning application in special learning launcher can be restricted, and the device limits the specified application to be executed. Thus, we can build a exclusive learning environment.

4.1   Function Design

The dedicated learning launcher is similar to the common Android launcher and responsible for the management of applications in Android systems. The main functions of a dedicated learning launcher can be divided into four parts: application management, additional function management, shelf tab management and workspace switch.

Application management, application installation is when users download and install the Android click on the application, if the installation is successful, a new application icon is generated on the home screen. Launcher is responsible for icon management. Opening application refers to starting the application when the user clicks on the program icon. When unloading the application, dragging the icon to the bottom of the screen, trash instruction will be displayed.

Additional function management: (1) create and delete shortcuts, press the blank screen at the bottom of the screen will pop up a window asking if you want to add a shortcut; delete shortcuts of applications with the same mode of operation; (2) widget management, share the same operation as shortcuts management; (3) folder management, share the same operation as shortcuts and widget management; (4) wallpaper management, launcher displays special learning wallpaper, performs wallpaper updating and other functions.

Shelf tab management, the background of the home page is a bookshelf, there are four buttons: preview, class, homework and review on the upper part of the shelf. When the user clicks a button, the system will be switched to the corresponding functional area. The system contains a total of 11 workspaces, each application will be run in the corresponding workspace to ensure that students learn and work in a closed environment.

Workspace switch: in our custom dedicated learning launcher, a total of 11 working areas is set, by sliding left and right, a user can choose different work areas. When the system is starting, the system launch the very first workspace on the left by default. When students doing homework assigned by class, teachers and parents can set the corresponding password to lock other workspace to avoid interference from other entertainment applications.

4.2   Launcher Design Overview

The overall architecture of the dedicated learning launcher uses the MVC (Model View and Controller) framework. The MVC framework realize the code decoupling of data module and view module through the controller module: changing the view display will not result in changes in the logic and processing code of the data layer, also a different form of expression can be specified for the same logic or action. The division of each module for the learning launcher is clear, the data management module comprises a control module, the data support for the view module is also guided by a control module; the degree of association between the control module and view module is relatively higher, and the user's touch operation between the view module and control module is influenced by each other, control module is required to be responded to user touch operations

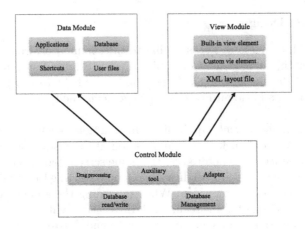

Fig. 1. The structure of MVC

The relationship between the three modules, the data module, the view module, and the control module, is shown in Fig. 1.

The detailed function of each module is described below:

View module: this module is responsible for Android's UI interface display, each display page is managed through the layout file, and layout file format using XML format, each of which is an element of display control. When writing a view module for a dedicated learning launcher, we can use the Android system's own view elements (such as buttons, text boxes, etc.), or expand the default view elements as needed. However the default view elements provided by the Android system are small, the extensibility is good, and program developers can extend and modify them according to their needs.

Data module: this module is primarily responsible for managing information about installed applications on Android devices and information about plug-ins and widgets in each workspace, including desktop icons, location information, and so on. The data of the Android application is actually maintained by the Android system, and the dedicated learning desktop calls the interfaces of the Android system to access these application data. Data is managed by using the SQLite database.

Main control module: The main activity for dedicated learning desktops, whose roles are connector between data modules and view modules. When the view module receives the user's touch operation, the control module is responsible for calling the corresponding interface to perform data processing. When a new data is generated in the data module, the control module is responsible for displaying it on the view module. The operation of the control module is triggered by view element. In this module, dragging and dropping processing component is responsible for the user's touch operations; adapter component is responsible for providing data support in response to list views; database read and write component is used to access the database; database management component is used to load and update a variety of data items.

4.3 View Design

In Android systems, the design of human computer interaction interface can be described statically through XML files or using Java code to generate dynamically. In the dedicated learning desktop, the designed UI is of great numbers, so we adopt to take the XML file as primary and Java code dynamic generation as a secondary strategy to generate the views of the dedicated learning desktop. Most pages only need to control their hidden and display properties. This layout enables using XML file descriptions; there are a few dynamic interfaces that require a mixture of Java and XML to modify layout in real time. In this study, the custom learning launcher is tailored for learning and education as shown in Fig. 2. The UI interface contains four buttons for selecting four types of learning applications that students are using. When a type of learning application is applied, the system automatically shields the rest of the non learning class applications.

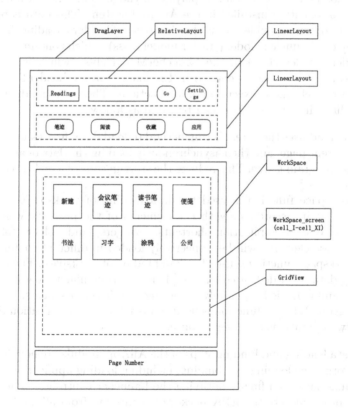

Fig. 2. Layout design of customized launcher

4.4   Data Storage and Management

When customizing start launcher, we use SQLite (database management software) to manage appropriate data, and the learning data in dedicated launcher needs to be managed. Application data refers to the location and related information of the applications installed in the Android system. App shortcut (application icons) refers to the program icons corresponding to the application, stored in SD card with their paths Folder means that you can put the same type of program icon in a folder, where each folder's location information is managed by the database. Wallpaper refers to wallpaper data, each workspace can set only one wallpaper, storage locations and other information are managed by the database. Button means in the launcher, we need to manage the data of the four tag selection buttons on your home page, similar to the management of the program icons.

In the start-up and initialization process for learning the launcher, the main work is to load the UI data and displayed on the screen, UI data refers to the data of the application installed in the Android system. This data is read with the help of content provider from the database. The data loading function is handled by the LauncherModel (starter model class), which contains an internal class Loader (loader class) in the LauncherModel class, which is used to do specific loading. A thread is defined in the loader class - LoaderThread (load thread) for asynchronous execution of load actions. The corresponding function call procedures in the flow chart can be listed as follows:

- loaderThread uses the thread's run method to load data, first loading the data of the current page, and then asynchronously loading the data of another page until the program is free. This reduces the startup time of a dedicated learning launcher.
- loadWorkspace function is used for data loading of workspace. Workspace data load is in accordance with the elements of the property were loaded, including Widget application shortcuts, (widgets) and Folder (folder) elements, these elements will be respectively loaded in different containers.
- bindWorkspace function is used for data binding of workspace. The workspace binding data for a dedicated learning launcher is similar to loading the data process and is loaded separately according to different elements.
- loadAllAppsByBatch function is used to load and bind application data, and these two operations are done at once.

The data loading and binding steps of the AllApp module are not the same as those of workspace loading and binding, including loading application data first, then binding data, and finally notifying the Launcher controller. When loading data, the program gets the APK package information from all of the installed applications from the application manager. The data loading and binding of AllApp module is different from workspace: the data loading of AllApp module will complete the operation of data binding at the same time of loading.

The Workspace class contains three types of data, ItemInfo, FolderInfo, and LauncherAppWidgetInfo, corresponding to application shortcuts, folders, and

Widget data, respectively. The data loading process first read data from the special desktop database, and then store the data according to the elements of the three attributes in the ArrayList array; the process of data binding is the view elements of these three ArrayList elements in the queue and the establishment of special learning desktop association.

Between the Launcher and LauncherModel objects interact through the Callbacks interface: LauncherModel Callbacks interface definition, and the Launcher class implements the Callbacks interface and realizes the corresponding function call interface. LauncherModel calls this interface in the function that loads the data, in this way feedback data and status to the Launcher. Once the data binding is complete, the Launcher can run, and when the uninstall program or the folder is deleted, it triggers a change in the database and eventually feeds back to the display interface. This series of operations is accomplished by matching the controller launcher class between the UI and the data model LauncherModel.

4.5   Customized Launcher

The special learning task in the custom launcher customization level of the Android system and Android application layer system layer, are not related to the Linux kernel layer. However, in order to replace the default launcher, we still need to recompile the Android system image.

5   Rethinking of the Home Key

Note taking is an essential part in most knowledge learning conditions. In the traditional paper-based learning mode, paper textbook and paper excise book make it easier for users to do writing behaviors. By taking advantages of web technologies, many web-based learning supporting tools has taken place to make online learning more convenient for modern students. However, Taking notes on a website through computers is limited by the input devices. Keyboard and mouse cannot transfer a paper-based learning style to web-based learning. Indeed, we need smart devices equipped with materials which can write and draw on it. Consider that the iOS devices cannot be customized or tailored easily, we choose Android devices to realize our goals.

Students may need to take notes whenever they are learning. On a regular Android tablet computer, the process should be performed as follows: exit currently used program, open a dedicated note application, and then log in. This process is troublesome. In order to improve efficiency, we need to add a mechanism for "note taking and wake up the note-taking application in time" for the system. No matter what application the system is running, when you need to take notes, you can achieve a wake-up call to note-taking application software any time.

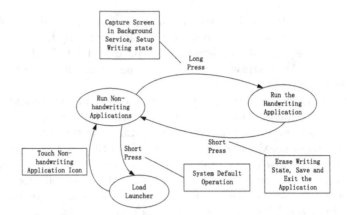

Fig. 3. State transition with customized operations

5.1   State Transistion

Home key on the current android devices is the main physical button. It performs an interruption function of running application. In native Android operating systems, the response events of the home key includes long press and short press. Long pressing the home key is used to display all of the applications that have been opened recently, and short pressing the home button is to return the Android system launcher from the current application. The home Android button operation status transition diagram is shown in Fig. 3.

Because the home key possesses high priority in the Android, we can achieve a wake-up call by customizing the home key's operation flow. When the user is using other APP, he may need to mark on a particular screen. He can choose to press the home button long enough. At this point, the system will save the current program's running state and screen the screenshot. Next, wake up the note taking program and take the previously saved screenshot as the background information for the notes. At this point, the user can annotate and take notes of the picture just now. When the user completes the note operation, and then through the short press home button, the system will store the note information, and then return to the previous application, and restore the program's full running state.

5.2   System Analysis

The customization of home keys runs through the hardware layer, the Linux kernel layer, the framework layer and the application layer of the Android system. The structure of the android system and module we modify are shown in Fig. 4. More specifically, our customized design is shown in Fig. 5.

Unlike common event monitoring and response events, listening to the home key event is intercepted by the system at the framework layer and send a broadcast.

Therefore, we need to add a listening module at the framework layer and add the background service module on the application layer.

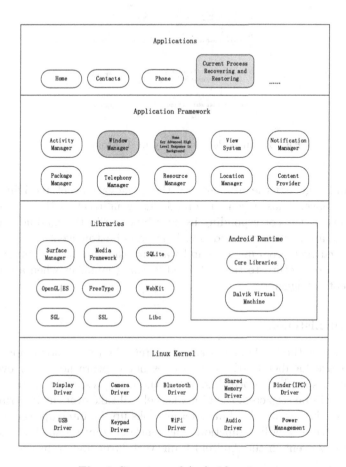

Fig. 4. Structure of Android system

After the hardware layer detects the change of the electrical level of the home key, the response pulse signal is generated, and the corresponding interrupt number and interrupt processing function provided at the Linux kernel layer will be executed. The kernel's interrupt function will number the home key's interrupt event and send it to the upper layer of the Framework, where the Android kernel performs event handling over the Linux kernel.

In the framework of the system at the entrance of the home key events, interceptor performs an interception, and then sent to the broadcast to frame layer, so HomeWatcher module should be treated in a broadcast event, broadcast receiver calls different functions according to the corresponding event listener. In the application layer, the home key monitors service module in the background is responsible for writing long press event and short press event handlers in the

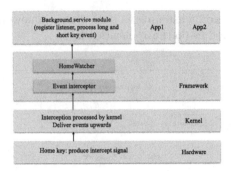

Fig. 5. Embedded home key in Android system

listener, and registers the listener into the broadcast event receiving module mentioned above. Thus, when the broadcast event receives the corresponding keystroke event, the corresponding listener function in the module is executed and the software logic is executed. The long press button event in this module is to save the current program state and wake up the handwriting program; load the launcher and return to the dedicated learning launcher when a short press button event is triggered.

5.3 Event Listener

The home key is the fundamental key of current Android system, and the ordinary keystroke handler (onKeyDown) does not capture home key events and performs corresponding processing. When the user presses the home key, interrupt events will be triggered, the Linux kernel will take over the interrupt generated by home key event. The Linux kernel looks up the interrupt vector table to find the interrupt handling function. The function converts the home key event to normal key event in the Android framework layer and transfers to Android system software layer.

In the Android system, when software layer receives the Linux kernel layer to home key interrupt event, the window process management service will take charge in the incoming event, and make judgement and dispatch by interceptor function. If the event belongs to KEYCODE_HOME, KEY-CODE_MENU and KEYCODE_SEARCH, then the event will be sent to phone window manager for processing. After series of call such as home hotkey processing function, eventually closing window function of activity management service will send the system an broadcast, the content of which is Intent.ACTION_CLOSE_SYSTEM_DIALOGS.

In this paper, when dealing with the key events of Home keys, the Home-Watcher module is used to encapsulate the broadcast receiver, which receives the broadcast in the system, and then processes the corresponding long press or short press events. There are three main classes that need to be discussed: Home-Watcher, interface onHomePressedListener, and the inner class of HomeWatcher

InnerReceiver. The onReceive function of the broadcast receiver is responsible for processing received system broadcasts and calling the corresponding listening function according to the registered listeners. As HomeWatcher users in this system is a background service module at the application layer, we need to monitor interface and listener registration to the HomeWatcher instance, so, when the broadcast receiver received event, we call the listening function defined in the background service.

MainActivity will instantiate a onHomePressedListener instance and the instance of the listener is registered to the HomeWatcher object to be able to monitor events through the set method of the HomeWatcher object. When the HomeWatcher's internal class InnerReceiver processes event requests, the Main-Activity object is notified by the registered listener object, and the corresponding event processing code is executed.

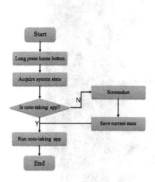

Fig. 6. Long press response

Fig. 7. Short press response

5.4   Background Service

The function of the backstage service module is to handle the long press and short press key events of the Home key. This section explains in detail the flow of algorithms for long and short events, with the two main functions being onHome-Pressed and onHomeLongPressed. The onHomeLongPressed function handles the long press key event of the Home key, and the onHomePressed function handles the short press key event of the Home key. To mark the running status of the Android system, a flag bit is added to the system to identify whether the current system is running the note application. The flow chart of the algorithm of onHomeLongPressed function as shown in Fig. 6, in the key of Home monitoring module monitors the Home key to long and then notify the backend module according to the key event, onHomeLongPressed function call background service module into the press button event process. First get the position and determine whether the currently running application notes application, mark the state of the system if it is, the current function did not continue to run the application notes; if not, the screenshot, and save the current state of the program, and then call the application notes.

The flow chart of the short event handler function onHomePressed is shown in Fig. 7. First get the position and determine whether the currently running application notes application, mark the state of the system if it is, first save the notes and the current state of the program, and then restore the state in the system before running application notes (the system state is stored in the specified file); if not, the loading of special learning launcher.

Fig. 8. Customized launcher

6   Evaluation

In this section, we conduct a thorough test of the customized Android online learning system from two aspects of functionality and performance. The test results show that the customized launcher can focus on learning applications in the course of learning, shielding the entertainment applications, and thus ensuring the efficiency of learners in the learning process. And can be a quick key to wake up note function, improve the efficiency of learning and product experience.

First, we tested the overall functionality of the system. When users are using the customized system for online learning, system switches launcher and hides non-learning class applications automatically as shown in Fig. 8. Besides, through the client, online learners can log into their accounts and receive the job assigned by the teacher. And they can directly finish the homework on the tablet. For example, fill in the blanks for digital homework, upload short answer, either in handwritten on a tablet computer format or writing on paper and then upload pictures.

After students press the Home button while doing their homework, the system will save the current screen and then wake up the 'note-taking' application. Demonstrate here in the first workspace (learning workspace). When you just wake up your note application, it's in graffiti. If you need a long period of operation, you can click the 'nail' button in the bottom right corner to secure the current graffiti interface. If you need to take notes, you can click the two buttons at the top or right of the screen to add paper to the left and right sides, and take notes on the new page added. When the note-taking actions are finished, users press home button to return to the previous application.

In addition to functional testing, we also conduct a thorough evaluation of the performance. In the embedded system, the task response time refers to the self processing request handler to interrupt a corresponding execution time interval. Interrupt response time refers the time period from the interrupt trigger to the execution of the first instruction of the interrupt service routine. In this system, the concept of the response time of the Home key function is wider than the above two concepts, and its meaning is: from the user's length, pressing the Home button to the system to fully wake up the time of writing the handwriting program. The response time can be divided into two stages: (1) the user presses the Home key of the Android system to deal with the Home key and broadcasts (analogy to the interrupt response time); (2) the HomeWatcher module receives the broadcast to the backend module generated by the system to complete the corresponding operation (analogy to interrupt processing time).

To test the response time of the customized Home key. In the background service module, the short and long press events are used to start and end the event function, and the system time is acquired by using the API provided by the Java, thus the processing time of the Home key response is obtained. Here we did four rounds of experiments, each of which was written with a primary key, and the soft pen was written 3 times, in milliseconds. At the end of each set of experiments, the machine should be restarted for another set of tests.

After analyzing the data on the table, we have made a comparison of the performance tests, as shown in Fig. 9. It can be seen that the performance of note taking prompt arousal mechanism is acceptable. The Android customization scheme proposed in this paper is in accordance with the requirements and feasible. According to the test response time for customizing the launcher function and custom home key event, the performance of user customized solutions is acceptable.

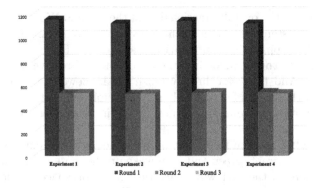

Fig. 9. Home key test

7   Conclusion

After analyzing the application scenarios of the online education digital operating system, this paper proposes a Android customization scheme including education software ecology and terminal operating system. Research on two key problems of the scheme in this paper: the first is to isolate special learning and normal entertainment desktop, we implement and add a new Launcher starter system; second is the Home key senior response mechanism, the main goal is to let students in the learning process take notes anytime. By taking function test of Launcher and the performance test of home key response mechanism, the solution proposed in this paper is feasible.

Acknowledgement. This work is supported by the Natural Science Foundation of Tianjin (No. 16JCYBJC15200, 17JCQNJC00300, 15ZXDSGX00020) and the funding named "Research on Visualization Framework and Device Oriented Group Teaching" of Tianjin Read Electronic Co., LTD. The corresponding author is Ye Lu.

References

1. Allen, I.E., Seaman, J.: Class differences: online education in the United States, 2010. Sloan Consort. 30 (2010)

2. Brunsmann, J., Homrighausen, A., Six, H.W., et al.: Assignments in a virtual university the WebAssign-System. In: Proceedings of the 19th World Conference on Open Learning and Distance Education, Vienna, Austria (1999)
3. Ngai, E.W.T., Poon, J.K.L., Chan, Y.H.C.: Empirical examination of the adoption of WebCT using TAM. Comput. Educ. **48**(2), 250–267 (2007)
4. Allain, R., Williams, T.: The effectiveness of online homework in an introductory science class. J. Coll. Sci. Teach. **35**(6), 28–30 (2006)
5. Cheng, K.K., Thacker, B.A., Cardenas, R.L., et al.: Using an online homework system enhances students learning of physics concepts in an introductory physics course. Am. J. Phys. **72**(11), 1447–1453 (2004)
6. Anderson, T.: The Theory and Practice of Online Learning. Athabasca University Press, Edmonton (2008)
7. Henderson, S., Yeow, J.: iPad in education: a case study of iPad adoption and use in a primary school. In: 2012 45th Hawaii International Conference on System Science (HICSS), pp. 78–87. IEEE (2012)
8. Schlosser, L.A., Simonson, M.R.: Distance Education: Definitions and Glossary of Terms. IAP, Charlotte (2009)
9. Chen, J., Chen, P.H., Li, W.L.: Analysis of Android kernel. Modern Comput. **11**, 034 (2009)
10. Shanker, A., Lal, S.: Android porting concepts. In: 2011 3rd International Conference on Electronics Computer Technology (ICECT), vol. 5, pp. 129–133. IEEE (2011)
11. Brahler, S.: Analysis of the Android architecture. Karlsruhe Institute for Technology (2010)
12. Yaghmour, K.: Embedded Android: Porting, Extending, and Customizing. O'Reilly Media, Inc., Sebastopol (2013)
13. https://www.kantarworldpanel.com/global/
14. Gamma, E., Helm, R., Johnson, R., et al.: Design Patterns: Elements of Reusable Object-Oriented Software. Pearson Education, New York (1994)
15. Yoon, H.J.: A study on the performance of Android platform. Int. J. Comput. Sci. Eng. **4**(4), 532–537 (2012)
16. Amalfitano, D., Fasolino, A.R., Tramontana, P., et al.: Using GUI ripping for automated testing of Android applications. In: Proceedings of the 27th IEEE/ACM International Conference on Automated Software Engineering, pp. 258–261. ACM (2012)
17. Zhao, Q.: Application study of online education platform based on cloud computing. In: International Conference on Consumer Electronics, Communications and Networks, pp. 908–911. IEEE (2012)

Author Index

Printed in the United States
By Bookmasters